"[This book] gave me deeper understanding of the extreme suffering of sexual violence survivors in our patriarchal societies where still today, the law of silence, denial, and manipulation rules alongside impunity and banalization of crimes and the guilt, solitude, and rejection in victims. Whatever your interests, discipline, persuasion, or profession, I am persuaded that reading this book will help you to better understand the victim in front of you or the survivor seeking your help."

Denis Mukwege, winner of the 2018 Nobel Peace Prize

"Muriel is a professional who is pushing forwards the understanding of victims of domestic and sexual violence with the determination of an activist."

Roland Coutanceau, psychiatrist

"Thank you, Muriel Salmona, for all the lives you've changed for the better, including my own; you are a beacon of intelligence, rigor, and kindness in this world."

Kate Rose

"Muriel Salmona, psychiatrist specializing in domestic and sexual violence, has developed the concept of traumatic amnesia. Since the lockdown, she has faced a surge of calls for help."

Le Monde

"Muriel Salmona: 'The tide is turning in favour of victims of sexual violence'"

l'Obs

"Muriel Salmona, the repairer of abused bodies and souls. She has become the voice of victims of domestic, psychological, and sexual violence, and child criminal exploitation … Through her association, she has above all succeeded in having the seriousness of assaults on minors recognized."

Le Temps

"Muriel Salmona fights internationally to defend victims of sexual abuse and works in particular with the University of Liège as well as with the Nobel Peace Prize winner, the Congolese gynecologist Denis Mukwege."

Le Soir

"Muriel Salmona exposes 'a veritable code of silence, which prevents victims from being genuinely saved and efficiently helped.'"

Economie

Sexual Violence, Dissociation, and Inequality

Sexual Violence, Dissociation, and Inequality is a book about traumatic memory—or how lived trauma is repeated by victims as if happening again.

The author, internationally renowned psychiatrist Muriel Salmona, lays out a convincing argument for the ways in which victims are neurologically compelled to relive trauma and how, with proper treatment, they can fully heal. Informed by decades of clinical practice, research, and activism, Salmona explains how victims' behaviors are rooted in neurology as normal responses to abnormal situations. In contrast to a climate of victim-blaming denial, Salmona explains how grave the violation of victims' human rights truly is and what to do about it in terms of care and prevention. She explains in clear language how to reconstruct victims' narratives, which are often clouded by traumatic amnesia, and thereby reconnect parts of the brain that were severed during the traumatic event.

This is a guide for professionals who work with survivors, for survivors themselves, and for anyone committed to understanding and reducing violence and inequality.

Muriel Salmona is a psychiatrist specializing in the care of victims of violence. She is the founder and president of the Association of Traumatic Memory and Victimology and a member of the International Mukwege Chair and the Independent Commission on Incest and Sexual Violence Against Children (CIIVISE). She was awarded the Legion of Honor in 2018 in recognition of her commitment to victim advocacy. Please visit her website to learn more: www.memoiretraumatique.org

Sexual Violence, Dissociation, and Inequality

A Guide to Understanding Traumatic Memory

Muriel Salmona

Routledge
Taylor & Francis Group

NEW YORK AND LONDON

Designed cover image: © Getty Images

First published in English 2025
by Routledge
605 Third Avenue, New York, NY 10158

and by Routledge
4 Park Square, Milton Park, Abingdon, Oxon, OX14 4RN

Routledge is an imprint of the Taylor & Francis Group, an informa business

© 2025 English translation, Kate Rose and Muriel Salmona
Foreword by Dr Denis Mukwege

Originally published in France as: Le livre noir des violences sexuelles
by Muriel SALMONA
© Dunod 2019 for the second edition, Malakoff

Library of Congress Cataloging-in-Publication Data
Names: Salmona, Muriel, author.
Title: Sexual violence, dissociation, and inequality : a guide to
understanding traumatic memory / Muriel Salmona.
Other titles: Livre noir des violences sexuelles. English
Description: New York, NY : Routledge, 2025. |
Includes bibliographical references. |
Identifiers: LCCN 2024028226 (print) | LCCN 2024028227 (ebook) |
ISBN 9781032802619 (paperback) | ISBN 9781032802626 (hardback) |
ISBN 9781003497516 (ebook)
Subjects: LCSH: Sex crimes--France--Psychological aspects. |
Sexual abuse victims--France. | Sexual abuse victims--
Rehabilitation--France. | Psychic trauma.
Classification: LCC HV6593.F7 S2513 2025 (print) |
LCC HV6593.F7 (ebook) |
DDC 362.8830944--dc23/eng/20240823
LC record available at https://lccn.loc.gov/2024028226
LC ebook record available at https://lccn.loc.gov/2024028227

ISBN: 9781032802626 (hbk)
ISBN: 9781032802619 (pbk)
ISBN: 9781003497516 (ebk)

DOI: 10.4324/9781003497516

Typeset in Palatino
by KnowledgeWorks Global Ltd.

Author's Dedications

To Jean-Pierre, my husband, who always believed in me with unconditional love and support, at my side helping me with all my actions and projects, and who was an assiduous first reader and excellent editor of this book. Our passionate exchanges and his questions, sensibility, and intellectual rigor have constantly nourished my research and elaboration, and I can never thank him enough; with all my love.

To our children, Laure, Maud, and Rémy, and their partners, Jean-Fabrice, Théo, and Marine, for their love, human qualities, precious help, and constant support. With them I found the force to fight bitterly to make a better world for them, authentic and filled with love, where they can fully be themselves and be happy. I hope to have succeeded a little bit; with all my love.

And I would like to give a special mention to our three adorable grandchildren Noam, Lila, and Alexis for all the joy and wonder they have brought us since their birth, and their fantastic parents Maud and Théo for Noam and Lila, and Rémy and Marine for Alexis; they give me the strength to continue my fight for a better world in which they can grow up in safety, with all my love.

To my mother, recently deceased, to my father and aunt, who died prematurely, and to all those who disappear too soon from our families, with special thoughts for those who were deported and assassinated by the Nazis; I honor their memory.

To all those who've been with me by my side to offer advice and support throughout my research and engagement. Thank you for believing in me, all my friends, colleagues, members of the organization Traumatic Memory and Victimology, and to all those who fight within institutions or organizations and on social media for a fairer and more equal world that respects everyone's rights.

To all my patients, victims of violence. Through these pages, I honor you and your incredible strength and courage. Thank you for taking this long road with me over 20 years and for everything we've learned. My biggest reward has always been that magic moment in psychotherapy when you meet yourself as you truly are, free of the permanent terror stemming from violence that used to haunt your life. Finally, you are free of the destructive acts and statements of torturers who colonized you and all the murderous remarks, injustices, and betrayals of those who should have been on your side: the moment when you finally come alive to yourself, free to exist, love, create, and live your own life.

To all victims of violence. May this book be as faithful a mirror as possible, so that you feel less alone and can find your dignity and worth. May it testify to your struggle and your courage, giving you hope. Violence is a scandal, an instrument of oppression, and a destruction that must be denounced again and again... That you are abandoned to your own devices is shameful, and we must lift our voices loudly about it until we are heard. Together, we must fight for a society that shows enough fairness and solidarity to never leave a single victim without care, protection, justice, and compensation.

To the deceased Alice Miller, who tirelessly witnessed the suffering of beaten, terrorized, humiliated, and abandoned children and gave voice to them, "to break down the wall of silence and join the child waiting on the other side." She was the first to shed light on the endless repetition of violence that society doesn't want to see or hear and who gave us a message of tremendous hope: through awareness of the consequences abuse has on children and on the adults they become, we can break the cycle.

To all feminists, who were the first to break the silence about sexual violence and its frequency, severity, and impact. They fought for justice and offered political analysis of sexual violence's role in domination and oppression. I honor them.

This book is dedicated to all of you.

Muriel Salmona, Bourg la Reine, France

Translator's Dedications

To my elder brother, Nick, who suffered from abuse and trauma. When I learned of his premature death, a fire was lit in me, and it fueled the translation of this book. I honor the kindness of your spirit that could never be corrupted and remember the boy you were. I offer this translation to protect others like you from a similar tragedy.

To my son, Zengan, for having opened a world of love to me and for all the joy and growth we share every day. Thank you for giving me the wonder of your thoughts and presence.

Thank you to Mary Daly, with whom I studied at Boston College, for giving me valuable clues in understanding reversal and making sense of the world. Your words spin on, noble crone, across space and time!

Thank you, Muriel Salmona, for all the lives you've changed for the better, including my own; you are a beecon of intelligence, rigor, and kindness in this world.

I dedicate this translation to all of you with my love and friendship,

Kate Rose, Flagstaff, Arizona, USA

Contents

About the Author

Dr. Muriel Salmona is a psychiatrist specialized in the care of victims of violence. President and founder of the organization Traumatic Memory and Victimology,[1] She is an active contributor to the international Mukwege Chair[2] and the French CIIVISE, which combats child sexual abuse and incest. For her extreme dedication to victims, she was awarded France's highest recognition, the Legion of Honor. She is the author of many books, articles, and research studies and has had a tremendous impact on policies, laws, and attitudes for protection and care for victims, especially victims of intimate partner, sexual, and child-abuse violence.

About the Translator

Kate Rose holds a PhD in French and comparative literature from the University of Montpellier, France. She teaches in Flagstaff, Arizona, where she uses Muriel Salmona's research to give writing workshops on healing from trauma. Her own research and creative writing, largely informed by Salmona's work, can be read at nau.academia.edu/KateRose

She hopes this book will help bring about justice, understanding, and healing for victims and is eager to work with others on this and to give talks and trainings. Contact her at katerose88888@gmail.com.

Translator's Note

In French, words somewhat arbitrarily have genders, and the word "victim" ("*victime*") is feminine. Therefore, in the original, victims are referred to as "she," although this could mean a victim of either sex. Similarly, the word "*aggresseur*" (which I translate as "perpetrator" or "abuser" according to the context) is masculine in French. Muriel Salmona cites definitive statistics showing that the majority of violence is committed by males against females and that this is symptomatic of profound inequality and misogyny; however, she also states that male victims deserve the same consideration, just as it is no less serious when women are the abusers. Salmona provides evidence that the neurology of psycho-trauma is the same in men and women, though the social conditions are not.

Usually, I refer to the victim as "she" and the perpetrator as "he," though in many cases, either could be male or female. This is to respect the statistical reality and the connotations of the original French. I have occasionally changed the pronouns to remind the reader that there are also male victims and female perpetrators, and when this does happen, it is no less serious in terms of psycho-trauma.

The word "abuse" does not exist as such in French ("*abus*" downplays the violence). I have translated the French term "*violence*" with "abuse," "violence," or "aggression" according to the context.

Preface

By Nobel Peace Prize laureate Dr. Denis Mukwege

On my nightstand, you will find this book.

Dr. Salmona's brilliant analysis of PTSD, traumatic memory and dissociation, and cognitive and behavioral disorders in victims has pulled back the thick curtain that until recently kept the truths about victims beyond our grasp.

Sexual Violence, Dissociation, and Inequality has given me a deeper understanding of the extreme suffering of survivors in our patriarchal societies. Still today, the law of silence, denial, and manipulation rules alongside impunity and banalization of crimes and guilt, solitude, and rejection in victims.

Whatever your interests, discipline, persuasion, or profession, I am persuaded that reading this book will help you to better understand the victim in front of you or the survivor seeking your help.

This book has made a substantial contribution to the holistic care approach we have been developing to best treat victims of sexual violence for the past 20 years at the Panzi Foundation and Hospital.[3]

This is why Dr. Salmona and I work together to improve our practice and lead an international plea for the voice of victims to be heard and acted on and the perpetrators of incest, rape, and sexual assault finally be held accountable by the courts.

I wholeheartedly recommend this book, and I am confident that the English-language edition will spark understanding in many more people. This book is a key and a beacon of light for those determined to move society forward toward equality, safety, autonomy, and women's empowerment.

Dr. Denis Mukwege
Bukavu, DRC
September 15, 2021

Preface

By translator Dr. Kate Rose

This book is both timely and, unfortunately, timeless. I hear people asking why there is violence and hatred. This theme emerges when there are acts of harm perpetrated against communities or individuals. This can be anything from desecration of a synagogue to assault of a Black person by police, or it can be the murder of a woman in prostitution or the gruesome slavery of kidnapped children. People ask this same "Why?!" when examining historical tragedies such as trans-Atlantic slavery or the Holocaust. We see horrors in the news every day. We ask: Why? Why? Why? Some have ceased to ask. "That's just the way it is," they say. "That's just human nature."

Here, you will find strong evidence that this is not the case. *Sexual Violence, Dissociation, and Inequality* explains these "mysteries" in light of neurological discoveries and sociological realities. Dr. Muriel Salmona has connected the dots like no one before her, and the image that emerges is both disturbing and heartening: We see the extent of the problem—bigger than we ever imagined. Yet, through doing so, we also see that violence is not inevitable or natural.

Sexual Violence, Dissociation, and Inequality: A Guide to Understanding Traumatic Memory focuses primarily on sexual violence, of which females are by far the majority of victims and males of perpetrators. This is not natural; a combination of neurological and sociohistorical realities has left this virtually unquestioned for millennia. We are all conditioned, no matter our gender, to put women (and children) last. With bold integrity, Salmona reveals female realities in a book that is feminist because it presents rigorous scholarship that does not succumb to conditioning or norms. She is not afraid to swim against an overwhelming tide and is as passionately an activist as a researcher and practicing psychiatrist. This rare combination gives way to a book like no other that reaches unapologetically to the heart of today's concerns in the world. Everyone who wants peace and safety for themselves and future generations should read it.

Salmona elaborates on the neurological underpinnings of behaviors in both victims and perpetrators of sexual violence. The socio-neurological paradigms she reveals shed light on all forms of discrimination (sex, race, religion, orientation, ability), as she provides a compelling and truly revolutionary framework for understanding inequality.

In addition to offering powerful overlooked evidence and astute analysis as to why violence and inequality persist, *Sexual Violence, Dissociation, and Inequality* is of inestimable value to professionals in regular contact with victims. Salmona explains how victims' behaviors are rooted in neurobiology as normal responses to abnormal situations. Amid a climate of victim-blaming denial, Salmona explains how grave the violation of victims' human rights truly is. Their "character flaws" are actually symptoms of trauma and should be taken as strong evidence that they were wronged, not as an excuse to discredit them. Most unprotected of all are children. Often prisoners of their tormentors, they are the perfect victims with the least risk of getting their criminally abusive parents caught.

The current norm in the United States is that although trauma-informed care is sometimes available, it is lacking crucial pieces of awareness offered by Salmona. In particular, she responds to the psychology of perpetrators: Their cruelty, intentionality, criminality, injust impunity, and (most significantly) the neurology of why they became abusers based on their own trauma. The words Salmona chooses are crucial: Perpetrators are called criminals (and not simply "bad parents" as they might be called in normative care). They broke laws that were in place and should have been enforced, meaning the victim's human rights were severely violated. This is a social-justice approach to care. It teaches victims that they are not failures; it is society that failed them.

Salmona's approach includes social-justice but also intricate studies of the brain. Although it involves "talk therapy," it is a more objective approach than psychoanalysis insofar as the pathway to healing does not mainly target victims' thoughts, feelings, or interpretations, except to legitimate that these are fairly standard relative to what happened. For example, claustrophobia is a normal response if someone has been nearly choked to death. Therefore, the symptom of claustrophobia may be used to trace back to an act of violence that has been forgotten (amnesia being the norm for severe violence and abuse).

But here's where Salmona really goes deeper than psychoanalysis: Reconstituting what happened and understanding its behavioral manifestations as normal responses to horrific abnormalities allows victims to "turn off the alarm" (amygdala), which is otherwise susceptible of going off at any time and resubmerging the victim into the physical state they were in at the time of the original violence. If untreated, the only way to "shut off the alarm" again is to repeat the trauma.

This finding is proven by neurological studies, yet before Salmona, no one has brought to the surface how significant this really is. Taking it even further, Salmona discovered that tracing all symptoms of trauma allows the victim to translate the raw emotion/alarm into a coherent narrative (reconnecting the amygdala and the hippocampus, severed during the trauma). Thus the violence can be correctly related as what was done to them, not what they are; they decolonize themselves. There is objectivity in this approach, not only in how consistently symptoms play out in victims but also in the contextualization of what happened to victims as part of a larger epidemic tragedy and social injustice.

This book swims against the current in many ways. The language here is very clear. We talk about victims, whereas it is popular to use the term "survivors." Far from meaning victimhood will stay with someone their whole lives, Salmona emphasizes that a crime was committed. This shifts the responsibility onto society. Whereas it is fashionable today to talk about "survivors" rather than victims, using the term "victim" is a conscious choice that emphasizes that there are also perpetrators and that sexual violence is a crime. "Survivors" could be of natural disasters, but victim implies that there was human agency: Someone intentionally set out to destroy them. This essential piece of the puzzle (the perpetrator's mind) is usually overlooked or downplayed, even in trauma-informed care.

Similarly, terms like "mother" and "father" are rife with contradictions, as they imply what society wants to believe: Parents want what's best for their children; if they don't, they are those exceptional monsters we sometimes see on the news, far from our lives, the aberrations that confirm the rule. In reality, many people have children to serve as medicine and slaves to treat their own traumatic memory. They don't believe their lies, and they know exactly what they are doing. Systemic injustice is rarely denounced, and Salmona highlights the necessity of this for healing.

Salmona's approach to treating victims' advocates other language choices that clearly distance themselves from myths and norms designed to silence and pathologize victims. Victims' behaviors are normal responses to abnormal and incredibly unjust situations; they are less about them and more about how they were "colonized" by the violence and how the authorities did not do their jobs to protect them. This is a radical approach to care for victims, and Salmona has helped many over decades of clinical practice. This includes fully curing people misdiagnosed with schizophrenia, ADHD, and other disorders without the use of medications. The responsibility shifts: In conditions usually attributed to the patient's own erroneous brain chemistry or random causes/no cause, traumatic memory is clearly identified, its behavior patterns elaborated, and it's finally treated as such.

Adequate measures not only for care but also for prevention can be found in this book. It is interesting to read it in light of the #MeToo movement, which heightened awareness of how pervasive and pernicious sexual violence is. #MeToo started in 2017, and there were numerous international offshoots, such as #MeTooInceste and #MeTooMedia in France in 2021. These movements finally identified sexual aggression as a form of systemic violence entrenching a sexual caste system of male privilege. Finally, the public at large was confronted with the truth:

Sexual violence is not only severely devastating to victims; it is also a form of and means for discrimination. This touches society as a whole insofar as it perpetuates male domination, often through insidious myths about sexuality and the nature of men and women.

Although #MeToo was important, the victims who were able to testify are only the small tip of an immense iceberg. The majority of victims, those who are the most vulnerable and the most in danger, remain gagged and invisible. Most are terrified victims under the fist of traumatic amnesia or control, with no tools or resources to identify what they have suffered and are suffering, let alone express it on social media. Many have known nothing else since childhood and have normalized the violence and exploitation that characterize the bulk of their lives. Victims are most often alone to repeat the cycles of victimization they have been groomed for, usually since childhood. This fits with gender and other roles and myths society imposes. This means unimaginable suffering but also a tragic loss to society.

The information and analysis Salmona provides is based on solid neurological evidence too often relegated to little-read academic papers and decades of clinical practice. It is of universal importance, though there are some specificities of the United States situation. For example, the United States has fewer social services than in France (heavily subsidized daycare, allowance for children, universal healthcare…). Lack of such services creates the most strain for single parents, 80% of whom are single mothers.

Social services are all the more less likely to detect abuse because they disproportionately scrutinize poor single mothers of color, although they are not statistically more likely to abuse their children than rich white couples. Abuse happens equally across socioeconomic and racial categories. This means that worthy mothers struggling to get by have their children taken from them and often abused in the foster care system. The other side of this same coin is that social workers almost never investigate parents in a higher socioeconomic bracket. I myself come from a family of a wealthy, educated white couple, and the abuse that went on was well-hidden by them but among the worst imaginable.

We need better measures to identify victims and bravely act on their behalf, even if this involves confronting powerful narcissists to rescue powerless children. The law needs to be applied, and this means equally for everyone, rich or poor. Working in a high school, I see students with obvious symptoms of trauma that are not being treated as such. They are blamed for their behaviors. These are considered parts of their personalities, not symptoms of what happened to them. Parents are generally believed—after all, they come across as the rational ones. Rarely are "troubled" students asked what is going on at home. In spite of the law, this is still implicitly considered a personal matter. This basically means people can abuse their children as much as they want (especially if they are rich, white, and good at hiding it). Narcissistic parents look great and are in stellar health because they are treating their own trauma through using their children, substitutes and surrogates to suffer in their place. This is how abusers treat the trauma they endured. They change the roles but not the script.

Fortunately, only a slim minority choose the path of using others. Because traumatic memory is almost always unacknowledged, even by health professionals, victims are left to their own devices. The way our brains are wired requires victims to relive the trauma either as victims or as perpetrators. Traumatized men are groomed to take the latter path and women the former, explaining persistent inequalities. The vast majority of victims have a strong ethical sense and would "rather" become victims again. (Let's recall that this neurological imperative is no weakness on their part; it is the normal response to abnormal violence.) A small number choose to become perpetrators instead, feeding the cycle. There are always plenty of victims available to them among adults who have already been victimized or among children. This is because society mostly allows this through inadequate detection and rare/unequal application of relevant laws.

It is, however, possible to treat traumatic memory so that victims recover fully. This involves piecing together what happened to them in all the details and the resultant feelings and behaviors. It involves recognizing the injustice of it and that their responses are normal. It involves decolonizing them from the trauma and the roles imposed by the perpetrators for perpetrators' own benefits, treating their own traumatic memory. This therapeutic approach involves no medication and is cumulative, so that the treatment (taking the form of conscious work reconstituting and demining with a compassionate professional until they learn to do this fully alone) does not require long-term care. It just requires that professionals be trained in this, which they are currently not, and that victims have access to their services. My hope is that all professionals read this book and teach it so that it becomes part of the standard curriculum and also that it reaches victims and their loved ones directly.

Until this happens, the usual case is that victims have no idea what happened to them, why they are different, why they have so many problems. Just as society and their loved ones blame them for their symptoms (unrecognized as such), victims internalize the blame (just as they took on the roles forced on them by their aggressors for their own survival). Even if people around victims do know that something horrible happened to them, victims are often told to get on with life—forget about it and move on. This is the most counterproductive advice possible.

In Salmona's illustration of this, victims are hiking up a mountain with a backpack full of rocks while others' packs are empty. No one sees the disadvantage they are at. They are told to keep up, don't slow everyone down; if by grueling exertion, they do keep up or even go past their peers, it is at great expense to their health and they have furnished unrecognized superhuman effort.

These past decades have seen great strides for victims but also tremendous backlash. New ways to discredit victims have emerged, such as theories about embedded memories. The majority of victims experience traumatic amnesia, and this increases the younger the victim was at the first act of violence and also with how severe the violence was. This is especially tragic insofar as many victims do not understand where their behaviors are coming from. They believe a society that they should just get their act together and move on.

The most vulnerable victims (who don't have access to the media) are the ones who should be protected and supported as a priority, and yet they are those who are least identified and spotted; denial remains in control. #MeToo has helped people finally realized that a large number of women and also some men have suffered sexual violence, often since childhood. They had to survive this violence and its consequences in total isolation, and most suffer constantly and are still in danger. Their tormentors, most often relatives, were never prosecuted.

The testimonies of victims that emerged as a result of #MeToo are countless and received enormous media coverage. They were corroborated by numerous investigations and by the expertise of organizations and professionals. It has therefore become difficult to ignore the scale and seriousness of sexual violence and the failure of governments to prevent it, protect victims and their rights, and punish the guilty.

After #MeToo, it has become impossible to ignore the cascading injustices, the enormous harm suffered by the victims, and the inhuman nature of sexual violence. We could have expected the public authorities to fight this violence and its impunity as a priority. This would mean measures to improve protection, care, and legal support for victims. It would include massive mobilization of legislative, human, and financial resources commensurate with the seriousness of sex crimes and their consequences.

This did not happen. Victimization surveys in France show us that sexual violence continues to increase every year. Worldwide, sex crimes against children are exploding on the internet: 100 million images and videos were recorded in 2023, compared to 1 million in 2014. Victims of sexual violence are still not being protected. The detection of violence by professionals should be systematic, but it is rare and incomplete. The provision of care is scarce and difficult to access, and health professionals are poorly trained. They are not aware of most of the findings in this book, though these are based on decades of research published in peer-reviewed papers. A bridge was missing between these findings and their application; this book is, finally, the bridge.

We know that sexual violence causes psycho-trauma that, if not specifically treated, has serious long-term consequences. For over 70% of victims, mental and physical health are severely impaired. Half suffer serious impairment in their studies and professional life, with a huge increase in the risk of poverty, homelessness, and addiction, and (significantly to Salmona's research) of experiencing violence again (MTV/Ipsos, 2019). The World Health Organization has recognized since 2010 that the psycho-traumatic consequences of sexual violence are a major public health problem and also that specialized treatment for psycho-trauma is effective and makes it possible to avoid the majority of the consequences. Lack of specialized care leads to huge loss of opportunity for the health and quality of life for victims.

Ignoring or blaming victims is easier than confronting a major social problem. This includes in mental health fields as well as in child protection, education, and the criminal justice system, wherein victims' psycho-traumatic disorders should be considered as forensic evidence. This is because psycho-traumatic symptoms are universal and pathognomonic (they are evidence of trauma). Instead of confirming their testimonies, such evidence is actually used against victims. It is used to under-mine their character. Evidence of past abuse discredits them, as do lapses due to traumatic amnesia. Whereas mixing up details, drawing blanks, or having vague, mixed-up recollections actu-ally indicates that something very serious happened (based on neurological understandings of trauma), such symptoms often are used as pretexts for dismissing acts of violence.

The rate at which sex criminals are brought to justice has always been low, and it is further decreasing. The figures in France are scandalous (but not exceptional): Only 0.6% of all rapists are convicted. Convictions for rape decrease each year (40% fewer in 2018 than in 2008). These shocking figures have had no media or political impact. They have led to no emergency measures to correct this obvious violation of international law (which obliges nations to pursue and punish sex offenders). Four years later, in 2022, amid general indifference, we learned that convictions for rape further decreased by 31% between 2019 and 2020. In 12 years, the number of convictions for rape decreased by half (Infostat Justice 2018, letter from the national observatory on violence against women n°17, November 2021).

Impunity contributes to the continuation of a profoundly unjust, unequal, sexist, and patriarchal society because it sends a message of tolerance to criminals and a message of abandonment to the victims whose rights are violated. Impunity encourages perpetrators to treat their own traumatic memory through committing these crimes. Again, this is one of the most astounding and overlooked findings of Salmona's research: The psychology of the perpetrator.

Impunity represents a powerful obstacle for victims who want to assert their rights. This alone is an unacceptable injustice. It also means that in society as a whole, there is a system of inequality in which those who hold privilege can freely use those who do not. They use them to treat their own traumatic memory, but this is excused by myths of inferiority (as we can see in the case of racism as well as misogyny). Impunity considerably aggravates inequalities, discrimination, the vulnerability and precariousness of victims, and it allows privileges and domination to be maintained. Laws exist but are not applied.

Salmona's work is crucial in asserting that victims' human rights are being violated. This is rarely stated clearly even in trauma-informed care in the United States, though it is a key component of Salmona's clinical practice. It is time to shift from a psychoanalytical approach that listens passively to victims to help them explore their feelings to a social-justice approach that clearly tells victims that they were wronged. Again, what happened to them was not, for example, "bad parenting" but criminal acts of torture on par with the most psychologically damaging (combat, torture, and sexual violence, particularly within the home).

It is time to train trauma-informed professionals to help victims trace each symptom to each traumatic event, overcoming amnesia, so they can fully understand themselves and reconnect the "alarm" and the "narrative" centers of the brain. This is the goal of Salmona's revolutionary approach to trauma-care, and it has been extremely successful, including in treating patients who were said to be (for example) schizophrenic, incurable, and needing to be medicated for life.

Research has proven the severity of sexual violence and its consequences. Nonetheless, just as society as a whole perpetrates myths and stereotypes that support rape culture, professions and institutions do the same. When it comes to sexual violence and its victims, they ignore both laws and research. Professionals repeat stereotypes about female and male sexuality, women as sex objects, sexuality, and violence. They subscribe to society's glamorization of "sexuality" that violates and degrades women and blame victims for their behavior, scrutinizing their appearance, history, and contact with perpetrators.

The pervasive rape culture severely harms victims by accusing them of false allegations, parental alienation, false memories, and so on. Pornography is rampant and freely available online, with children watching it from ever younger ages (average age of first viewing: 11). Pornography is not mainly just sexualized images anymore. Mainstream pornography categories feature gang rape, incest, underage, and racialized characters of women. This is where most children learn from their most vulnerable age what sex is, including roles for men and women. This early grooming or training is the cornerstone of a world that blames and delegitimizes victims, casting doubt on their testimonies and experiences while exonerating aggressors.

Violence—particularly sexual violence—is an instrument of power. It produces inequality, discrimination, and subjugation. At the core of this mechanism is traumatic memory. This original finding of Salmona is a game-changer that could revolutionize prevention and care for victims and lead to true equity in society.

Today, we cannot say that the reality of sexual violence and its psycho-traumatic consequences is still ignored because of lack of evidence. The research exists but is most often set apart in different disciplines and read only by isolated specialists. This book is relevant to specialists, to victims and their loved ones, and to anyone concerned with justice and equality, with detailed information and an accessible tone. The availability of information is not, however, the only hurdle on the path to justice for victims.

The evidence and knowledge accumulated over more than 20 years is irresponsibly disregarded by many professionals.

Australian criminologist Michael Salter notes an *active production* of doubt and ignorance with the aim of contesting the growing professional and public recognition of sexual violence against children. He identifies this as anti-epistemology. Anti-epistemology recognizes that gaps in knowledge and silences in discourse are not simple absences but rather the product of power relations (McGoey, 2012) and intensive processes of *delegitimization and production of ignorance* (Nelson, 2016). This means that power structures determine how knowledge is used and whether it is used. The challenge is not only to reveal the realities of traumatic memory to professionals and patients. It is also to combat the fact that the distribution and application of knowledge is, unfortunately, controlled by dominant institutions in their interests. This includes a large number of abusers in positions of power.

If we want the world to show solidarity and justice to victims of the serious human right violation that sexual violence is and for such crimes to be recognized, psycho-trauma must be taken into account. An absolute priority is to recognize that psycho-trauma is the logical and universal consequence of violence. It is necessary to inform the public and train professionals on the mechanisms of psycho-trauma (traumatic immobility, traumatic memory, and dissociation) and its serious repercussions on the health and lives of victims. This will make it possible to finally provide effective care, serve justice, and prevent huge suffering and loss of opportunity. Knowledge of psycho-trauma will finally overcome myths and sexist stereotypes at the origin of the almost systematic questioning of victims' words. This will finally restore victims' rights and dignity. This is the fight that Salmona is leading with Dr. Denis Mukwege, 2018 Nobel Peace Prize laureate, and what this book seeks to do.

Letting violence go unpunished, not protecting victims and not treating their psycho-trauma, generates violence in an endless cycle, from person to person and from generation to generation. The first risk factor for suffering or committing violence is having suffered it. Fighting violence means above all protecting victims, caring for them and providing them with justice. It is urgent to take action. It is time to stand in solidarity with victims and commit to the fight against sexual violence and all other forms of injustice.

Dr. Kate Rose

Notes

1   *Created in 2009, this organization and its website (memoiretraumatique. org) present data and resources for victims, professionals, and organizations. Its goal is to improve protection and care for victims of violence through better informing the public, training relevant professionals, and educating victims about the little-known neurological processes and resultant behaviors that are likely to "colonize" their lives. The underlying commitment is to end all forms of violence through widespread and accurate understanding of its mechanisms and adapted and relentless action, recognizing how severe the consequences of inaction continue to be.*

2   *"The Mukwege Chair aims to develop interdisciplinary research in the field of sexual violence against women and to bring together the knowledge on this issue from different partners and universities in Belgium and around the world." chaire-mukwege.uliege.be/cms/c*

3   Founded by Dr. Mukwege for survivors of the sexual violence used massively as a weapon of war in his native Democratic Republic of Congo, the Panzi Hospital treats both physical and psychological damage and helps victims rebuild their lives and communities. For more information on this incredible initiative and the global campaign to end rape for which Dr. Mukwege received the Nobel Peace Prize in 2018, go to panzifoundation.org

Introduction

Why is it important to be informed about sexual violence and its traumatic impact on victims? Since the first publication of this book in 2013, the #MeToo movement exploded. This hashtag, first appearing on social media in October 2017 during the Harvey Weinstein scandal, has had striking success in liberating the words of women who suffered sexual violence. Starting in the United States and spreading globally through successive waves—even to the least likely places—this historic advance has not stopped since.

It all began with a study published in the *New York Times* on the many actresses sexually assaulted by the most powerful producer in Hollywood. Although this had been known for decades, with several victims having already accused Harvey Weinstein, nothing had been done. Denial and the law of silence allowed the producer to continue sexually attacking actresses without any consequences. This scandal brought to light the frequency of sexual violence that women endure in the film industry, the seriousness of it, and the culture of denial and complicit tolerance. When victims' testimonies were finally in the media, there was so much outrage and solidarity that more women felt safe and legitimate in exposing the violence they too had endured. Words spread like wildfire, and women told their stories with the hashtag #MeToo. Suddenly, these women were heard, believed, and recognized, and the aggressors, so long protected, were finally questioned. A wind of hope and solidarity reached women throughout the world.

In France, the struggle against sexist and sexual violence was declared a national priority in November 2017. However, the hashtags #MeToo and the French #Balancetonporc (literally "denounce your pig," coined by journalist Sandra Muller) had

DOI: 10.4324/9781003497516-1

difficulty taking off. Victims' testimonies and accusations were framed as slander when the aggressors were named, and none of the public figures accused were affected. They continued their careers in prominent positions, even receiving sympathy. Sandra Muller was accused of slander by the man she named. (She was found guilty, though the case was dismissed on appeal.)

The voices of the most vulnerable and discriminated victims were silenced, though they represent the majority of cases (children, disabled and/or institutionalized people, minorities, and other marginalized groups). Many large-scale studies have shown how widespread discriminatory sexist violence sex and crimes against children are. The outpouring of influential testimonies, books, articles, plays, films, documentaries, and podcasts has revealed many institutions to be infected with sexual violence (the Church, the arts, sports, universities…). Research has now exposed astonishing numbers to quantify the prevalence and impunity of sexual violence amid overall indifference and rape culture.

It took legal scandals in France to bring to light the incredible lack of punishment that pedo-criminals (those who commit sex crimes against children) benefit from and the horrific mistreatment of victims. These scandals finally moved the general public, especially the case of Sarah in Pontoise and Justine in Meaux, little girls of 11 years old considered by the courts to have consented to be penetrated by 27- and 22-year-old men because there was no law about the age of consent in France. In 2017, we launched a manifesto against the lack of punishment for sex crimes and to better protect and respect the rights of victims. We demanded a national plan with eight urgent measures, and this was signed by 29 NGOs and nearly 106,600 individuals. It was presented to the head of France's Commission for Equality Between Men and Women. They followed through on some of our recommendations, such as the creation of an effective online platform to report sexist and sexual violence and the establishment of ten new centers to treat psycho-trauma (still far from the 100 we discussed).

A law was drafted and voted on in 2018 (Schiappa Law), but due to a lack of political courage, key measures were not taken.

Though the limit for reporting child sex crimes was extended to 30 years after the victim reaches adulthood, we did not obtain imprescriptibly (no time limit) for all cases or even for repeat crimes or in the case of traumatic amnesia. The law especially failed to put in place the age of consent as promised by the government, and even the president himself, to protect minors under 15 years old and incest victims. This was a huge disappointment since without an age of consent, the law could continue to consider children of any age as consenting to sexual acts.

The year 2020 was a turning point for exposing pedo-criminality and the propaganda that makes it tolerated. Vanessa Springora's memoir *Consent* accused a man who abused her when she was underage, famous writer Gabriel Matzneff. As Matzneff's writings celebrated sex with minors, she was accusing an entire intellectual and literary milieu that condoned sexual abuse under the pretext of elitism and sexual liberation. However, most pedo-crimes remained in the shadows, especially those committed within families, until early 2021 when Camille Kouchner published *La Familia Grande*. She exposed the repeated rape of her twin brother by their stepfather over the years and broke the silence on the ultimate taboo of incest.

It was time that victims of incest were no longer gagged! In one weekend, over 80,000 tweets were posted under the hashtag #MeTooInceste, with international echoes. The media rushed to the side of victims and gave them and those fighting for them large tributes. The exemplary media coverage of Camille Kouchner's book offered incest victims unprecedented legitimation and safety to tell their stories. They were finally heard. The idealization of the family, along with the denial, law of silence, and anti-victim propaganda of abusers and their accomplices—previously effective in disappearing crimes and reducing victims to silence—were shaken by this unprecedented clamor.

Society seemed to finally wake up and discover, horrified, the seriousness of this "cruel, degrading, and inhuman crime," as the European Court has called it. France's president himself responded by posting a video on Twitter in which he recognized the urgent need for radical social change. He committed to believing and protecting victims of childhood sexual violence and punishing perpetrators, putting an end to their impunity. His words were strong: "We are here. We hear you. We believe you. And you will never again be alone... These testimonies, these words, these screams—no one can ignore them any longer. Now it is time to take action to protect our children from sexual violence." Following this, the government and lawmakers sought reform, which led to what we were demanding for so long: A specific and enforced protection of children from sexual violence. This included voting in an age of consent of 15 years (18 years in the case of incest).

This decision, taken just three months after #MeTooInceste and including the creation of a new government agency called the Independent Commission on Incest and Sexual Violence Against Children (CIIVISE), is a historic advance, but it leaves much to be desired. The new law excludes many children from reinforced protection. The few measures planned to detect incest in schools and reimburse psychological care do not address the total failure of institutions to combat sexual violence. The measures mask how catastrophic the situation is.

The government has failed in all its obligations to prevent violence, protect and care for victims, and punish abusers. We need to find out the exact scope of the problem in order to implement solutions and necessary reforms. The government must take responsibility for having failed in its obligations and must be aware of this and make amends for those who were abandoned, endangered, ignored, unprotected, with no treatment, care, justice, or compensation. Their rights were trampled, and they endured a cascade of injustices, overwhelming prejudice, and scandalous loss of opportunities for health and social integration.

There is still a long road ahead to overcome denial, the law of silence, rape culture, sexist stereotypes, and theories that blame the victim. Many people still do not know about the psycho-traumatic consequences of sexual violence and the tremendous prejudice done to victims. Adding insult to injury, many are made to feel guilty about their own misfortune and portrayed as unworthy, illegitimate, and not deserving of solidarity.

For the past 30 years, there has been much propaganda based on stereotypes, false ideas, and lies. This persists despite groundbreaking advances in the understanding of sexual violence and the severity of its consequences. This ubiquitous propaganda infects institutions and leaves victims unheard and ignored. It also blocks the path to reform and awareness needed to protect victims, treat psycho-trauma, and make sure that justice is served. To get beyond this, it is necessary to inform and train people nonstop and to fight against inequality and discrimination, especially for victims' rights to be believed, protected, cared for, and compensated.

None of this is simple. Despite impressive progress these past decades, denial, silence, impunity, and rape culture are fed by sexist stereotypes and hateful anti-victim theories that persist in the face of scientific discoveries and advances. Sexual violence continues to be seen through the deforming lens imposed by perpetrators and their accomplices. It is essential to gain justice for victims, legitimize their words, and recognize their suffering. If now most people agree that sexual violence is a serious and traumatic violation of rights, dignity, and physical and psychological well-being, it is because of the hard work feminists have done over decades.

In France, over the past 30 years, a huge amount of work has been done by feminist organizations to inform people and organize actions to end sexual violence. They succeeded in getting hotlines put in place, such as "women-rape-information" (women anywhere in France can dial 39-19 or 119), and (in 2018) a government platform to report sexist and sexual violence through an online chat button operating 24/7. In the United States, Rape, Abuse & Incest National Network (RAINN) offers constant support to sexual assault victims through an online chat and a free hotline (800-656-4673). France's triannual government plans have included combatting violence against women since 2011 and now specifically mention rape and sexual aggression. These are national priorities for the five-year plan of current president Emmanuel Macron. In 2017, sexual violence against children was finally considered for the first three-year plan, and in 2018 and 2021, new laws to reinforce prevention of sexual violence against children were voted in, with an agency for incest prevention (CIIVISE) created in 2021.

In France, sexual aggression is now legally considered a misdemeanor to be handled by the magistrates' court (*tribunal correctionnel*) and rape is among the most severe crimes handled by the circuit court (*cour d assises*). There have been many recent actions that led to improvements in the 1980 law, which defined sexual aggression and rape as violations or sexual penetration using violence, constraint, threat, or surprise:

◆ There is now a more complete and precise definition of moral constraint and surprise (with the laws on February 8, 2010 and August 3, 2018), with the crime of rape considered: "Any act of penetration of any nature or any act of mouth-to-genital contact" (according to the April 21, 2021 law) "committed on another or on the perpetrator through the use of violence, constraint, threat, or surprise."

◆ The April 21, 2021 law added crimes of rape and sexual aggression specific to minors when committed by adults according to an age of consent of 15 years if the age difference is five years or more and an age of consent of 18 years for incest committed by a family member or someone having authority in law or in practice over the victim. These new crimes and misdemeanors specifically about adults abusing minors do not require proof of violence, constraint, threat, or surprise for victims to press charges.

◆ Since 2006, rape between spouses was legally recognized.

◆ Prostitution is now recognized as sexual violence, and since 2016, the "customer" is punished. Using prostitutes under 15 years old legally qualifies as rape or sexual aggression.

◆ The definition of sexual harassment was extended to create a new misdemeanor called "sextortion."

◆ The time limit for reporting doubled for adult victims in 2017, from three to six years for misdemeanors and 10 to 20 years after adulthood for rape and aggravated sexual assaults; in 2018, this was extended to 30 years for rape. In 2021, this was further extended in the case of repeated sexual misdemeanors by the same attacker on multiple underage victims (the limits for reporting rape and sexual aggression were prolonged).

◆ We know much more about sexual violence and its heavy impact on victims' mental and physical health than we did two decades ago, following major studies in France and internationally. We have now been able to prove how serious and widespread sexual violence is. We can identify the psycho-traumatic disorders that all victims are likely to manifest and find concrete evidence of neurological damage. We are familiar with the neurobiological mechanisms and resulting symptoms and have devised specific treatments that work. Since 2018, we have finally been able to open 15 psycho-trauma centers in France (out of the 100 we are asking for).

The scientific and sociological advances in research have unfortunately not resulted in significant changes in practice. This is due to the law of silence, denial, and almost total impunity for abusers. Lack of training for professionals, absence of recognition and protection, and abandonment of sexual violence victims remain the norm.

Not recognizing the realities of sexual violence—its frequency and severe traumatic effects—means it is considered as isolated incident rather than systemic sexism. Rape culture—with its false representations and stereotypes that imply the victim is lying, provoked the rape, or consented—continues to guarantee almost total impunity for perpetrators. Sexual violence is, however, considered under European law as a cruel, inhuman, and degrading form of torture—a definition gaining ground internationally. The World Health Organization has classified sexual violence as a major social and public health problem since 2010. Sex crimes are among the most serious crimes, and nations are required to prevent and punish them no matter who the perpetrator is.

Even when sexual violence is recognized, its psycho-traumatic consequences are not, and specific, effective treatment is rarely offered. Lack of knowledge concerning psycho-traumatic symptoms explains why victims are most often misunderstood. They are blamed for reactions and behaviors that are the normal psycho-traumatic consequences of sexual violence (McFarlane, 2010). This guilty ignorance is responsible for the discrediting of victims' words during police and court procedures. Standard reactions to trauma such as tonic immobility, traumatic memory, and dissociation are more often used to discredit victims than as evidence.

The most traumatized and endangered victims are likely to also be the most dissociated and anesthetized emotionally, which means that those assigned to protect and care for them rarely fear for them ("she doesn't seem to mind, so why should I?"). Traumatic dissociation is wrongly perceived as an absence of suffering and sensitivity or as an intellectual limitation. Tragically, the dissociated victim receives indifference at best from those assigned to her case or her care, and she is also very likely to be mistreated and revictimized by those designated to help her.

Why is this still happening when objective evidence exists to describe psycho-traumatic disorders clinically and we have effective tools to diagnose and treat them? Specific therapies can reintegrate traumatic memory as autobiographical memory through repair of neurological damage, thanks to the brain's neuroplasticity (Elhing, 2003). Full recovery is possible without medication or medicalized procedures, with the help of specially trained, caring, and socially engaged professionals knowledge-able about sexual violence and traumatic memory.

Reluctance to implement this valuable knowledge is largely due to ignorance and societal misrepresentations. Many people are unaware of these facts:

◆ Sexual violence happens everywhere and is usually committed by a man close to the victim: 90% of cases for adult victims and 94% for child victims, according to the 2018 ONDRP and 2015 IVSEA studies.
◆ More than 1 in 6 women and 1 in 20 men have been victims of sexual violence (CSF, 2008).
◆ The majority of victims are children: 81% of sexual violence victims were under 18 when the abuse began; 51% were

under 11, and 21% were under six years old. Nearly 60% of rapes are of minors. Eighteen percent of women and 7.6% of men were sexually abused in childhood.

◆ Each year, 94,000 adult women and 16,000 adult men are victims of rape or attempted rape (United Nations statistics).

◆ Each year, 130,000 girl children and over 35,000 boy children are victims of rape or attempted rape (United Nations).

◆ Ten percent of French people have been victims of incest, meaning 6.7 million people ("Face à l'inceste"/IPSOS 2020). The average age of child victims is ten (CSF, 2008; OMS, 2014; IVSEA, 2015; VIRAGE, 2017; MTV/IPSOS, 2019). France is by no means an exception.

◆ Pedo-criminality is rampant on the internet! We cataloged 1 million photos and videos in 2014, 45 million in 2018, and over 70 million in 2019 depicting children (90% girls) younger and younger (3–13 years for 90% of them) exploited most often by members of their families (99% men) and enduring increasingly barbarous acts. France has the third largest number of sites and users in the world (second in Europe). Nine out of ten of the abusers are male, and 25–30% are minors. The vast majority are known by the victim, and over half are family members (IVSEA, 2015; VIRAGE, 2017; MTV/IPSOS, 2019).

◆ Fewer than 10% of rape victims report the crime, and under 1% of rapists are condemned (ONDRP, 2018, Infostat justice, 2018).

◆ Condemnations for rape have gone down 40% in the past decade (Infostat justice, 2018). Rapists are the most likely of any criminals to get away with it.

◆ Eighty three percent of sexual violence victims say they were not protected, and the least protected are also the most vulnerable and discriminated against: Children, minorities, and disabled people… (IVSEA, 2015).

◆ Having been abused or not abused in childhood is the main determining factor of health 50 years later if no specific care is given (Felitti and Anda, 2010).

◆ Sexual violence impacts the brain, provoking neurological damage and setting off neurobiological safety
mechanisms. This manifests as tonic immobility and
makes it impossible for the victim to react. Dissociation
anesthetizes her and traumatic memory forces her to
relive the violence for years or decades, if nothing is done
to treat it (Rauch, 2006; Salmona, 2013).

◆ For 95% of sexual violence victims, consequences on
mental health are reported as serious or very serious
(IVSEA, 2015).

◆ Forty two percent of sexual violence victims attempt suicide, with 50% in the case of incest and rape in childhood
(IVSEA, 2015).

These facts are too little known. United States statistics (cited
by RAINN) are similar or higher, and there are many countries
where sexual violence is even more prevalent. Our 2019 study
showed that the average French person still underestimates the
extent of sexual abuse, and most wrongly believe that rape is
usually committed by strangers in public places on sexually
attractive adult women. Their perception of sexual violence relies
on the myth of impulses and uncontrollable sexual desire that
the victim arouses through her behavior, what she is wearing, or
the risks she takes. Many people (over 75%) do not realize that
rapes occur in all social settings and are usually committed by
those close to the victim, who is most often underage.

Even if they know the law and definition of sexual aggression,
they are unaware of how rarely sexual violence is punished,
and they overestimate the number of crimes reported and of
perpetrators condemned. Ninety percent think that the number
of sentencings for rape has risen in the past ten years when it has
actually gone down 40% (MTV/IPSOS, 2019)!

This persistent denial is part of rape culture and explains why
the vast majority of victims must survive alone with no protection, justice, or reparation for the sexual violence they most often
endured repeatedly since early childhood. Alone, they endure
the catastrophic consequences of psycho-trauma on their health
and lives without help or adequate care. This abandonment of

the vast majority of victims represents a loss of opportunity and a severe violation of their human rights. It is urgent to put in place adapted and accessible care by trained specialists for all victims. "This is a global problem of public health of epidemic proportions that requires urgent action," declared Dr. Margaret Chan, director of the World Health Organization, in 2013.

If victims were informed about the neurobiological mechanisms, symptoms, and typical consequences of violence and offered specific assistance and care, they could escape from hell and finally find relief. As this victim of incest in childhood related in an email to our organization:

> Reading your article on traumatic memory and dissociative mechanisms allowed me to understand what I hadn't before: the reasons behind my self-destructive behaviors. I was finally able to talk with those close to me. This is quite a relief. I am returning to myself and putting all the guilt that I accumulated behind me regarding my risk-taking (drinking myself unconscious, unsafe sex…). I am much gentler with myself and my two children.

It is essential that those close to victims and the professionals who care for them have the tools to better understand, protect, and support victims. As for perpetrators, such tools could also help them confront the serious consequences of their acts. Everyone should have these tools to help prevent, combat, and punish all forms of violence.

To abolish sexual violence, we must combat denial, the law of silence, false ideas, impunity, and inequality that leave most victims unrecognized, unprotected, and uncared for. Currently, most victims do not receive any specific treatment or guidance that takes into account what we know about neurobiology, and their abusers walk free. It is necessary to spread the information far and wide about the law, human rights, the realities of sexual violence, and its consequences. Everyone needs to know that sexual violence has nothing to do with sexuality. It is a massive weapon of domination, destruction, submission, and social control.

Sexual violence is above all male violence against women; it is sexist, hateful, and discriminatory. It is part of a patriarchal context of force and inequality in which children and the most vulnerable are discriminated against. Girl children are the most harmed: Victims are 83% girls and 17% boys. Disabled children are 4–6 times more often victims than abled children; orphans, institutionalized, and racialized children are also targeted (VIRAGE, 2017; ONDRP, 2017; MTV/IPSOS, 2019; Danmeyer, 2016).

Everyone needs to know that there are serious long-term consequences on the life and health of victims, which makes sexual violence a major human rights issue for society and public health: It is most urgent to address it.

Everyone needs to know what traumatic memory and traumatic dissociation are, without which victims will never be fully understood or recognized, nor will the seriousness of violence be taken into account. One of our goals is to create awareness that leads to public outcry against sexual violence so that it is no longer tolerated and perpetrators are no longer free to continue their abuse. There needs to be solidarity with victims so that they are no longer alone and can get help, justice, and compensation. As the title of the 2015 UNICEF France report states, "every child counts," and most victims are children. Every woman and man also counts and must be protected from sexual violence; this is an urgent priority. I hope this book will contribute to awareness, prevention, and healing.

1.1 In a Victim's Own Words: The Need for Competent Care

May 2012: "I saw a psychiatrist for the first time at age 17 while hospitalized for anxiety attacks and hallucinations.

Shortly thereafter, I requested psychotherapy because I felt very badly and often thought of suicide. Every week, I saw a psychologist at the psychotherapy center near my home. She didn't speak to me or answer my questions. She just listened.

I had many more stays in mental hospitals, around 15 total, lasting a few days to several months, due to anxiety, hallucinations, dissociation, and some suicide attempts. I was treated by the psychologist and various local psychiatrists for around 7 years.

After this, I lead a mostly normal life until the day I separated from my partner, after enduring several years of psychological abuse. I collapsed. I sought help and began psychotherapy with a professional specializing in couples. She didn't talk to me or answer my questions; she just listened. I saw her every week for 6 years, during which the physical, psychological, and sexual abuse I endured in the past surfaced in my memory in invasive ways. I suffered from serious physical and mental disorders and was again put in a mental hospital.

I thought I was crazy, but at the same time, I wanted to know exactly what illness I suffered from. I needed to put a name to it. I got an appointment with a specialized service at Sainte-Anne hospital to get a diagnosis. The psychiatrist saw me for 15 minutes and told me I was borderline. I read a lot about this but did not recognize myself in it.

My therapy continued, and I still wanted to know what I was suffering from. I found the internet forum of Alice Miller and participated in it. Alice Miller is the therapist who spoke out against the mistreatment that adults, usually parents, often inflict on children. This was the first time I could talk about the abuse and have people actively listen, believe, understand, and get angry. These people were not therapists, but with them I began to dismantle the abuse that had become part of me. I understood that abuse in my childhood and adolescence were at the origin of my disease, and that I was not crazy but rather a victim.

I got in touch with an organization for mistreated children and adult survivors. I was able to see a therapist for the first time who would exchange with me and answer my questions. But one year later, she moved away.

When this happened, I hadn't been leaving home except to see my therapist, go to work, and do groceries. It was difficult for me to use public transportation. I stepped away from the world. The symptoms came back, and I suffered from disabling physical and mental disorders. I had to find a psychiatrist to help me. The next one was with me for 7 years. It wasn't easy, because anytime I had a breakdown, she'd offer me long-term or permanent medication. I always refused this, because my goal was a shorter treatment and full recovery.

I started a new therapy with a psychologist from an organization that assists victims of family violence. Faced with my questions, she suggested that I might be suffering from post-traumatic stress. I didn't know what this was and wanted to learn more. I searched and read everything I could about mental trauma, post-traumatic stress, and victims' lives.

Through my research, I found out about a center specializing in the treatment of psychotrauma. I called to make an appointment and get a diagnosis. They refused to see me, without any explanation. This refusal hit me hard, and I felt discouraged and exhausted. I lost trust and felt I was treated as less than human.

Around 2 years ago, suffering from invasive breakdowns at any moment and still seeking a diagnosis, I found the website of the organization Traumatic Memory. All the information I read there corresponded exactly to what I was feeling and to the hell I was living. It was amazing to learn that my terrifying physical and mental disorders were normal. To know how my brain and body were working during and after the abuse provided unhoped-for relief.

It meant I was not crazy. Physical, mental, and sexual abuse were at the origin of my disorder, and that didn't stem from me: I was normal. I had just developed traumatic memories that could be treated, and I could be healed.

Since my first meeting with a psychiatrist, 36 years have gone by. During these years, I met with 21 psychiatrists and 10 psychologists, without ever finding what I needed: 36 years of selftorture, searching, struggling, hope and loss of hope, and overwhelming solitude.

Today, I hate it that victims still have to be extremely lucky to find treatment with someone truly competent and be able to recover and thrive."

1

The Consequences of Sexual Violence

DURING MY FIRST CONTACT WITH a medical environment, I was revolted by the indifference and insensitivity with which many doctors treat patients who are victims of violence, especially sexual violence.

This indifference and insensibility, along with a cruel lack of caring, shocked me even more while I was an intern specializing in psychiatry. I naively expected that psychiatrists would be especially active in fighting against violence and caring for victims, on the contrary, denial and minimalization of victims' suffering were the norm in the psychiatric institution.

1.1 A Public Health Crisis That Doctors Ignore

Today, the situation has not changed much. Doctors, in general, and psychiatrists, in particular, still have little interest in victims of sexual violence. This is even more incomprehensible in that the serious consequences of violence on health have been scientifically proven through research over the past decades. Studies done internationally show the frequency of violence has serious impact on the physical and mental health of victims. Psycho-traumatic disorders have finally been identified and classified as normal, defining neurobiological consequences present in all victims of

DOI: 10.4324/9781003497516-2

violence. The neurobiological mechanisms at the origin of such disorders are now well known (Yehuda, 2007; MacFarlane, 2010). Sexual violence, along with acts of torture, is the most psychologically damaging form of violence. For a rape victim, the risk of developing post-traumatic stress is 80% for adults and nearly 100% for children, compared with an average of 24% for all traumatized victims (Breslau, 1991; Rodriguez, 1997).

Since 1996, then in 2014, the World Health Organization declared that violence is a major public health problem in the world. The ACE study in the United States, led by Felitti and Anda (1998, 2010), surveyed 17,000 people and published results in the most prestigious international medical journals. They showed that 50 years after having endured violence and serious neglect in childhood, people present a considerably higher rate of early death, organic pathology (heart attack, hypertension, diabetes, bronchopulmonary disorders, sexually transmitted infections, chronic pain, and so on), mental pathologies (post-traumatic stress, suicide, depression, anxiety, panic attacks, personality disorders, insomnia, problems with memory and concentration, etc.), addictions (alcohol, drugs, tobacco), eating disorders, unsafe sex, and risk of new violence throughout life (as victim or perpetrator) (WHO, 2010; IVSEA, 2015, Hillis, 2016; Fulu, 2017). Abuse and neglect in childhood can decrease life expectancy by 20 years, depending on what happened (Brown, 2009).

Recent evidence documents the biology of violence, showing that traumatic stress endured in response to violence can harm the brain's architecture, the immune system, metabolism, and inflammatory responses (Anda, 2010). Early experiences of violence can cause lasting neuronal, endocrine, and immune system damage, and it can even increase the genetic alternation of DNA (Anda, 2010; Perroud, 2011; Danese, 2012; Heim, 2013).

Most doctors' lack of interest in the consequences of violence on health leads to a considerable loss of opportunity in victims of sexual violence. Victims are usually abandoned or mistreated by doctors. Knowledge and new discoveries in this field are not very widespread. Only few universities often train in psychotrauma and it is not part of the medical school curriculum even for students specializing in psychiatry. A study by France's

Interministerial Mission for the Protection of Women Victims of Violence and for Combatting Human Trafficking (MIPROF) conducted an investigation in 2013 with 1,472 medical students (all years) and found that 82% of them received no training about sexual violence, while 95% think that doctors have a major role to play for victims, and over 95% want to receive training to detect and treat violence and its consequences. Doctors are often in contact with victims, so it would make sense for them to be informed and perhaps read some of the hundreds of publications and studies readily available on the internet. Few do so. Most doctors, like the rest of the population, adhere to stereotypes and the law of silence and denial.

1.2 Non-Assistance to Those in Danger

It is rare that doctors are capable of identifying the standard psycho-traumatic symptoms in their patients and linking them to violence endured. Even rarer are those who know how to treat them—and the right treatment in time could prevent much damage and a lifetime of suffering and loss. Treatments can avoid almost all negative consequences on life and health, including premature death and new violence that feeds the cycle.

Most doctors consider that violence is not serious and that victims are somehow responsible for it, so it's up to them to live with the consequences and find their own solutions. The assumption is that they let it happen, were weak, or made poor judgments—live and learn. Doctors routinely ignore psycho-traumatic symptoms and prefer to consider victims fragile and torn by inner conflicts. This is easier than naming the intentional destruction of sexual violence. Victims are unfairly considered responsible for their own suffering.

Victims need a totally different discourse. They need competent doctors who express solidarity and a humanistic discourse that recognizes violence and suffering. They need to speak out against sexual violence and remind victims that what happened to them was criminal so that victims can extract themselves from the violence and start piecing themselves together.

What victims should hear from doctors is, "We're going to protect you, make you safe, help you, and heal you. The symptoms you experience are the usual consequences of violence, and we can treat them. Your suffering is normal, legitimate, and proportional to the seriousness of the violence endured. The one who abused you had no right to do that; it's very serious and nothing could justify it; it is punishable by law, and you have the right to press charges ..." This is even more important than creating a warm and welcoming atmosphere, as recognizing the reality of how serious violence is and giving relevant information is already therapeutic. A treatment specifically centered on sexual violence is by far the most effective.

Perpetrators must be held accountable and the harm done repaired. In a democratic society every person has the fundamental right to safety, life-saving care, and justice/application of the law. A society that allows violence to happen and abandons victims is profoundly unjust and unequal. It is a society of hierarchical privilege, and the law of might makes right.

1.3 Is Sexual Violence Inevitable?

Many doctors think that sexual violence only concerns private life. They think it is about family norms, conflicts, preferences, or passionate love relations; conveniently, it is none of their business. The Hippocratic Oath that they take comforts them in this if they can ignore the law: "When allowed into homes, my eyes will not see what goes on there."

Often, doctors subscribe to catastrophic societal norms about sexuality. They think that sexual violence is about seduction and is part of human nature, thus condoning pornography, prostitution, and harassment. For them, it is not violence but sex, and it would be unreasonable, outdated, or prudish to oppose it. Some wrongly think that giving patients explanations about psycho-trauma or asking them to talk about the abuse would make them feel worse. For agitated patients, doctors are more likely to medicate, sedate, or even restrain or lock them up than they are to seek antecedents of trauma and make connections. Although today's doctors are more respectful than in the past, we still have a long way to go. Some doctors treat sexual violence victims as less than human.

Mental and physical suffering in victims is hugely underestimated by doctors, who often consider it exaggerated or unimportant. Patients are thought to be lying or to have ulterior motives. Some doctors even take advantage of their position to further sexually abuse patients.

1.4 Discourse of Denial

A doctor specializing in psycho-traumatology was working in a rehab center for drug addicts and recently told me that while their team was being inspected, she spoke of the incest a patient was victim of in childhood. The supervisor responded, "Incest is good sometimes," while a psychologist from the team said: "so what?" He'd been assigned to this patient for two years and didn't know or care about the incest that would, however, explain her addiction. This same doctor spoke callously about the trauma of a young woman addicted to crack and still experiencing sexual violence. The woman could only say "he helps himself" to describe the violence, not able to name it; the supervisor remarked, "I doubt that. She's not so young anymore."

Too often, doctors impose treatments that are totally inappropriate, paying no attention to patient's needs or opinions. They think they know best and don't hesitate to preach and moralize, totally removed from patients' reality. They destabilize and humiliate victims and confuse them even more.

Such doctors, when faced with a six-year-old boy presented as disobedient, insomniac, a runaway, masturbating compulsively, and exposing himself are likely to tell him, "It's not okay to do that," and to tell his parents that they need to impose their authority better so that the child will obey. Finally, a sedative or amphetamines will be prescribed for the boy's attention problems without anyone asking what the child endured to cause such behaviors. If his mother tries to speak about molestation by an elder brother of 13, they sweep away the information—that has nothing to do with it, just child's play.

If the patient is a 14-year-old girl failing in school, disobedient, "gothic," suicidal, using drugs and alcohol, scarring herself, suffering from anxiety, depersonalization, and eating disorders, others will make light of it as just part of adolescent boundary-pushing and thrill-seeking. But they will also lecture her: "That's dangerous. You're worrying your parents, who do everything for you ...." Or they might hospitalize her for months with heavy medication. They never ask about violence, although asking is all it took for this patient to finally speak about incestuous rape by her father at the age of 7. If this same adolescent became pregnant from this incest and went to a doctor to ask for an abortion, the doctor might still ask no questions about possible violence and instead make her feel guilty about not using conception, as if she just had to be more responsible and informed, or shame her "so it doesn't happen again."

To a young African woman, 19 years old and recently arrived in France, who screamed while in labor and was seized with terror and distress so strong, she asked to be killed, and who did not want to take her newborn into her arms, was treated with total ignorance and condescension, called hysterical and, not holding back their racism, they said, "It's cultural." They didn't bother to take into account that this young woman had been through the trauma of genital mutilation and was forced into a marriage where she was repeatedly raped by a man 40 years her senior.

The indifference and incoherence of doctors is rooted in sexism, and it disgusted me during my medical studies. With other students and a few remarkable doctors, we formed a movement to fight abuse of power among doctors and for radical change in doctor-patient relations. Many years later, there has been some progress, but most doctors are still indifferent to violence.

The most brutal shock came when I was an intern in a mental hospital in 1986. I wasn't prepared for the tremendous violence of this closed universe, especially since a revolution in psychiatry supposedly took place in the 1960s. This had made it appear an appealing field for us students.

During the "revolution," many humanistic intellectuals and psychiatrists such as Lucien Bonnafé helped gain a new vision of the mentally ill and psychiatric care centered on the whole person. They rethought "craziness" in political and sociological terms as the symptom of dysfunction produced by alienating systems. The discovery of neuroleptics, a new and highly efficient medication to treat delusions, was associated with new sectors of care and development of medical-psychological hospitals and day hospitals. This made it possible to treat mental patients not only in "asylums" but also "beyond the walls," avoiding that they be locked up for life.

However, in spite of these tremendous improvements, most patients who were "locked up" in psychiatric hospitals were still considered incurable and interested almost no one, except when they presented bothersome behavior disorders that were necessary to calm using physical and chemical straightjackets. Though "asylums" changed their names and were called "specialized hospitals," the conditions remained those of immense ghetto villages shut off from the outside world in which patients had no rights. There was institutional violence from care workers, and the law of might makes right among inmates. There was a black market for drugs and alcohol, and violence against the most vulnerable, including sexual violence, was everywhere and never spoken about, including rape and prostitution.

The mentally ill are a population separate from others, not part of the "us" of care personnel, the "sane." This underclass of people do not benefit from the same rights and can be deprived of freedom without having committed any crime or misdemeanor. They are exposed to much violence and danger in the name of their supposed welfare, safety, and health. Mental illness was considered endogenous (caused by factors within the organism), meaning not due to things that happened, and medical treatment consisted of making the most obvious symptoms disappear through medication and isolation.

The violence endured by most mental patients that I came across during my internship was never considered, although it was very serious, including torture, rape, and attempted murder, most often from early childhood. This was never connected to their mental state, although post-traumatic stress had already been identified by the medical community. It was not, however, normally studied by doctors, even psychiatrists, or used for diagnostics and therapeutic orientation. Victims of violence unjustly found themselves excluded, locked up, and condemned to a life of suffering, with fewer rights than the criminals who abused and destroyed them in the past (which no one asked them about).

1.5 The Deception of Psychoanalysis

Psychoanalysis often appears as a seductive alternative to conventional psychiatry. It uses a gentler approach centered on talk therapy, letting the patient speak, viewing her as a subject, and interpreting her symptoms and behaviors. Psychoanalysis, however, cares little about the actual violence patients have been victims of. It connects their suffering to inner conflicts and asks them to consider their subconscious impulses, desires, and fantasies, with no attempt to gain justice or find links between symptoms and violence endured. It can be helpful for some patients if done with a well-intentioned therapist, but it cannot cure traumatic memory.

The central concept of psychoanalysis, the Oedipus Complex, and the Freudian vision of sexuality were always problematic to me. From the beginning, I simply could not believe they applied to everyone. They seemed unjust and incoherent, whether for patients or for myself. They seemed outdated and constructed on a sexist vision of male-female relations and a catastrophic view of sexuality. Sex was viewed as an inherently violent and predatory impulse that needed to be contained and sublimated through civilization and education.

As a young feminist, I was enraged by the tranquil misogyny of psychiatric institutions. They took certain "fantasies" and "personality traits" to be innate in women without asking whether these might be the consequence of omnipresent sexual and sexist violence. Furthermore, faced with many patients who were survivors of incest, I found the Oedipus Complex not only useless but also profoundly unjust and intolerable!

1.6 Taking Sexual Violence into Account

The work of psychiatrist Sándor Ferenczi, a marginal disciple of Freud, became known in France starting in the 1960s. In 1932, he wrote about "the confusion of tongues between adults and the child" and how it leads to abuse. He reintroduced Freud's theory of seduction against the will of Freud, who abandoned it in 1897.

Freud first considered that "seduction"—in reality sexual aggression inflicted by adults on children—was at the root of neurotic and especially "hysterical" behavior. This finding, however, revealed sexual violence to be both rampant and very harmful; it meant that many of his patients had been sexually abused in childhood. So, Freud then denied this disturbing and consequential finding by developing notions of fantasy and the Oedipus Complex. The sexuality of children, considered as traumatized by adult aggression in his first theory of seduction, became, in the new theory of impulses, traumatized for the child due to sexuality's own nature.

Ferenczi was the only direct disciple of Freud who recognized the seriousness of sexual aggression—most often incest—endured by his patients as children. He was the first to, with extreme benevolence, look into sexual trauma in childhood and how it becomes adult suffering. He described the consequences with precision, proposed radical new treatment, and spoke out against adult behaviors that traumatize children. Most psychoanalysts ignored his findings for over half a century, and only recently have they become a reference in caring for victims of abuse.

1.7 Care for Victims: A Personal Commitment

Since adolescence, my plan to become a doctor was largely due to a thirst for justice in understanding and healing victims of violence. Many painful experiences are at the origin of this plan.

The first concerns my relations with the adult world during childhood and early adolescence. This was a world of all-powerful violence in which the lives and words of children could be ignored, including their suffering and their needs. Adults showed shameless dishonesty and incoherence toward children, scorning their ability to see that the emperor has no clothes. I saw that girls were considered inferior and were sexualized and taught to hate their bodies; they could mainly hope to be a seductive object and servant for men, and access was barred to many professions.

I made a solemn contract with myself that I would never become like those adults, flaunting an incoherence and indecency allowed by their position of power. I would never give up working toward a world of truth and justice, where children would have rights and women would be considered equal to men in all ways: A world of coherence and without violence.

When I was 13, I found out about the unthinkable genocide of Jews during the Holocaust by reading first-hand accounts and history books on my parents' bookshelf. This was a terrible shock, at the origin of many nightmares in which I identified with the victims. What despaired me the most was how survivors were treated after the camps were liberated. They were condemned to silence, anonymity, and horrific suffering and solitude. They were told to turn the page and go on with life in a society reconstructing itself. Not helping victims seemed to me gratuitous violence and serious injustice that added to the monstrosities endured. I promised myself I would do something about this.

After I graduated from high school, my father died at 48 years old from stomach cancer due to excessive smoking and drinking—a kind of drawn-out suicide. His depression and addiction were clearly linked to the personal history I pieced together: Unhappy childhood with abusive mother, incestuous nanny, and absent father, then an adolescence full of failure despite his intelligence. To escape this family in which he and his sister were slaves, he joined the army at age 19, just after WWII, and spent two years in Indochina. He came back even more traumatized and destructively alcoholic and did odd jobs to survive. At 24, he met my mother, "the only love of his life"—his life buoy. He became totally dependent on her. He didn't want any children so that he wouldn't have to share his wife—medication-crutch-bandage—with anyone. Finally, he accepted my unplanned birth, and both my mother and I were prisoners of his open wounds. Despite our efforts, it was impossible to heal these. He died much too young, but in time to know that I graduated high school and was going to study medicine. His slow death by self-destruction enraged me. He died from what had happened to him: That was clear to me, although I was the only one; doctors claimed it was due to his personality and his genes. It was his history that should have been treated. Since then, I've worked for over 20 years treating patients by uncovering with them their past, connecting it with their symptoms, and explaining the neurobiological and behavioral consequences of trauma while fighting for justice and an end to all forms of violence.

2

The Shattered Mind

2.1 Mechanisms of Traumatic Memory and Dissociation

Violence, especially sexual assault and abuse, has overwhelming power to immobilize victims and colonize their psyches. It also affects witnesses, loved ones, and professionals working with victims. Understanding how violence and trauma play out in the brain is crucial for victims to overcome their colonizing and numbing effects. Awareness of victims' normal physical and psychological responses to violent attacks or abusive acts is necessary to prevent lasting trauma. However, most people—including professionals who assist victims— are not familiar with how psychological trauma works. This means that victims are not given adequate support from those around them. No one can understand their behaviors, and no one wants to think about the horrors they endured. Victims are told to forget the past and move forward. They are most often silenced, or they choose to keep their suffering to themselves for fear of traumatizing those around them. Many stay quiet because they do not want to risk being misunderstood, not believed, or mistreated by those who are supposed to help and heal them.

DOI: 10.4324/9781003497516-3

2.2 The Brain on Psycho-Trauma

Most people do not realize that the psychological harms of violence are rooted in neurobiology. They are classified as psycho-traumatic disorders, such as post-traumatic stress disorder (PTSD), listed in the *Diagnostic and Statistical Manual of Mental Disorders* (fifth edition). In reality, these "disorders" are the normal and universal consequences of violence (McFarlane, 2010). Since the 1980s, they have been recognized by the international scientific community as pathognomonic, meaning that the "disorders" are characteristic of traumatizing violence and are diagnostic evidence of trauma. The effects of trauma are recognized as proportional to the severity of violence but also to its unexpected, unpredictable, and/or life-threatening aspects. The destructive intentions of the perpetrator and the inexplicable, incoherent absurdity of his (or her) actions correlate with more severe effects. Victims are typically disbelieved and neglected, which adds to the disorienting effects of trauma.

Psychological trauma, or psycho-trauma, is defined as an "effraction of the psyche through the overwhelming of defenses by violent stimulation from an aggressive or life-threatening act or an act that targets physical or psychological integrity of an individual exposed as a victim, witness, or assailant" (Crocq, 2007). Psycho-trauma paralyzes the victim's psyche, an effect referred to as "tonic immobility." With rape victims in particular, tonic immobility is a common response: The victim becomes stunned, petrified, and incapable of defending herself (or himself) mentally and physically. Corroborating previous findings, a large-scale Swedish study has shown that tonic immobility occurs in 70% of rape victims, and it also increases the victim's likelihood of developing PTSD.

Tonic immobility is not widely recognized. Therefore, added to victims' suffering is the misunderstanding of their own response; they might feel guilty and confused about "not fighting back." The law traditionally upholds that if a rape victim is not screaming and fighting, she is actually consenting, or at least was not very troubled by the rape—when it is actually the opposite:

Tonic immobility is evidence of the attack's life-threatening severity.

When tonic immobility sets in, the victim freezes and can no longer use mental representations (analysis, understanding, and decision-making) to play a defensive and modulating role in the face of intense stress. This stress is the normal adaptive mechanism for any human faced with extreme danger. It is a "neurobiological, physiological, and psychological alarm acting to defend the individual from an aggression, threat, or unexpected situation" (Crocq, 2007).

2.3 Scanning the Brain for Evidence

While traumatic violence is occurring, the paralysis of psychological defenses (tonic immobility) leads to excessive stress that can cause neurological damage. The damage is reversible if specific treatment is given. Important discoveries were made in 2003–2005, with key neuroscientific studies that include clinical input. These have allowed for better understanding of the brain's reactions and functional impairments resulting from trauma (Schin, 2006; Yehuda, 2007; Salmona, 2008). Violent disturbances produce altered states of consciousness and problems with emotional memory, and they are at the root of many (misdiagnosed) psychological disorders and much mental anguish.

The specific brain disturbances that occur during and after traumatic violence or abuse are now well documented, and they are both neurological and psychological. They include significant malfunctions of emotional circuitry and memory. Tangibly marking the brain, these effects have been identified on MRIs. Neuroscientists have used the quantity of synapses to show a decrease in activity and volume of some brain structures and hyperactivity in others, as well as changes in emotional response and memory-related circuitry (Rauch, 2006; Nemerof, 2009). Recently, epigenetic changes have also been shown in victims of childhood sexual abuse, with the modification of a gene (NR3C1) involved in control of responses to stress and secretion of stress hormones (adrenaline and cortisol); such changes can be transmitted to the next generation (Perroud, 2011).

A study published in 2013 in the *American Journal of Psychiatry* showed MRI evidence of anatomical differences in specific cortical zones of adult women survivors of childhood sexual abuse. Remarkably, some cortical zones are significantly thinner than those of women who were not abused, and these correspond to the somatosensory zones of the parts of the body targeted during the abuse (such as genitals, anus, and mouth). These cortical zones are even thinner in victims of extreme abuse (Heim, 2013).

Abuse and violence are transmitted among family members and across generations through little-known but scientifically proven mechanisms. I will now elaborate on these using a clinical and theoretical model that I developed through a synthesis of research in psychiatry, social sciences, and neurosciences, and through decades of clinical practice.

2.4 The Response to Ordinary Danger

When faced with a dangerous situation, we are all programmed to set off an immediate, automatic, and involuntary survival-based emotional reaction. This reaction is governed by a small subcortical structure called the cerebral amygdala ("amygdala" refers to its almond shape) (Ledoux, 1997). This emotional reaction serves as an alarm and prepares the organism to exert exceptional effort to escape a danger by fighting it, avoiding it, or fleeing it. To do this, the cerebral amygdala orders the secretion of stress hormones adrenaline and cortisol by the adrenal glands. These hormones allow for the mobilization of a huge quantity of energy by increasing the oxygen and glucose available in the blood. The heart beats stronger and faster, blood flow increases, breathing becomes heavier, and a state of hypervigilance begins. Then, the cerebral cortex analyzes available information about what happened (experiences, lessons, spatiotemporal indications), and these are stored in the hippocampus.

The hippocampus regulates memory, learning, and spatiotemporal orientation. It is another small cerebral structure and functions like software that can encode, classify, and store experiences in memory; it is necessary to refer to past events. Assisted by the hippocampus, the cortex elaborates survival strategies and makes decisions that are best adapted to a given situation.

As with other alarm systems, once the emotional response (amygdala) is set off, it does not shut itself off automatically. Only the cortex, assisted by the hippocampus, can modulate the alarm according to the situation and the organism's energy needs and can shut it off once the danger is no longer present. In a normal situation (not of traumatic violence), all sensory, emotional, and intellectual information is processed, encoded, and stored by the hippocampus in the circuits of memory. The event is recorded, integrated in the neural circuitry, and available to be retrieved and narrated. At first, the telling might stir up an emotional reaction, but this diminishes over time. However, the emotional memory of the event remains active to serve as a reminder of a dangerous experience to avoid. If you get stung by a wasp, the sight or sound of a flying insect will provoke an emotional reaction to inform you of a danger, which you will then identify by remembering the sting. Through identifying the insect, you can protect or reassure yourself depending on whether it seems dangerous or not. Such recollection of an event is called autobiographical memory.

2.5 Shutting Down: The Normal Response to Abnormal Violence

When traumatic violence occurs, all emotional response mechanisms are interrupted. Faced with extreme danger, the cerebral amygdala flares up, and an automatic emotional response sets in. The incoherence of the violence and of the attacker's determined and incomprehensible will to destroy her (or him) reduce the victim to emptiness. The violation rips through her psyche like a tidal wave and sweeps away all mental representations and certitudes, and nothing can stop it. The cortical activity of the victim is paralyzed, and she is in a state of shock (tonic immobility). Thus, frozen, the cortex cannot analyze the situation and respond in a beneficial way.

Scientists have conducted experiments that have proven the existence of this cortical paralysis. In one study, MRIs and functional magnetic resonance imaging (registering fluctuations in blood flow to determine which brain areas are active) were used on a Vietnam veteran with PTSD and on someone who had not experienced trauma. Researchers had the two people listen to a neutral narration in which there is a sudden interruption describing wartime violence. This triggered an emotional response in both people but an analytical response only in the non-traumatized person. In the person with no prior trauma, the MRI shows numerous cortical zones activating in response to stress. These are mainly in the prefrontal cortex and the hippocampus, which allow for analysis of the situation (in this case, only a narration) and then modulation and diminution of the emotional response. These enabled the person to develop a reassuring interior monologue and to decide to complain about the disturbance after the study. The traumatized person's brain, however, showed a total absence of cortical activity on the MRI, with no zone lighting up. The person froze up and was unable to calm the emotional response that the narration of violence provoked (Bremner, 2003). This causes tonic immobility or total lack of response.

When tonic immobility occurs (during extreme stress, including combat and rape), the cortex freezes, and the victim is paralyzed. She cannot scream, speak, or rationally organize a defense (and this is often later held against her). Because the cortex shuts down, it cannot control the emotional response. As the violence increases, secretions of stress hormones adrenaline and cortisol also rise. The organism rapidly finds itself in a state of extreme stress (Shin, 2006).

2.6 Life-Threatening Dangers from Within

The state of extreme stress entails cardiovascular risks and the threat of severe neurological damage. This is due to the increase in stress hormones (adrenaline and cortisol) released into the bloodstream. At a high dose, these stress hormones become toxic to the organism. An excess of adrenaline can provoke sudden death through myocardial infarction (heart attack). Cortisol (in large amounts) is neurotoxic and can provoke neuronal damage responsible for epilepsy, loss of consciousness, amnesic ictus, and comas.

As many as 30% of the neurons in some cerebral structures can be destroyed or damaged by the psychological trauma of an attack or abuse, with a significant decrease in dendritic spines and neural connections (Woolley, 1990; Yehuda, 2007; Nemeroff, 2009). The victim is in danger of death not only from the criminal intentions of the attacker but also from the internal risk created by the extreme stress that the attack provokes. The neural damage can result in absences, epileptic seizures, unconsciousness, and lacunar amnesia (as with cranial trauma). Lacunar amnesia and neurological damage were shown to occur in mice experiencing trauma, with an excess of glucocorticoids (equivalent of cortisol in mice) in a 2011 study by the neuroscientific team of the French National Institute of Health and Medical Research in Bordeaux (led by Aline Desmedt, with whom I collaborate); results were published in the peer-reviewed journal *Sciences*.

> Amnesia can be partial or complete. There may be occasional episodes of forgetting, or the entire period before and after the attack could be a consistent blank. With traumatic amnesia, the victim no longer remembers a large or small part of what happened, and the severity of the aggression correlates with the resulting amnesia (the worse the violence, the less it can be consciously recalled). This little-known fact has huge implications for criminal justice as well as for mental health.

2.7 The Brain's Short-Circuit: A Powerful and Tragic Defense

When being violated, the victim is in extreme cardiovascular and neurological danger. To prevent irrevocable damage or death, the brain uses a remarkable defense: Disjunction. Just as an overcharged electrical system short-circuits to avoid blowing up or burning out anything plugged in, the brain trips the emotional circuitry by urgently secreting neurotransmitters (endorphins) and substances similar to hard drugs morphine and ketamine—a powerful cocktail (Zimmerman, 2010), as morphine and ketamine are often used together to treat undue pain after surgery (they are also NMDA receptor antagonists).

Disjunction ("short circuiting"/disconnection) is a survival mechanism that brutally interrupts connections between amygdala and other brain structures. In the case of traumatic aggression, the isolated amygdala's alarm keeps ringing and cannot be switched off; vital information is blocked. Disjunction finally shuts off the alarm, stopping the life-threatening risks of heart attack and severe brain damage due to the over-secretion of stress hormones. Secretion stops suddenly, and there is no longer a risk of imminent death. But another consequence of disjunction is that the cortex no longer receives information on the person's psychological, physical, or emotional state. The cerebral amygdala can no longer transmit information to the hippocampus so that it can process the memory and situate it spatially and temporally. Traumatic disjunction has neurobiological consequences at the root of psycho-traumatic disorders and myriad health problems that typically go unrecognized as rooted in traumatic memory and dissociation.

Disjunction places victims in a sudden state of emotional and physical anesthesia. Victims continue to experience the aggression but no longer feel anything—a state called dissociation (Van der Hart, 1992). Victims describe dissociation as a feeling of unreality, indifference, or insensibility as if they are absent or have become simple spectators of the situation. (Dissociation can occur both during a violation and when traumatic memory is triggered.) This is due to the self-induced emotional and physical "anesthetization" linked to disjunction, with a sensation of bodily death. The immediate consequence of dissociation is that the victim is even less capable of defending herself (or himself).

The interruption of connections between the amygdala (alarm) and the hippocampus (narrative memory) is at the origin of traumatic memory. Disconnected from the amygdala, the hippocampus can no longer encode, integrate, or store in memory the violation, which means it cannot become a normal autobiographical recollection. The attack remains a trapped event that cannot reach the status of narratable personal history—and this trapped, ongoing presence of the violence is what I have named a traumatic memory. Traumatic memory functions as a time machine that can at any moment force victims to relive the emotional and sensory experience of a past traumatic aggression. They are unable to consciously control their cortex. This results in immense suffering and forces victims to put in place survival strategies.

We will now explore the protean manifestations of traumatic memory and traumatic dissociation, including key survival strategies and behaviors: Avoidance, control, hypervigilance, dissociation, and anesthetization.

3

The Time-Machine from Hell

TRAUMATIC MEMORY IS LIKE A landmine that explodes as soon as you step where it is buried—whenever a situation, thought, or sensation recalls (consciously or not) a past traumatic aggression. If left untreated, traumatic memory can last for years, decades, or a lifetime. It generates a permanent sense of danger and insecurity in victims, as if they live permanently in the middle of a minefield. Traumatic memory is a raw emotional and sensory recollection of violation that stays trapped in the cerebral amygdala (alarm system). The superior cortical functions cannot control it, and thus, it escapes all attempts at analysis or transcription into autobiographical discourse. It cannot be narrated but only relived as uncontrollable and unstoppable "hallucinations" (Janet, 1928; Van der Kolk, 1991).

Traumatic memory is different from autobiographical memory, which is conscious, declarative, worked through, revised, and modified as time goes by. With autobiographical memory, the emotional intensity of past events decreases over time. The content can be transformed or even falsified. Memories of events that had a strong positive or negative emotional impact are eventually less emotional and based on intellectual representations rather than raw sensory experiences. We might remember the intensity of physical pain or a pleasant warmth from the sun, but we do not feel these in the same way as when we originally experienced them. We might remember the quality of light or the sounds and

DOI: 10.4324/9781003497516-4

sights of a storm and reconstruct them mentally, but they will not come to us exactly as they were.

In recalling a traumatic memory, however, the traumatizing event is relived identically, without reconstruction, and it remains unchanged even after many years. Time does not diminish the intensity and realness of sensations and emotions. The reminiscences are intrusive and fully invade the consciousness of victims, forcing them to relive the attack or abuse in the present with the same terror, pain, perceptions, and physiological responses. Traumatic memory flares up spontaneously through mental associations and stimuli or contexts reminiscent of the original violence.

The victim might be aware or unaware of the link between present stimulus (trigger) and past trauma. The memory might be viewed as a complete or partial "film" of the traumatic event or be totally abstract (with the victim not recognizing that she has already endured this same sensory and emotional experience). Recollections take the form of sudden flashbacks; dreams and nightmares; sensory experiences that seem to be illusions or hallucinations; and/or painful psychological, emotional, somatic, and motor experiences (Steele, 1990). They replay the intense psychological and physical distress and suffering of the initial violation.

Any dimension of the trauma can be reactivated and relived, including the aggression itself (transporting victims back to a time and place), the emotions and sensations (terror, pain, fear of death), and anything about the attacker (insults, lies, threats, smells). This traumatic memory of the perpetrators' violent acts colonizes victims and results in confusion between their own selves and their attackers/abusers. This often entails feelings of shame, guilt, and perplexity as perverse and violent words and feelings surface in victims and are wrongly perceived as their own. These come from the abuser and constitute an additional torture for the victim.

3.1 A Ticking Time Bomb

Traumatic memory is an emotional and sensory abscess. It is a swelling cyst of recollection that forces victims to keep viewing the "film" of an attack or abuse with all the sensations of it happening all over again. This involves an uncontrollable neurovegetative storm (sweat, paleness, tachycardia [accelerated heartbeat], muscle spasms, sensations of throat constriction with difficulty breathing) and motor reactions (automatic defensive motions, immobility, stiffness, bulging eyes, open mouth), absence, loss of consciousness, and/or dissociative symptoms.

This torturous time machine traps sleeping victims in nightmares and "hallucinations" and pollutes their waking hours with associations, emotions, and sensations that bring past violence into the constant present. A word such as "rape" or insults overheard, even if not directed at the victim, can set the machine in motion. Catalysts (triggers) can be anything: A sudden noise, a door slamming, a falling object, a shout, a firecracker; a certain smell, silhouette, or texture (blood, sweat, sperm) reminiscent of the attacker; a violent scene in real life or on TV; a stressful test or job interview; a strong emotion or surprise (even positive); a headache, pain of birth, sensation on the skin (rubbing, caressing), insect crawling, dizziness, nausea from fatigue or illness; feelings of suffocation when underwater or something covers the face; feelings of confinement when in an elevator, train, airplane, or MRI scanner; a situation not understood or that seems incoherent or unfair, even if not directed at you; a person or animal in danger or very vulnerable; a context, place, date, or time of day; weather (very sunny, windy, rainy, stormy, very cold or hot); and so on. This long list is far from covering all potential triggers of traumatic memory (reliving the aggression).

When traumatic memory sets in due to any association, it suddenly invades victims' fields of awareness without any warning or any possibility to defend themselves or to avoid it. Victims are forced to relive past violence as if it is happening again with the same terror, distress, shock, pain, and despair. It plunges victims into the spatiotemporal dimensions of the trauma—a virtual reality so palpable that past trauma eclipses the present moment. Victims experience the intolerable sensation of reliving a violation with the original intensity. The same vital risk and sensation of imminent death arise with the same paralysis of the psyche (tonic immobility). This can result in new trauma through emotional overload.

Traumatic memory is an emotional memory that can take the form of recurring nightmares. These can be so violent that they cause immediate disjunction. Even so, once awake, the victim might not remember the details and just feel that it was a rough night. Others might witness and later inform victims of the agonizing screams, sobs, and thrashing. "Nightmares" might actually be hallucinations between dream and wake states. In these, victims relive the violence with an intensity and terror so real that it can provoke states of psychomotor paralysis or somnambulistic (sleepwalking) movements as the victim is forced to act in invisible scenes. These can recur over a long period, often several decades. They are extremely agonizing and can make victims dread the sleep to the point of avoidance through total insomnia. These nightmares or hallucinatory states typically plunge victims into a severe state of perturbation and anguish for the entire day that follows.

The partner of a young woman who was victim of particularly horrific paternal incest with acts of torture as a child describes her nights: "She disjuncts almost every night in the way you describe in your article... wandering ghost phase... phase of violence toward herself or me...violent sexual phase (a sort of temporary 'nymphomania' that can last for two hours), phase of returning to childhood, crying, calling to her mother for help, screaming at her father... What I hear in the night goes beyond any understanding. For some time now, I have succeeded with gentle words and actions in calming this last character. I take 'the child' in my arms, reassure her, and caress her, and she goes back to sleep... Toward the end of each phase, she wakes up and never remembers anything. Never!" Similarly, partners and children of those who survived Nazi camps can hear them scream and cry every night. They relive hell and seem to clearly hear the yelling of the SS and dogs barking, smell the ovens... (Zadje, 1996).

Daytime traumatic memory can take the form of hallucinations in which the "film" of the violence plays out as flashbacks in which the victim is trapped and forced to relive the same situation over and over. Usually, however, the memory is fragmented into emotions, sensations, and illusions without the context of the traumatic event. It can take the form of an idea, tension, gut feeling, fear, despair, pain, noise, or vision. There are bodily manifestations of stress (sweat, goosebumps, uncontrollable shaking), expressions of terror (bulging eyes and mouth open for a scream that cannot be released from a stiff, frozen body), and involuntary behaviors (shudders, jolts).

Imposing itself as a tangible alternate reality, traumatic memory can easily lead to suicide attempts, frenetic fleeing, aggressive defense reactions, and calls for help. The replay is sometimes longer, stretching on for hours or even days, with victims' present lives held hostage by past violations (colonized by trauma). In my clinical practice, I have watched patients relive the terror they felt while being attacked, with uncontrollable trembling, extreme paleness, eyes rolling backward, and revulsion with retching. Some relive almost being suffocated to death by a shocking holding of breath, and I have seen patients dissociate fully, immobilized, and absent.

3.2 Misunderstood Flashbacks

Fragmented memories are often misinterpreted. A victim's (relived) anger or rage is taken at face value in the present, and ordinary outbursts or aggressive actions are not linked to past events and lingering effects of trauma. A sudden feeling of aggression might be wrongly attributed to a trivial present situation itself, when really it is just pulling the trigger for traumatic memory. Recollecting/reliving of past emotions might be misinterpreted as present anxiety attacks, panic attacks, or even cardiac problems. Memory-based pain is often misidentified as physical in origin. It is often so extreme (sharp abdominal or chest pain, for example) that a victim seeks emergency medical or even surgical care—and when examined, no physical problem is found. Thus, victims risk receiving pointless treatments and even surgeries.

When survivors think of rape or picture images from a rape scene, this might be misidentified as their own fantasies or desires. Sensory or kinesthetic recollections of sexual molestation might give the false impression that a survivor is sexually excited by a situation that has, in reality, triggered traumatic memory; she is actually recalling the perverse excitement of the abuser, not of herself (a "colonizing" effect of trauma). An unrecognized scene of sexual assault could wrongly be perceived as her own desire to "let loose." The deadly insults of the perpetrator ("you are ugly, stupid, mean, worthless, a loser; you're only good for this; you love it, don't you, the blows, getting fucked up; you don't deserve to live") replay like a broken record every time traumatic memory is triggered. This might lead victims to think they really believe this about themselves, which leads to risky behaviors and suicide attempts.

Images, phrases, and sensations that invade a victim's psyche are often misdiagnosed as delusions with visual, auditive, and kinesthetic hallucinations; the reality is that these are recollections. One example is of a WWII veteran who was part of the first D-Day (June 6, 1944), during which nearly 90% of soldiers were killed or wounded. During the 50th anniversary commemoration at the original site called Omaha Beach, a canon was fired. This triggered his traumatic memory, and he was immediately blown back in time to relive being on a ship fired at by Germans. He started to scream and run in zigzags under the bewildered gaze of attendees. This is similar to the reaction of a patient who, hearing me say the word "rape," flung herself violently backward with an anguished expression, eyes fixed on an invisible scene, and jerked her left arm back and forth with her fist clenched. She was reliving her rape at seven years old, during which the rapist immobilized her arm. She had succeeded in grabbing the knife with which he'd threatened her and tried to defend herself by stabbing him. I gently called her name and asked her to look at me, and she was able to leave this scene after a few seconds. She was exhausted, and it took a while before she could explain to me what she had relived. On the palm of her hand (which had become so rigid during the explosion of traumatic memory that it was difficult for her to open), her nails had left deep marks.

Every Friday and Saturday night, this patient woke up screaming from a terrifying nightmare that she did not remember, her bed a battlefield, and her naked without knowing why. She would feel unbearable distress and the urge to commit suicide through strangulation, which she attempted several times with a scarf. The rape was at a summer camp on the last night of her stay, a Saturday, and the attacker, a large adolescent, undressed her completely, raped her, and attempted to strangle her. The emotional response set off by traumatic memory is so violent that it can result in another trauma. As with the original assault, it can include tonic immobility, overload, and vital risk, followed by disjunction. Through this reliving, traumatic memory perpetuates and feeds itself, growing bigger. It is so unbearable and traumatic that the victim will do anything to escape it. This is why hypervigilance, control, avoidance behaviors, and finally (a last resort) disjunction and dissociation are so common in victims.

For those close to victims, witnessing the explosion of traumatic memory is frightening and disorienting, especially when they do not have clear and accurate explanations for what is happening. It is shocking to see the disjointed and unpredictable transformations, especially when there are screams, expressions of terror and panic, and violent movements. It can be traumatic for the witnesses, especially if they are children. Traumatic memory is the encrypted phantom described by Nicolas Abraham and Maria Torok in *The Shell and the Kernel.* Children of victims traumatized by unspeakably horrific abuse—even if unaware of it—are confronted with the presence of this phantom. It haunts them and has psycho-traumatic consequences (as with children of Holocaust survivors).

Symptoms of traumatic memory are unconsciously absorbed by these children and confront them with emotional awareness of the violence the adult survived. Children might even be traumatized indirectly by the past violent acts inflicted on the adults in their lives (though never directly witnessing these or experiencing traumatic violence). They might develop avoidance and control behaviors or even dissociative behaviors that put them in danger. The child is not traumatized by the parent who is a survivor but by the perpetrator's incomprehensible violence. This psycho-trauma is not inscribed in the child's body—the body has not endured any of it—but rather in his or her ideas, emotions, and representations of the world. Similarly, the child of an executioner, even if this role is kept secret, is haunted by the phantom of violence committed by the parent. Violent acts create traumatic memory in the one committing them too, doubled by traumatic memory of any abuse endured in the past.

3.3 Colonized by Traumatic Memory

Traumatic memory devastates victims' self-perception and jeopardizes the feeling of certainty that humans need, so that victims endlessly doubt and question everything. Reason can no longer be relied on, as a situation said to be safe could trigger a panic attack, and a person loved and normally trusted might suddenly make a victim feel completely insecure without any apparent reason, to the point where it is necessary to flee the relationship. Victims who consider themselves peaceful in nature might suddenly find themselves invaded by extremely violent images and unsurmountable rage without knowing why. They might think of themselves as deeply romantic and sentimental, yet crude and violent sexual images impose themselves on their thoughts; they might feel sexually excited by pornography, even though they hate it. They might love their children more than anything and yet be invaded, with tremendous agony and without apparent reason, by extremely violent images in which they see themselves killing, harming, threatening, throwing out the window, or sexually assaulting the children. Believing themselves to be courageous and down-to-earth, they might find themselves having inexplicable fears (as might a small child), feel extremely vulnerable in ordinary situations, feel terrifying anxiety about something insignificant, and be petrified by a very simple problem. Wanting to always be very kind, they might find themselves lashing out horribly for nothing, for a small annoyance, and insulting people with words that they would normally never say. They might believe themselves to be happy and well-adjusted, and yet a huge depression could brutally fall on them with ideas of suicide. Suddenly, they are unable to project themselves into the immediate future and feel that it's all over, though there is nothing that would seem to explain this state. Thinking of themselves as mentally solid, they might suddenly start to see monsters or menacing shadows, hear voices, or feel objects penetrating their bodies. Although they usually enjoy eating, it might suddenly make them feel disgust or nausea. Knowing themselves to be in good health, they might be bewildered to find themselves agonizing over searing pains with no apparent cause, sensations of extreme discomfort, and the feeling that death is near.

All these symptoms of traumatic memory place victims in a state of total insecurity. They can count on nothing since even if everything appears perfectly calm, the worst can happen at any moment with a panic attack and dreadful thoughts invading them. Everything can crumble, pivot, or switch instantly without warning; anything can become a threat. Victims feel themselves to be different from others and unable to advance normally in life and maintain their grip on reality. They think they are instable and hard to get along with. They must then put in place avoidance and control strategies and turn away from many situations and potential plans. Their self-esteem is catastrophically low. They are ashamed of themselves, what is going on in their heads, what they cannot manage to do, not being who they want to be, and not being like other people. They feel guilty. They constantly torture themselves and scrutinize their own behaviors.

Through traumatic memory, perpetrators are eternally present in victims' lives and continue to impose the same atrocities, toxic remarks, and deliberately induced suffering with the same perverse pleasure in destroying their prey and imposing their mystifying scripts (Sironi, 1999). Perpetrators sense that the violent acts they commit will linger on in this way, and it is part of their motivation and satisfaction. Having lived through trauma in their own past, they gain the relief of reenacting it—only this time, they are in the controlling role and no longer the victims. The script is the same, but the roles change. Fortunately, it is only a small minority of victims who become perpetrators; however, it is enough to feed the cycle.

The earlier the abuse happened in victims' lives, the more they must construct themselves around incomprehensible emotions, feelings of terror, and perverse words and deeds. They must battle these without understanding what they are and where they come from. Traumatic memory haunts victims, taking them over so that they cannot be themselves—or worse, they believe there are two of them or even three: A normal person (which they are), a worthless loser who is afraid of everything (what the abuser said they are), and a guilty person that they are ashamed of and who deserves to die (the abuser in them). The worthlessness and shame are scripted by the abuser and replay in victims' minds until they become terrorized and confuse it with themselves.

3.4 Traumatic Memory in Young Children

Traumatic memory is much more serious in babies and children than in adults due to fragility, dependence, powerlessness, lack of experience, physiological and psychological immaturity, and the process of growing, becoming someone and constructing a self. The central nervous system's immaturity makes children's brains much more sensitive to the effects of stress through the excessive secretion of cortisol, with higher risks of damage to neurons (especially dendric), with neuronal death, and epigenetic modifications of neuronal DNA. Some parts of the brain, particularly within the limbic system, prefrontal cortex, and hippocampus, can lose volume and stay atrophied for as long as the victim remains unprotected and does not receive adequate specific care. However, children's nervous systems are highly malleable, and with appropriate care, their neurons can recover very well.

In children under two, the hippocampus—cerebral structure that functions like software for memory and learning—is very underdeveloped. The hippocampus is necessary to record events in memory, integrate learning, and situate yourself spatio-temporally. It is due to this immaturity of the hippocampus that children cannot remember anything from birth to two years of age. The absence of memory does not mean that the child cannot be traumatized by violence; *it is exactly the opposite*. This is because the cerebral structure governing emotional response, the amygdala, is active and functions even before birth, starting in the seventh month of pregnancy. The emotional response of small children is more intense than that of adults because there are fewer possibilities to modulate the response. Their cerebral cortex, the modulating structure, is less efficient because it holds fewer capacities for analysis and other resources that adults have. It also cannot rely on the hippocampus to draw on memories and lessons that would be useful for understanding and categorizing a situation (of abuse, for example). The emotional circuit is less modulated and at even higher risk of overcharge, so that there is considerable cardiovascular and neurological danger (neurotoxicity and hyperexcitation that can cause epileptic seizures and loss of consciousness). The safety mechanism of disjunction is also set off and results in dissociation and extensive traumatic memory.

These neurological facts mean that very young children are highly impacted by abuse. Even if they don't consciously recall anything, they are invaded by symptoms due to the traumatic memory of what happened. This traumatic memory colonizes them and forces them to relive the same terror and pain that they felt during the abuse. Their psychological development is infected by traumatic memory and the survival strategies they put in place to escape it and anesthetize themselves. These might lead to personality, behavioral, and/or cognitive disorders that might, when invasive enough, be mistaken for psychotic or borderline states, severe obsessional and attention deficit disorders, and mental deficiencies. Due to an inadequate understanding of psycho-traumatic disturbances, child victims are usually misdiagnosed and given ill-adapted treatment unlikely to foster lasting recovery. After two or three years, if the hippocampus becomes functional, the abuse could also be forgotten partially or fully through psychogenic amnesia of survival, which is frequent.

4

Traumatic Dissociation

DURING ABUSE OR ASSAULT, PARTS of the brain's emotional cir-cuitry suddenly switch off to avoid death, just as an electrical system short-circuits to avoid the explosions of overload. I refer to this as disjunction. With disjunction comes a physical and emotional numbing or deadening (anesthetization). At the height of terror, anguish, and insurmountable stress, the pain abruptly stops (disjunction), but the abuse continues. The victim still sees the abuser raping or otherwise harming her and still hears him yelling and threatening, but there is no longer an emotional con-notation to what she sees. She feels nothing

This emotional anesthesia clouds everything in strangeness, unreality, or derealization. The traumatized victim feels like she is not actually living what is happening. It feels as if she is not part of it but merely an onlooker observing from a distance or even totally transported to another time and place, as if already dead. These common reactions during a traumatic assault are grouped under the term "peritraumatic dissociation." In a confused stupor, the victim experiences a dream-like state of modified consciousness with reflex actions (on autopilot), hallucinations of leaving the body and floating above it, spatiotemporal and perceptual distortions with time slowing down or speeding up, distances and proportions shifting, and objects moving around. In this early phase, these dissociative peritraumatic phenomena might last minutes, hours, or even several days, occasionally months, as the victim lingers in a confused or discordant state.

DOI: 10.4324/9781003497516-5

Such states include incongruous feelings such as hilarity, excitement, or an astonishing calm and serenity linked to massive emotional anesthetization. The victim's discordant emotional states provoke inappropriate reactions from those around her, such as worry (about the symptoms and not the cause), dismissal or disbelief about what happened, lack of empathy, or even mistreatment or non-assistance to a person in danger. (Translator's note: In France, people are legally required to assist those in danger, sometimes called "duty to rescue" in English.)

During a terrorist attack, a mother with her six-year-old daughter found herself fully dissociated in front of the dead body of her child. She was convinced that since she felt absolutely nothing when seeing it, the torn-up body could not possibly have been that of her daughter. For three months, she was sure that her daughter had run away and that it was urgently necessary to find her.

A woman opened her door for her next-door neighbor at 10:00 p.m., thinking that his wife or children needed help, and he pressed a hand to her mouth and raped her before she could move or scream. For an entire year, she was in a state of dissociation. She remained disconnected, on autopilot, and emotionally anesthetized. She could talk about the rape in a detached manner without showing any emotions, as if it did not concern her. During this time, she was not able to report the crime.

A young woman, only 20 years old, succeeded in escaping from the man who had just raped her. She only realized during a police investigation several months later that there was a gap of several hours between the moment she escaped by jumping into a bus and the moment when a bus driver saw her at a bus stop, disheveled and covered in blood and called 911. She thought that she had simply ended up at the last stop of the bus she had leaped into for her escape. She had actually wandered for several hours and must have taken another bus and walked in autopilot without anyone caring about the state she was in until a bus driver finally called for help. In the last two examples, the police clearly did not understand anything about post-traumatic dissociation in victims when they said their statements were incoherent and, therefore, they must be lying.

A young patient who survived the Bataclan theater massacre (a mass shooting north of Paris on November 13, 2015) lay flat in the orchestra pit after a bullet had entered her rear and came out of her abdomen. She was there until help arrived over two hours later and didn't move or feel any pain.

As soon as emotional anesthesia and the dissociative state disappear, the victim often experiences an emotional onslaught and is flooded with intense physical pain, severe anxious distress, behavioral disfunction, and intense neurovegetative symptoms (tachycardia, sweat, trembling, feeling choked). The overwhelming stress can manifest as extreme agitation, logorrhea (excessive talking), crying, shouting, violent outbursts with self-harm (pulling out hair, scratching, or hitting oneself), and the pressing and uncontrollable need to run all over the place or hide. In contrast, it can also provoke a stupor with psychomotor paralysis, including mutism, retreat, and opposition. Along with these effects, there might also be physical responses such as temporary blindness, deafness, and muscle paralysis, as well as extreme somatic disruptions linked to the intensity of stress, including arterial hypertension, tachycardia (accelerated heartbeat), extrasystoles (irregular heartbeat), heart pain, difficulty breathing, asthma, breakouts on skin, pruritis (itching), hair falling out, tinnitus (ears ringing), aversion to food, nausea, vomiting, diarrhea, allergies, and genital pain.

4.1 The Dangers of Depersonalization

When abuse is ongoing or when the victim is still regularly confronted with the abuser (as with incest or family/domestic violence), the dissociative symptoms might become permanent and necessary to survive in unbearable conditions. The victim of abuse finds herself disconnected most of the time and is said to be "spaced out," "not all there," or "head in the clouds." She is unresponsive and appears incapable of concentrating and paying attention to what is around her. Sometimes this stuporous state that makes her seem intellectually limited. To her, it seems as though thoughts and feelings float around her, do not belong to her, and that she has no identity. This is called depersonalization.

Child victims of severe physical or sexual abuse are often permanently dissociated and wrongly labeled mentally disabled. Their unresponsiveness and emotional anesthetization put victims in even greater danger of additional abuse and abandonment, as their apparent absence of emotion makes it so the mirror reflex of empathy doesn't work at all. When faced with dissociated victims, no one spontaneously feels any emotion or any concern for them. They are easy to forget. As they do not react in the face of abuse, the abusers set even fewer limits, and the abuse is more often repeated. These victims are also used as scapegoats in their schools, institutions, and workplaces. They might be victims of repeated gang rapes and can be easily trapped in prostitution networks.

If the violence only occurred once (a rape by a stranger or a terrorist attack, for example), it does not happen anymore, or there is a stretch of time between attacks, peritraumatic dissociation fades, and reality begins to return. But every time it explodes, traumatic memory of the violence makes victims relive the state of overwhelming stress. From this, new dissociative symptoms arise due to disjunction of the emotional circuitry.

Dissociative symptoms due to traumatic memory include sensations of unreality, confusion, and depersonalization so that victims feel like spectators of their own lives. Their own life events pass them by, and they feel inept in their relations with others. Emotional and physical anesthetization function in parallel with dissociative symptoms, further widening the gap between oneself and others. Emotional anesthetization and the depersonalization that goes with it make victims feel inauthentic as if they are playing a role.

When traumatic memory flares up often, with frequent dissociative incidents, it is impossible to find the appropriate register of behavior, which is extremely painful and troublesome. Victims are there watching and listening to themselves speak as if it were another person, permanently distanced from themselves. As no natural, spontaneous response is available to them, they are forced to invent a stance, a response, and an emotional state and perform these. They are at constant risk of overacting, responding excessively and histrionically, or underacting and appearing cold, unreactive, or disconnected. The solution might be to closely follow what others do, observing and imitating them to be more or less in sync. To avoid always being chameleons (like Woody Allen in the film *Zelig*), victims must establish consistent and convincing roles for themselves. To do so, they must fight the effects of dissociation. They act as the person they think they should be or that others want them to be, molding a character that sometimes takes on a life of its own with coherent behaviors and narratives. However, this character might correspond less and less to the victim's own inner world. Victims might need to lie to uphold the fabricated normality while becoming increasingly convinced that they are faking it. Dissociative symptoms are thus at the root of extreme difficulties in seeming to have oneself together, and victims may feel that they are only borrowing personalities and have none of their own. They might also act *as if* well-adjusted while feeling an internal void—sometimes called an "as-if personality."

Internal void and tragic despair are hiding behind the curtains of this successful show of well-adjusted normality. Traumatized children and teens, unable to establish normal relations with others, often develop an imaginary second life that they tell no one about, even when it almost fully absorbs them. There might be imaginary parents, friends, intimate companions, and pets, each with a specific personality, and they experience intricate dynamics and events that are much richer than in real life. Sometimes, they give life and words to a doll or stuffed animal or allow a real animal to speak. Such children appear to be always elsewhere, spaced out, or absent.

4.2 The Dangers of Disembodiment

Emotional anesthetization is dangerous. It cuts victims off from their spontaneous emotions and does not allow them to react appropriately in risky situations. They might find themselves being seriously violated and not react at all. Without protest, they endure the unendurable. Vulnerable to abuses of power and to sexual predators, they might have such a high threshold for enduring discomfort and mistreatment that when faced with people who are perverse, unhealthy, unhinged, or dangerous, they "don't feel a thing." An anesthetized victim might be the only person to accept a very abnormal proposal or to receive insults with a permanent smile pinned on her face. This is the case with prostitutes, almost all of whom are in a state of dissociation with significant emotional and physical anesthetization. Fully dissociated, they might feel little disgust, rejection, and pain during sex acts imposed by the situation of prostitution.

Due to dissociation and emotional anesthetization, victims find themselves in extremely dangerous situations while appearing indifferent even as physical attacks occur. They experience anosognosia (denial of their bodily reality), which also leads those around them to deny it, as the natural triggers of empathy for a victim are hijacked by emotional anesthetization (if she doesn't seem to mind, why should anyone else?). Her signs of not caring what is happening to her should, on the contrary, be taken as indicators of serious abuse, past and present.

Dr. Judith Trinquart has studied the consequences of repeated unwanted sexual acts on prostitutes. These acts often involve abuse and violence. Trinquart has identified in prostitutes a kind of dissociation that she calls disembodiment or bodily disinvestment. It signifies the loss of ownership of one's own body:

> Originally a protective mechanism, it leads to very negative outcomes for prostitutes' health. Their threshold for enduring pain is far beyond the norm. They no longer receive their bodies' warning signals and do not know when they need treatment. This is why, even when they have adequate access to health services and specific assistance, they do not seek necessary medical attention. Their bodies do not belong to them and become objects that they neglect. A customer beats her up, but she does not feel the blows or the pain; or she gets tuberculosis and coughs horribly for eight months but only goes to the hospital when in the terminal phase. This is not a

conscious desire for self-destruction; it is an automatic reflex of self-neglect. They are anesthetized and no longer aware. Their bodies have become mere instruments and objects of loathing. They lose the sense of protecting these bodies. Some of them cannot anesthetize themselves fast enough, so they sink into alcoholism and drugs to endure the unwanted sex and everyday acts of violence
(Trinquart, 2002).

Similarly, many homeless people develop a certain indifference to the extreme conditions of their lives, including high tolerance for physical and emotional pain, constant danger, and freezing temperatures. Tragically, this indifference is reflected back at them by the world. This might lead to the extreme situation of those they called "musulmans" in concentration camps and especially extermination camps such as Auschwitz. They seemed already dead, indifferent to everything, and fully disconnected from those around them. They were in the final stage of post-traumatic stress and complete dissociation that comes before death. But without going so far, traumatized victims constantly submerged in intolerable suffering often find themselves, through consuming psychoactive medications, drugs, or alcohol, in an almost permanent state of dissociation. They are in a sort of walking coma, anesthetized and indifferent to everything.

4.3 Dissociated Victims: Preferred Prey of Perverts

Confusion and disorientation linked to dissociative symptoms lead to cognitive difficulties and constant doubts about what is perceived, heard, said, and understood. This puts victims at greater risk and makes it difficult for them to have their needs and certainties respected. Dissociated victims are easily influenced and "hypnotized." They are often pre-programmed and on auto-pilot. They have no self-confidence and find themselves caving in to desires of others when pressured to do so.

There is a huge risk that they will become the chosen victims of predators on the lookout for them. The more dangerous the person in front of them, the more he revives the traumatic memory of a victim. He chose her because what she says and does is out of place and out of touch. Through acting out his domination of her, he causes her to dissociate, putting her in a hypnotic state that makes it impossible for her to think and defend herself.

She breaks down. She becomes confused and totally disoriented, and therefore extremely vulnerable. The victim thinks this incapacitated state is due to her stupidity, inferiority, or pathological shyness. It is actually directly linked to the setting off of safety mechanisms when faced with the danger of the person she is facing. These mechanisms could be a useful alarm if the victim knew about them. Instead, she gives him the benefit of the doubt when interpreting this dangerous and perverse situation. He is often perceived by the hypnotized victim as superior, important, and much more intelligent than she is, or even someone fascinating that she might think she is in love with, due to the dissociative mechanisms we will now examine.

4.4 Dissociation and the Risk of Downplaying Violence

Dissociative symptoms cause some victims to place the traumatic events they have endured very low on the emotional scale once some time has passed. The violence is trivialized ("a good thrashing never hurt anyone") or even sometimes elevated to the status of lessons learned. The anguish and distress originally felt are forgotten and replaced by the memory of dissociation and emotional anesthetization that followed disjunction. Often during the first psychotherapy session with patients suffering terribly from numerous anxio-depressive symptoms, when asked what childhood was like, they will say it was fine or even "idyllic and wonderfully happy." In later sessions, they reveal tremendous mistreatment, including physical violence and severe neglect. It is not that the patient wishes to hide these facts or has forgotten them. It is that they feel what happened through the lens of anesthetized emotional memories. The trauma endured seems superficial now—no big deal, no harm done. They cannot make any link between emotional agony as an adult and the tortures of childhood.

One patient, a young adult who avoided any intimate relationships and had incapacitating anxiety along with nausea, vomiting, and social phobia that made it impossible for her to go to the bathroom anywhere except her own home, could not see the conditions of her childhood and adolescence as abnormal. She even thought that her symptoms might be due to the over-protectiveness of her mother. What she described, however, was absolutely shocking: In an incestuous universe with no privacy, she was forbidden to close the door to the toilets, the bathroom, or her bedroom—all doors wide open at all times—with a sick father who constantly exposed his naked body while casually describing all his urinary and digestive symptoms. A lot of work had to go into reidentifying the abuse, reinterpreting the facts, rediscovering the initial feelings, and re-expressing them in the safe space of therapy without her dissociating again, to finally do justice to the mistreated child of the past and allow her to disarm her traumatic memory.

4.5 Emotional Anesthetization: A Critical and Misunderstood Phenomenon

When faced with victims of domestic violence, medical, social, and law-enforcement professionals are often confused, as dissociated victims show no emotion when talking about the very serious violence they endured. They might try to persuade those attempting to help them that they are used to it and don't really mind. They are strong, and nothing can get to them, they say. They sometimes even say that it would not be very serious if they were killed. However, most of them consider that it's not the same for their children—violence toward them is very serious, and they should never have to endure it. Others are as anesthetized for their children as for themselves and are incapable of sensing the danger or realizing its devastating effects on their children. They are only evaluating the situation through their anesthetized emotional responses.

As loved ones or professionals, we must not be misled by the apparently positive outlook of some victims. Those who seem the least affected, disturbed, or anguished are not necessarily the least traumatized. They might be in a deep state of dissociation and emotional anesthesia and in even more need of care. When paramedics arrive at the scene of a serious accident, they have been taught that the most obvious victims—screaming, flailing, and covered in blood—are not necessarily the most seriously injured or in immediate danger. A silent person alone in a corner might be at much more at risk of dying within minutes due to internal hemorrhaging. Professionals need to be aware of this.

Another important phenomenon to be aware of, on a professional and personal level, is that we do not spontaneously have the mirror reflex of empathy when faced with dissociated victims. Instead, our natural impulse is to reflect back to them their indifference and lack of emotion concerning situations that should seem extremely troubling. Emotional anesthetization in the victim intercepts empathetic response in others. Only when we are aware of this can we modulate our response to provide adequate care and support? Those who care for victims must think rationally about the situation and, having prior knowledge of this phenomenon, recognize how their empathy reflex has been skewed. Only then can they reconstruct appropriate emotions to act in favor of victims.

Sometimes therapists or other professionals find themselves dissociating when listening to patients talk due to their own past trauma. Therapists might find similarities or associations with a patient's narrative that trigger their own traumatic memory. In some cases, violence endured by the patient is so shocking and atrocious that hearing about it can be traumatizing, even for a therapist who has no prior trauma. If professionals are not aware of such phenomena and of their own past trauma and repercussions, and if they have not developed the ability to identify and modulate or shut off their emotional responses, they might find themselves traumatized vicariously. They might also have ill-adapted responses that could constitute mistreatment and/or endanger the patient.

When listening to a certain patient, such professionals might succumb to uncontrolled anxiety, irritability, or even aggressivity. With a lack of empathy or benevolence, they might reject the victim or react with confusion or even numbness/banalization of violent acts (with comments that are unfortunately common, such as, "that's not very serious," "that was just child's play," "he didn't realize what he was doing," "you must have misunderstood") or indifference linked to the professional's own dissociation or emotional anesthesia. Such situations often lead to a lack of recognition or identification of violence and the dangers the victim survived—nothing will be done about the violence either to help the victim or to punish the perpetrator. The wrongness of what happened will be ignored, adding to the victim's trauma. Too often, professionals who are supposed to support, protect, and heal victims abandon them and sometimes even inflict new abuse on them.

4.6 Anesthetization Serves Abusers

As with victims, abusers also experience dissociation and emotional anesthetization, but they use these symptoms to serve their interests and control others. To play a role that is highly effective in duping victims and those around them with subtle but persuasive acts, abusers shift according to what circumstances require. One side of them masquerades as the friendly neighbor, the impressive professional, or the perfect father, and on the other side is the merciless dictator, the ruthless monster, the extreme sexual pervert, the raving lunatic. She might be the ideal friend, the devoted professional, the admirable mother in public, for her display window, and behind this, a woman with no conscience or compassion who does not hesitate to manipulate, betray, attack, or mistreat her children. When in public, she masks herself in lies—she is a complete fraud arranging everything so that she can, at no risk, secure herself a pool of victims at her disposal. They are often handed to her on a silver platter because she "is so kind to everyone" and "can do no wrong." The victims are totally disoriented by the shift from the "nicest person in the world" to the most hideous person imaginable (and back again). What can they make of this? Which one is real? What can they do about it? How can they not feel they are being very unfair when they denounce someone who was "so nice to them, so helpful, so loving?"

Even if the victims, against all odds, remain convinced that they are dealing with someone deeply perverse and have the courage to tell someone and denounce the abuse, they are at high risk of not being believed. Abusers' own emotional anesthetization makes violence and instrumentalization of others easy because they run no risk of feeling self-loathing or guilt, nor are they burdened with any compassion or empathy when faced with victims—factors that might otherwise limit the extent of violence they commit. The abuser is desensitized and can act without limits or conscience. The meticulous and sometimes well-advanced preparation for acts of violence already provokes disjunction, dissociation, and emotional anesthetization that facilitate the accomplishment of the attack (especially true of serial rapists and killers).

This explains why even after extremely serious violent acts repeated over long time periods, as in wars or state-sanctioned violence with crimes against humanity such as systematic rapes, torture, massacres, and genocide, the big war criminals and torturers still have no regret and do not feel guilty years or even decades later. They have stored up in their minds enough atrocities to feed their constant disjunction and emotional anesthetization.

5

On Your Own
Survival Strategies of Victims

5.1 Avoidance, Control, and Hypervigilance

To escape the atrocious suffering linked to traumatic memory, victims first put in place behaviors of avoidance, control, and hypervigilance. A flair-up of traumatic memory is true torture. Therefore, victims try to prevent this at all costs and avoid any stimuli that might set it off. They become hypervigilant, put in place avoidance strategies, and attempt to control their surroundings to be safe from anything that might remind them of the violence, even if not directly related. They might seek to avoid stressful or unpredictable situations, intense emotions, pain, and certain places or dates. They might be provoked by images, smells, words, voices, intonations, screams, noises, sensations, or touch. They avoid thinking or talking about these triggers. For victims who were not harmed from birth (for whom there is a before and after), they constantly feel in danger and lose all self-confidence; life has become a perilous minefield where nothing is as it was.

Reality can be even more dangerous if a victim is still enduring violence or threats. But even if the abuser is safe and the abuser is gone, traumatic memory can make her feel permanently in danger, with the threat of reliving the trauma at any moment. With traumatic memory dangling over her, she is unsafe

DOI: 10.4324/9781003497516-6

everywhere; her nights are foreboding, her thoughts potentially toxic, and her body at risk of reliving abuse at any moment. An unfortunate word or gesture from loved ones, even if perfectly innocent, might recall a detail of the violence, just as a TV or radio show or public lecture might be dangerous—everything carries a risk.

> Victims of violence do everything possible to restrict themselves to small, secure spaces innocent of any link to the violence—this means both physical and psychological spaces. Victims avoid thinking of anything that might have any connection to the violence so much that they might forget all or part of it. Entire stretches of life can disappear in this way, constituting what is called psychogenic amnesia; it sometimes lasts for decades. The mind systematically erases anything that could set off traumatic memory.

In this way, a young woman, 22 years old, did not remember when she was six years old, and her 16-year-old cousin sexually assaulted her. It was he who told her what he had done 20 years later. This young woman had a difficult adolescence of tremendous suffering, panic attacks, running away, trouble with schoolwork, recurring migraines, and especially serious sexual difficulties with vaginismus that made penetration impossible. She consulted many specialists about this. What her cousin finally revealed did not restore any memories in her, but gradually through therapy, symptoms, dreams, and sensory recollections allowed her to connect the dots and perceive the full picture of the traumatic violation; through doing so, she began to feel and live better than before.

5.2 A Disability in Personal, Professional, and Social Life

For a woman who was raped, going outside alone and encountering a man can put her in a situation of panic (she might only go out if someone accompanies her or she brings pepper spray, as many of my patients do). Being "trapped" in an elevator, airplane, subway, traffic jam, or classroom can be unbearable. Sleep is an ordeal (that she tries to put off as long as possible), and having sexual relations even with someone she loves is impossible except when she is totally dissociated. If she was kissed by force or raped orally, eating, swallowing, brushing her teeth, and going to the dentist are complicated sources of anxiety and nausea, and vomiting is unbearable. Someone brushing against her or being examined by a doctor can set off a panic attack. Having her period, defecating, having stomach aches or cystitis, or giving birth can all bring back the full torment of forced penetration.

Depending on when and where the violence occurred, a place, date, hour, season, day (often weekends, holidays, vacations), and atmosphere (night, very sunny day, rain, fog, snow) generate anxiety and are especially feared. Finding herself alone or without someone nearby to protect her can make her panic. I have many patients who were sexually abused in childhood when their mothers were gone, had massive separation anxiety as children, and found it impossible as adults to go out alone or stay home alone.

Stressful situations are very difficult for almost all trauma victims to manage, as they set off traumatic memory of extreme stress endured during the violence (they feel as they did when it happened). This involves neurovegetative hyperactive symptoms that are very disturbing, along with panic attacks, states of tonic immobility, and paralyzing psychological breakdowns. Victims find themselves unable to speak, respond, or act—they lose all their means. These reactions to stress are disabling, especially in situations where a lot is at stake for their academic or professional lives, such as oral or written tests, entrance exams, public speaking, or job interviews. These reactions of intolerance to stress can extend to an inability to answer the phone, write a letter, report, or thesis, or work with someone watching them. At their worst, they can make it impossible to have any professional or social life.

In social and intimate situations, these disproportionate reactions to stress make every encounter complicated and straining. To approach someone, talk to them, and declare feelings of love can be a terrible challenge, as can meeting new people for the first time or being in unknown situations. Being sick, going to the doctor, being examined, and medical procedures in general can be terrifying, and this is also so when a loved one is sick. Leisure activities can be contaminated by these reactions to stress, for example, the impossibility to tolerate suspense in a film or detective novel.

5.3 The Impact of "Educational" Violence

When parents physically or verbally assault children who haven't understood something or cannot answer a question, this leads to serious blockages from fear of making mistakes or not knowing something. These can paralyze the children's responses so that they cannot think straight and find answers when quizzed at school. They might then fail, which completes the cycle by provoking more abuse from parents. The petrifying terror of making a mistake or answering incorrectly, linked to traumatic memory of being raised with violence, can stay with people their whole lives and prevent them from voicing their own views and needs.

A patient who endured the crushing and tyrannical violence and domination of his father but who succeeded in spite of this at being an excellent student and brilliantly completed advanced degrees in literature, remained a little child terrorized by traumatic memory. With great literary talents and the desire to write novels, he could only experience this calling vicariously, "through citations," as he put it (citing a philosopher!). He moved forward hidden in the shadow of well-known authors that he could analyze and transmit as a teacher without the risk of exposing himself since he was not speaking in his own name. These avoidance behaviors have the advantage of allowing victims to never directly expose themselves while still being able to be themselves a little bit through the artist, writer, or philosopher they research, write about, or otherwise represent. For this patient, writing a novel was both his greatest desire and biggest fear. He had staked out a limited little life for himself in order to avoid any reminder of this, seeing very few people, avoiding strong emotions, and even depriving himself of friendships that would have given him too much joy and provoked an emotional response that would be too strong and thus a source of anxiety. He would not even allow himself to read books or poetry that he knew could be overstimulating.

5.4 The Restless Task of Avoiding Reminders

To avoid reminders at all costs, traumatized victims quickly figure out exactly which situations might ignite their traumatic memories. This includes situations they already experienced as well as those they guess might set it off or that they want to avoid, just in case. They will do anything to avoid these or, if not possible, to be ready for them and attempt to control the situation. This leads to debilitating phobic behaviors, reclusion, emotional withdrawal, limited thoughts and speech, and/or a state of constant alert with no possibility to relax. This explains sleep disorders, which are almost always present with traumatic memory—how can you fall asleep when it is impossible to let go and you are terrified of nightmares? It also explains the chronic fatigue and pain that victims always complain about. Being on edge, wound-up, and ready to flee to save your life is exhausting and leads to osteoarticular pain and severe headaches. Controlling the environment to detect any risky situation requires enormous mental effort and entails problems with concentration and attention because it is impossible to fully pay attention at work or when reading a book when you must at the same time survey everything around you. This mental effort is so taxing that any activity, even if it is pleasant and desired, is also feared.

To be able, in spite of all this, to at least live a little, victims self-censor constantly and stay in terrain that they have already tested and figured out in every detail. Usually, this terrain is extremely narrow, but at least victims can be relatively secure and feel a little bit of reassurance when living in it.

It might include home, loved ones, a few minor activities (always the same), TV shows, movies, or books known to be without risk, and a work situation that is not very stressful. If any change occurs—positive or negative—even a slight adjustment, everything crumbles. A move, pregnancy, birth, separation, departure, passing (especially of someone who protected them), loss of a pet, change of school, work assignment, job, or colleague… and everything has to start over. These changes are, as much as possible, systematically avoided. Sometimes, a new car, a new arrangement of furniture, and vacations can be just as destabilizing.

This explains the tenacious resistance of some victims to make changes that could be beneficial or even lifesaving, such as leaving a destructive family environment, separating from a violent partner or from ill-intentioned "friends," leaving a cult or a boring, horrible, or abusive job, or move out of substandard housing. A serious illness would be destabilizing not so much in itself as but rather due to an increase in vulnerability with many unknown and uncontrollable situations, stress from checkups, tests, and medical interventions, and other changes in lifestyle. This is why a traumatized victim might be in a paradoxical position of fearing an illness or treatment and yet being suicidal. Physical changes that others would hardly notice, such as slight hair loss in a man or the normal presence of a few wrinkles, creases, or spots on the skin, might be experienced by victims as horrible and catastrophic because they are definitive modifications to which they will have to adapt. Alterations in their physical appearance might make them feel even more vulnerable, and some avoid going out or covering up as much as possible.

For a teenage girl who was a victim of sexual violence, the physiological changes of puberty are usually experienced with severe anguish and a sense of danger. She might try to cover up the changes by wearing men's clothes or negate them through drastic diets and/or intense sports that make her body look prepubescent and stop her periods. Or she might try to muffle the changes by gaining a lot of weight and wearing baggy, shapeless clothing.

5.5 Nothing Makes Sense: Problems with Logic and Coherence

All avoidance and control behaviors are extremely disabling and most often not understood by those around victims, who get annoyed or judge them harshly when they urgently need help, support, reassurance, and security. Not recognizing symptoms of trauma, health professionals mislabel them depression, anxiety disorders, phobias, obsessive-compulsive disorder (OCD), or body dysmorphic disorder. They might even misdiagnose victims as neurotic or brand them as anxious, hysterical, phobic, or obsessional. Personality disorders might also be diagnosed in victims and treated only as such as if they arouse spontaneously with no connection to trauma.

Almost no one—including mental health professionals—connects these disorders (actually symptoms) to the lived experience of abuse and violence, to traumatic memory, or to survival strategies such as control and avoidance. The behaviors are perfectly logical and coherent to those who understand the constant danger lurking in victims' lives due to traumatic memory. Victims find themselves constantly walking on minefields where explosions can burst out from anywhere at any time. Every step they take risks setting off a hidden landmine. No one, when confronted with such a danger, could step forward except if totally unaware of the danger or totally disconnected (as we will see).

> The only options usually available are to freeze up and not take any more steps or to courageously explore the minefield step by step, very carefully, gradually identifying little secure spaces in which they can then circulate and avoiding unexplored spaces and those known to have landmines. For traumatized victims, the company of an experienced guide (a reassuring and attentive friend known to be stable, perceptive, and trustworthy) can be comforting, but even better is to be accompanied by a "demining expert" (a specialized psychotherapist) who

can teach victims to defuse or remove the "mines" themselves (the goal of traumatic memory- specific treatment).

Traumatized victims find themselves in a situation where making the slightest advance in life is ten times more exhausting and difficult for them than for someone who has not been traumatized, without any hope of assistance because no one sees any problem. It's as if to climb a mountain with a 1,000 meters (3,280 feet) of elevation gain, a climber with a traumatic memory carries a backpack ten times heavier than everyone else's packs, but no one knows or can see this difference (the packs look the same, but the victim's is filled with stones). Very quickly, no matter how much courage, endurance, or training she has, the victim lags behind, exhausted, and the group is annoyed at her "inability" to climb at the same speed as they do. She is unjustly perceived as lacking endurance and willpower and as complaining all the time—and how can she not feel like an incapable loser (especially when she might not understand her symptoms any more than they do)? She will painfully compare herself to others, even while realizing deep down that something is not right, because she knows she is doing her best.

It is easy to see why children grappling with traumatic memory are even more at risk, vulnerable, and dependent than adults, as traumatic violence can even stop the normal life course of adults and end their personal growth and creativity. The consequences for children are even more serious. An adult might somehow be able to figure out her symptoms, drawing from life experience and comparisons of life before and after the trauma. Adults can think back to who they were and who they wanted to become. A child, in a constant state of becoming, has no stable reference point. Children are forced to construct themselves however they can within a violent and incoherent universe of constant danger. Instead of discovering themselves and the world, they must focus on security and survival.

The abusers and their incoherent behaviors vampirize the child-victim's mental energy so that she (or he) spends all her time observing them to anticipate and avoid abuse. She develops adult abilities before her time and an abnormal awareness and knowledge of the aggressors' psychology. This includes deciphering how an aggressor is feeling, including the slightest changes in mood and the least annoyance or desire, which the victim will immediately attend to. She becomes the perfect slave: Submissive, devoted, and attentive only to the needs of others; she has no choice.

Children are forced to integrate an entire system of insane and tyrannical rules imposed by abusers within the home—a system totally at odds with the outside world. They acquire the resources and strategies to survive effectively within this family universe but do not develop the tools to live in the outside world. They feel like strangers to this world, so different in everything that they are terribly isolated. The only children with whom they have anything in common are other child victims with whom they can feel in familiar territory.

In addition to a family environment riddled with landmines, the child's own psyche becomes volatile as traumatic memory sets in. She must face not only the ongoing abuse but also survive with significant psycho-traumatic that becomes chronic and ingrains the patterns of abuse and violence into her own being. She must include these as part of her personality since she has no point of comparison. Her reactions, survival strategies, and symptoms linked to abuse and its psycho-traumatic consequences become part of her. She also incorporates the abuser's farces and behaviors (scorn, hatred, cruelty, excitement...). Normal development is not possible. As long as she is not protected and liberated from the traumatic memory of everything she was subjected to, significant developmental and personality issues are likely, including the feeling of not knowing who she is, whether she is a good person, garbage, a monster, what she wants or doesn't want, likes or doesn't like, and so on. (Her own identity is confounded with that of the abuser.)

Children possess fewer tools than adults for making sense of the world, as they have much less knowledge and experience; they are highly dependent on the protection and abilities of adults around them. Children's autonomy and freedom to organize the world around them to face dangers and protect themselves is also limited. Adults who are not abusive and could protect them usually have no understanding of what is going on. They have no insight into the actual conditions of these children. Instead, they devote tremendous energy to preventing them from mobilizing the avoidance, control, and protective behaviors that they need in place of the reassuring presence of caring and competent adults. These non-abusers are usually well-intentioned and want the children to gain autonomy at all cost—while the children feel in great danger—and develop like other children (who are not being abused and are unfettered by traumatic memory).

Such adults put traumatized children in tremendous psychological danger in forcing them to move forward and give up avoidance behaviors, which are said to be regressive (sleep beside an adult, suck their thumbs, and so on). Even more than adults, children may be driven to extremely harmful dissociating risk behaviors to survive and will feel even more painfully different from others without knowing why, progressively viewing themselves as disabled when facing life.

The abusers tend to favor traumatic memory and the resultant control and avoidance behaviors in their victims. They should control the surroundings so that nothing can destabilize the "master," and its responsibility is thrust on child victims to avoid any situation that might set off traumatic memory in the abuser. In a family situation, children might be ordered to not disturb or annoy adults and be trained to serve desires of parents, including their need for appearances and their need to dominate unquestioned.

The children thus develop abnormally acute abilities to analyze and observe, as they need to identify with the adults' functioning to better understand and anticipate whatever might provoke them. The children have no right to exist except under these conditions and are the perfect slaves: Kind, attentive, considerate, and submissive. Senseless violence falls on them so that the masters can "explode" without risk to themselves when their traumatic memories are sparked despite all efforts of the slave to prevent this.

As Sándor Ferenczi has written: "It is necessary to know the dangerous adversary perfectly and put yourself in his place constantly in order to gain any peace. You have to follow every one of his movements to protect yourself from them and try to appease and reason with the terrible tyrant." Such obligations to constantly put yourself in the abuser's place and be forced to understand and protect him at all costs make it so the interests of the abuser artificially become those of the abused child and lead to a loyalty in all circumstances and a "pseudo-attachment." For the child to feel safe, it is essential that the abusive parent feel good and not be annoyed. This task—of survival—becomes more and more important and goes before what should be the primary needs, desires, and interests of the child. This largely explains the Stockholm Syndrome.

5.6 The Stockholm Syndrome: Love Your Enemy

The Stockholm Syndrome was named after a hostage-taking incident in the city of Stockholm, Sweden. The hostages took the side of the terrorists to the point of turning against the police. This is what happened to women who were kidnapped as little girls and isolated and tortured for many years, such as Natascha Kampusch in Austria and Jaycee Dugard in the United States. After their liberation, they vacillated between hatred and pseudo-attachment toward someone whose least thoughts and emotions they had needed to adopt in order to survive. They became prolongations and coveted medicine of the abuser; refusing him anything became unthinkable. The abuser's interests necessarily became superior. Furthermore, the words repeated constantly by the abuser with the order to obey him, love him, and be loyal to him whatever happened, along with farces in which the victim was construed as having no rights and no worth, colonized the victim through her own traumatic memory and gradually transformed her into a devoted slave. Words lose their meanings, and for the victim, terror becomes love, and extreme stress becomes excitement and desire. For the abuser, hatred, violence, and destruction become love, and cruelty becomes desire or educative training in a constant perverse reversal.

5.7 Victims Are Conditioned to Stay Trapped

The tyrannical training imposed on children by abusers leads them to be over-sensitive to the least desires of others. As adults, they still believe it is necessary never to contradict or conflict with anyone, or they will feel in great danger. This is due to traumatic memory from childhood abuse at the hands of their oppressor each time they upset him or her. Such adults find it difficult to say no or to express their own needs or desires. This training is dangerous because it traps the now-grown child victims in constant service and attention to others. They are perfect potential slaves who can be used infinitely and appear to consent to numerous abuses—so kind, understanding, and emotionally intelligent...

Manipulators and abusers take advantage of this training to take control of victims and abuse them in ways that are difficult to discern or denounce. The victim's compliance and adaptability to every difficulty usually deter more obvious situations of violence (physical and verbal). The violence is no less, but it is more hidden, as psychological constraints force victims to submit without any objection to circumstances that deny their rights, dignity, integrity, and safety.

Within couple relationships, one partner might be trained in this way to make sure the violent partner is spared any stress, discomfort, and possible jealousy or frustration, including from sexual "needs" often used to gain dissociation. The partner formatted by trauma avoids claiming any autonomy that would lead the abuser to fear a loosening of his or her hold. Many women especially become slaves/medication fully devoted by force to their husbands, trembling at the idea of harming him or putting him "in danger" through filing a complaint or running away.

When victims do succeed in fleeing their abusers, they do not find themselves safe. Abusers who have lost their victim/medicine/drug find themselves feeling this withdrawal, which puts them in a state of severe tension where they will risk doing anything to get her back and will not let go. Acting out dissociating scenes, he might become extremely violent and dangerous, as many murders of women by intimate partners take place following a separation.

Escaped victims face not only dangerous threats and harassment from their ex but also the traumatic memory of violence endured is at risk of exploding and making them suffer more because they can no longer have any influence over the environment or behavior of their abuser (they think they see him leaping out everywhere, all the time). The end of (often daily) violence means that the almost permanent state of disjunction and dissociation it produced, and that anesthetized and disconnected them, fades. The angst linked to their traumatic memory might sometimes lead them to believe, quite wrongly, that it is the separation itself that is making them feel so bad. They believe that they cannot survive without their torturer and that they have him "under their skin" (as the song goes).

Constant vigilance and control behaviors can, paradoxically, become risk factors. As a victim constantly surveys everything around her in public, with all her antennas out, she is inevitably alerted to people with abnormal behaviors and attitudes or a worrying look about them, and she is attentive to their slightest movements or actions. This state of alert and this focus on unsafe people will identify her immediately to them as a victim and, therefore, potential prey. This is why a victim often finds herself targeted and approached by abusers who literally get their hands on them and don't let go, using dissociating strategies of infiltration/control/colonization (using tonic immobility and traumatic memory) and/or simple strategies of seduction.

Victims are not looking for abusers, though it might seem that way since they are so often trapped with them. It is not that they don't see it coming; they actually detect abusers too well, with their hypervigilant antennas deployed (their scanner, as one patient put it), when no one else would notice. Paradoxically, their ability to sense the danger puts them in danger. This detection sparks the traumatic memory of the abuser, which englobes not only the victim that he was but also all the terrorized victims that he has abused. This arouses in him the need to dissociate through committing new acts of violence. The victim's detecting process also informs him of the overdeveloped adaptive abilities that would make her a good victim for him.

Only a victim previously trained for her survival will survey the least acts and gestures of her abuser over time and endure this alone without seeking help. Such overdeveloped abilities are a guarantee of total impunity for abusers. The strategies that they use are based on the mechanisms of traumatic memory in their victims. Sometimes, a traumatized victim feels so much in danger (identified, approached, and attacked constantly) in spite of control behaviors that she does not go out anymore at all, does so only with someone or—last resort—when already anesthetized. She becomes anesthetized following dissociation gained by excessive use of alcohol, drugs, or risk behaviors such as wearing certain clothes or behaving in a dangerous way.

Avoidance leads to phobias, OCDs, emotional withdrawal, insomnia, chronic fatigue, development of an imaginary worlds, and ADHD, which are prejudicial to having a satisfying personal, social, and professional life. Even so, these control and avoidance behaviors are rarely enough, especially when new violence or big changes happen (adolescence, a romantic encounter, birth of a child, entry into professional life, losing a job…). Traumatic memory explodes, traumatizing victims again and leading to disjunction, emotional anesthesia, and a new traumatic memory.

Soon, spontaneous disjunction is not possible anymore, as a higher dose is needed of the addictive "hard drugs" secreted by the brain. The previous quantity of these drugs no longer produces the effect that it used to, and victims stay stuck in distress and the intolerable feeling of imminent death that can sometimes drive them to suicide.

5.8 Dissociation and Anesthetization: Anything to Avoid the Landmines

When avoidance behaviors are no longer enough or are not possible, victims often only have one solution to control traumatic memory: Behaviors of dissociation that they already experienced as effective while enduring acts of violence. To end extreme suffering and intolerable distress or to avoid feeling these again, victims seek the emotional anesthetization that will finally relieve them at any cost.

It often happens that victims can no longer protect themselves by using control and avoidance behaviors. This might be because they are prevented from using these—often the case for children and adolescents—or because new situations and life changes make them no longer a viable option. It also might happen each time victims must move forward in territory that is unsafe because it is unknown, are confronted with the risk of setting off their traumatic memory, or are exposed to their abuser or to new acts of violence.

Traumatic memory flares up again—they step on the mine, and it explodes. Recalling prior violence and the unbearable anguish, the victim's psyche is again in a state of tonic immobility, and the victim is unable to calm herself or to use her reasoning faculties to connect what she is experiencing to violence in her past. She panics, as this stress is beyond her control, and the distress is unbearable. Her cortex cannot eliminate or modulate the emotional response, which incurs a new "overload" and life-threatening risk. As with the initial violence, a new disjunction must occur. Each time, this reinforces traumatic memory, adding the trauma of this new disjunction to previous traumas. Moreover, due to the addictive property of drugs secreted by the brain, the disjunction is increasingly difficult to obtain. Eventually, the disjunction can no longer occur by itself, and the victim must provoke it. For this, she relies on specific patterns called behaviors of dissociation.

The traumatized victim quickly learns that some behaviors, such as banging his head against walls, hurting himself, putting himself in danger, getting drunk, taking drugs, screaming, being violent, eating nonstop, thinking about suicide or self-mutilation, or fantasizing about extreme violence calm him immediately. They stop the suffering by cutting him off from any emotion. These behaviors allow the victim to detach himself and be in a state of emotional indifference, or at least go for some time into another world.

What exactly happens? Disjunction happens due to the secretion of neurotransmitters that are endogenous drugs (produced by the body itself) classified as morphine-like (endorphins) and ketamine-like (antagonists of NMDA [N-methyl-D-aspartate] receptors) that have the same properties as narcotics. They can lead to addiction, tolerance, and dependence. When they occur frequently, disjunctions lead to habituation and need for the dissociating drugs secreted by the brain. The previous quantities of endogenous drugs no longer suffice to provoke disjunction and emotional anesthesia. A larger quantity of the drugs is necessary to gain the same effect. The existing traumatic memory, ordering the same dose of the drug, can no longer incur spontaneous neurobiological disjunction. Without this, the victim seeks a means to force disjunction of the emotional circuitry, and the means typically found are called behaviors of dissociation.

Behaviors of dissociation are backup mechanisms in situations of addiction and tolerance. They directly create a state of dissociation and anesthetization through anticipation of a situation that is likely to set off traumatic memory. They serve to provoke a larger secretion of endogenous drugs and further increase the stress level to finally allow for disjunction. Sometimes the victim adds to the endogenous drugs (produced by her own brain) exogenous dissociative drugs (alcohol, cannabis, heroine, opioids, LSD, ketamine, glue, etc.) in a quantity sufficient to finally provoke emotional anesthetization. Disjunctions and emotional anesthetization are no longer spontaneous when traumatic memory flares up; they now result from an intentional behavior, though victims are probably unaware of why they are doing this: To "trip the circuit" and obtain emotional anesthetization.

The behaviors that provoke disjunction are self-treating mechanisms of defense through anesthetization. They occur in situations of emotional overload and work by incurring surplus stress through risk behaviors and transgressions (risk of death through dangerous driving, extreme sports, anorexia and/or bulimia, unsafe sex, etc.). Personal risks might also take the form of careless spending, kleptomania, dangerous company, failure, neglect, and putting others at risk through delinquent behaviors, picking fights, and other violence. Situations of senseless terror (self-inflicted abuse, self-mutilation, running away) or terrifying thoughts and scenarios might also be sought for their ability to provoke an extreme and uncontrollable emotional response. Stimulating substances (such as amphetamines, ecstasy, cocaine, or crack) might also be sought for the high production of adrenaline that results. The emotional response is added to that of traumatic memory and produces an even stronger overload and therefore a larger secretion of endogenous dissociative drugs, which allows for disjunction to occur. These behaviors are stress addictions. Dissociating substances (alcohol, drugs, and some medications) directly provoke emotional anesthetization and a dissociative state and can be complemented by bodily techniques such as swaying, jolting, loud music, and self-hypnosis.

5.9 Dissociative Acts: Seeking Risk and Danger

Dissociative actions are those whose purpose is psychological or physical danger and heightened stress. They are deliberate, dangerous actions, most often repeated, that impose themselves as the only solution for traumatized victims faced with the unbearable effects of traumatic memory. Victims know the danger and senselessness of their actions but have no other means to escape a situation of overload. They cannot explain their actions but are forced by the urgency of a distress that nothing can calm.

Faced with the necessity of disjunction, a victim's need to hurt himself "naturally" arises: He bangs his head against the wall, hits, bites, pinches, scratches, cuts, or burns himself, or pulls out his hair. In dire need of something, the victim actively seeks to put herself in danger or to encounter the kind of violence she knows can appease her quickly. She might try to reason with herself, but most often, this is to no avail, and she knows she will descend into this vicious cycle again.

Dangerous and violent dissociative actions deployed in the service of disjunction, even when they are self-inflicted and harm no one else, are held against victims. Most people—professionals or not—would react to a victim in the middle of a traumatic memory explosion by using violent and dissociative actions themselves rather than calming words. They might try yelling, "slapping the victim out of it," throwing water in her face, shoving her under a cold shower, shaking her violently, locking her up, or threatening to abandon her ("If you don't stop screaming, I'm leaving!"). They might use violent means of restraint (ropes, straight jackets) or chemical restraint (powerfully dissociating psychotropic treatments). Such violence used to "calm" traumatized victims who "lose it" are unfortunately effective insofar as they do make the victims disjunct, which has the effect of anesthetizing them at the cost of aggravating their traumatic memory.

Victims gradually experiment with various dissociating actions and choose the most effective as well as the easiest to access, least costly, and most often least dangerous for herself and others. It all depends on what she has nearby and what will work best. It is very easy to have access to something to hurt or endanger oneself. It is easy for traumatized victims to strangle themselves with a scarf, put their heads under the water in a bathtub, self-mutilate with a razor or knife, burn themselves, or ingest a large quantity of food in a short time. Motor vehicles, especially motorcycles and scooters, are very effective for putting themselves in danger. Many sports, especially extreme sports, can be tremendous sources of risk situations. Alcohol is very easy to have on hand, with the first intake being very early, on average 8 years old in France, and 13 for the first time getting drunk. Studies show that those who have psycho-traumatic disorders have a significant risk of becoming alcoholics or drug addicts: 58% of men and 28% of women for alcohol and 35% of men and 27% of women for psychoactive substances. Almost 90% of severe alcoholics and drug addicts have traumatic pasts and histories of child abuse in particular. Clearly, people do not become addicted for no reason!

Another way victims anesthetize themselves through extreme stress is to scare themselves without putting themselves in direct danger and without using others, through detective novels or horror movies, but also through imaginary scenes where they are exposed to horrible dangers, murder, rape attempts, torture, or serious illness. These scenarios might become so invasive that they become delusions of persecution, especially among elderly women who endured incestuous abuse in childhood and were never able to talk about it.

One patient, over 80 years old, was regularly raped and tortured by her father from childhood until she was 20 years old. She survived these atrocities with no help, and once she was alone at home (her husband being hospitalized long-term), she developed a delusion that her neighbors were trying to enter her home to harm her. This elaborate delusion occupied her mind constantly, and every noise, smell, or coming or going of the neighbors was seen as attempted aggression. This included complex scenarios that generated extreme stress followed by anesthetizing disjunction and dissociation. Being alone at home awoke in her the danger that she knew as a child and adolescent when her father always took advantage of her mother and other family members' absence to commit his crimes. Her traumatic memory flared up and brought unbearable suffering and terror. Though at first, spontaneous disjunction put an end to this state, tolerance and addiction mechanisms soon set in and left her to deal with her distress with nothing to stop it. Imagining an intrusive and imminent danger increased the level of stress and allowed for provoked disjunction. She became a real addict to her delusions of persecution. Talking with her about the incestuous sexual violence she endured and giving words to name what she lived through, linking it to her symptoms, and having her talk to her daughter for the first time about what happened allowed her to slowly disarm her traumatic memory and calm her delusion without neuroleptic treatments.

The only freedom left for victims is to choose their dissociating actions, which makes the difference between those who stay in the position of victim through choosing actions that are dangerous for themselves and, as we will see, those who choose to become abusers. These victims-turned-abusers instrumentalize people or animals for disjunction by procuration (animals bear the brunt of the traumatic memories of some of their "masters," adult or child).

5.10 From Victim to Perpetrator: A Tragic Dissociative Mechanism

In terms of the stress produced, violence against someone else is as effective as violence against oneself, or even more so since it "benefits" from the supplementary stress generated by the horror of doing something immoral, atrocious, and criminal to an innocent victim. Such horror produces an even more severe psychological violation insofar as it makes no sense. It can be quite easy, for those who authorize themselves to do so, to keep close at hand another person to terrorize and harm.

Abusers rise from the ranks of former victims (usually abused as children). Among all the dissociative behaviors available to them, their favorite is to harm others. Someone who has not endured traumatizing violence has no reason to make others endure it and will get no benefit from this. Everything will prevent it, from fundamental ethics as a human being to natural empathy for fellow humans. The suffering of another would be unbearable, and the thought of the consequences of the acts would be a sickening, restless torment. Jorge Semprun described in *Literature or Life* the young German officer he found swimming in a river and then killed to take the weapons off when he was in the resistance movement during WWII. His nights were haunted by the officer and Semprun's own constant guilt. He thought about the life of this young German, his childhood, his family, the women he loved, the plans he had, and this tortured Semprun for years. This is a normal human reaction.

> As contradictory as it might seem, the inhuman violence against another is unfortunately possible because the abuser experiences it as very effective "treatment" for his own psycho-trauma. Inflicting suffering on another, abusers "treat" the psycho-traumatic consequences of the senseless and inhuman violence they previously endured (usually as children).

Victims are sacrificed to be used as medicine. Ready to explode at the moment of violence, with both victim and perpetrator beyond any tolerable threshold of stress, the perpetrator uses the victim to blow up in his place. This prompts his brain to produce hard drugs of dissociation that result in disjunction. The perpetrator saves himself from physical harm and from loss of dignity (as his chosen victim will endure these in his place). He actively seeks psychological harm through violation linked to the horrific nonsense of the violence committed. This creates extreme overload that trips his emotional circuitry. He will commit acts of violence intentionally not only when his traumatic memory flares up but also to prevent this from happening (as a precaution) and to gain emotional anesthetization almost constantly.

To use children, innocent by definition, as substitutes for self-harm and making them endure inhuman violence is extremely effective for obtaining disjunction. This is because the human psyche is not made to withstand violence that shakes the foundations of what it means to be human without risking total psychological destruction. Humans are normally incapable of committing *inhuman* violence. A loud alarm (emotional response) goes off immediately and is so insufferable as to make the inhuman acts impossible. However, when the alarm is actually sought because the inhuman violence was already endured, disjunction experienced, and traumatic memory put in place, everything is off track. The perpetrator can cross even the most impossible lines. No fear of physical or psychological death will stop him. He is already dead to the world and thus immortal. As Don Juan invites to dinner the statue of the commander he murdered, the fires of Hell do not scare him since he has already been there and back.

Victims of senseless violence have also met with death (a sort of physical death and especially psychological death faced with an absurdity that cannot be integrated). They come back as lifeless shadows of themselves. As long as incoherence is the norm in life, victims will feel already dead, like zombies or automatons. The violence killed them psychologically and devitalized them at the moment of psychological effraction. Since then, they have been eternally trapped in that moment when everything changed and locked into this unspeakable experience. The resulting disjunction and dissociation allow victims to set up appearances of self, but like ghosts, they go forward anesthetized and absent to life. Senseless violence makes victims into the living dead. Only a transfusion of sense could allow them to leave this hell and revive the psyche's tonic immobility. Specialized psychotherapy for traumatized victims and art are thankfully there to give back sense and coherence to many lives. Perpetrators are the real monsters; devoid of emotion, they think themselves immortal.

5.11 Reliving Traumatic Violence

Whether for victims or perpetrators, what is most effective to obtain disjunction and dissociation/anesthetization is to intentionally reproduce the initial trauma, though they do not understand why. This adds a "horror bonus" of incoherence. This "horror bonus" is terribly efficient for provoking tonic immobility in the psyche and disjunction in both perpetrator and victim. Reproducing the violence, committing or imitating an aspect of it, revives the initial traumatic act. When victims play around with suffocating themselves, for example, this can closely imitate an abuser's attempts to strangle, suffocate, or drown them. Children's sexualized games, their drawings, things they say, and how they expose themselves by stripping or masturbating in front of adults are also behaviors of repetition that are efficient for children to anesthetize themselves. Victims of sexual violence might use sexual self-mutilation, fantasies involving rape or other sexual violence, unsafe sexual practices, promiscuity, and/ or sadomasochism to gain this same anesthetizing effect.

Prostitution and pornography also replay scenes of violence. Prostitutes and "actresses" in pornography are trapped in the role of victims, while the consumers take on the abusers' role. This efficient dissociative role for porn users unfortunately explains pornography's success and expansion with more and more violent scenarios. Cults, gurus, dictators, tyrannical husbands, and gang leaders all recall and replay the colonizing control and tyrannical domination of violence within a family that the victim experienced as a child. Taking dangerous risks such as running away, self-neglect, and extreme experiences (hunger, cold, isolation, homelessness, drunken comas) all replay severe neglect, abandonment, and absence of care during childhood. Frequent accidents falls, and fractures replay physical violence endured in childhood (see the excellent work of Cornet, 1997). Eating disorders such as bulimia and anorexia replay force-feeding or starvation during childhood and sexual violence through oral penetration.

All risk behaviors that involve physical and psychological harm and degradation faithfully reflect the absence of worth that the children endured in the eyes of those who were supposed to care for them. All these risk behaviors have the self-treating goal of emotional anesthetization, but their repetition rapidly leads to dependence and aggravated tolerance (as with drug addicts and alcoholics, who are also enacting dissociative behaviors). This creates a snowball effect of risk, danger, and violence. It can generate a chronic dissociative state close to schizophrenia with total emotional indifference and experiences of depersonalization that are very dangerous for the victim. This chronic dissociation, involving both physical and emotional anesthetization, is found in extreme trauma that is repeated over time (situations of prostitution, homeless vagrancy, torture, sequestration, slavery, deportation, alcoholism, extreme addiction). Studies have shown that the risk of early death is high in such circumstances. When this extreme indifference sets in with those who commit violence against others, extremely dangerous perpetrators are made. Blatant lack of emotion and a smoothness in people who have committed criminal acts should tip off health and justice professionals.

5.12 Dangerous Behaviors in Adolescents

These dissociative behaviors are particularly apparent when victims of violence reach adolescence, especially when they are forbidden to put in place avoidance behaviors. They are very dangerous, causing many accidents on the road, at home, and in sports, which can be fatal (among adolescents and young adults under 25, the leading cause of death is accidents, and the second is suicide, much more frequent among victims). However, dissociative behaviors are just as dangerous through the intermediary of risk behaviors and severe neglect, such as overuse of alcohol, drugs, tobacco, unsafe sex, eating disorders, and bodily risks due to extreme sports. These continue into adulthood in a less obvious form, but they are just as catastrophic for health, life quality, and feeding the cycle of violence.

Dissociative behaviors are absolutely not understood by loved ones or professionals, and they are never linked to abuse. They are at the origin of what prevention campaigns seek to stop through fear (use of drugs and tobacco, spread of STIs, etc.). These are often ineffective or even counterproductive since they take no account of the traumatic origin of such behaviors or of their self-treating function when faced with the suffering and anguish that no one thinks to address. They take a moralizing and judgmental approach, employing tactics similar to threats and blackmail, totally ignoring the behaviors' origins in trauma. In adolescents, risk behaviors are often wrongly labeled as rites of passage, experimentation, exploration, pushing the limits, thrill-seeking, identity quests, or provocations and challenges when faced with the authority of the adult world. Only recognition of suffering, securitization, identification of lived experiences of violence, and treatment based on this can limit such behaviors and eventually allow victims to be entirely free of them.

5.13 Dissociation through Accumulation of Stress

We have examined the most violent dissociative behaviors, but there are others that result in dissociation through an accumulation of stress, such as gambling, compulsive shopping, and risky administrative and financial practices, as well as failure in studies or work. Some victims can no longer leave home without feeling in great danger. To be able to venture out in spite of this in dangerous territory (with men approaching them constantly), if they have to go out alone, they might put themselves in a state of dissociation and anesthetization through getting drunk or high or putting themselves in danger "before the time."

A 20-year-old patient who was victim of incest from her father from 8 to 14 years old could only go out after putting on garish makeup and ostentatious clothing. This clearly put her at risk, making her an immediate target as soon as she stepped outside. This generated significant stress, and the anticipation of possible scenarios of sexual aggression were effective in prompting an explosion of traumatic memory "in advance." Disjunction gave her the emotional anesthetization that she sought, allowing her to go out with the completely erroneous perception of being protected. Not surprisingly, she was accosted by predators and trapped by her behaviors of dissociation. The more dangerous the situation, with significant risks of aggression, the more she "added to it" compulsively to dissociate, overacting the role of "sex bomb," as she defined herself, making sexual remarks and carrying herself in a seductive way. The more afraid she was, the more she sought to dissociate to better anesthetize herself through putting herself in even greater danger. For this young woman, this ended many times in being locked up and raped, which, once she emerged from emotional anesthetization, put her in horrific pain and distress, only wishing to die so all that could finally end.

It is important to note that she absolutely did not want this violence and that she was terrorized rather than consenting. The sex predators discerned that she was vulnerable and terrorized, and they knew that she could not possibly want what they made her endure. In this situation of total inequality, some act with violence in the name of a false sexual "desire," which is really only the desire to destroy and annihilate the dignity of the other. They have absolutely no concern ever about the victim's humanity, but only about their own urge to be violent and use sexuality as a tool to procure without risk a highly effective drug to disconnect them. As for the woman, her body and psyche are directly subjected to being torn apart as an object that can be used, degraded, and considered as a place for "relief" where perpetrators calm themselves through unspeakable acts of horror. Just as with prostitution and pornography, men seeking dissociating violence can "buy themselves" a pretty young woman that they can pollute with their most demeaning "fantasies" and their most degrading acts, imposing themselves violently on her.

5.14 Addicted to Violence: The Traumatized Aggressor

As with the victim, the perpetrator needs to reenact traumatic memory to gain dissociation. Both experience an increase in dependence, tolerance, and addiction to endogenous drugs of dissociation. They need an increasingly large dose of the secreted substances to obtain disjunction, just as with heroin addiction (habituation and tolerance). Because the traumatic memory is constantly being recharged, it explodes more and more often, which creates an increasingly urgent need for disjunction (addiction).

The traumatized aggressor is a true addict to violence. The consequences of the new traumatic memory and the nonstop refueling and endless reactivation by situations or reminders of violent acts already committed results in a need of "treatment" through further violence. It becomes more and more severe through a drug-addicted mounting of horror. This is an endless process, the senseless violence being both the cause and consequence of a hellish self-engendered loop. Each time, the victim is the unwitting trigger of the perpetrator's traumatic memory of abuse he already made her endure and also the fuse for him to dissociate and anesthetize himself.

This is why imposing meetings or confrontations between victim and perpetrator puts the victim in serious danger of being retraumatized. She becomes dissociated and thus at risk for new acts of violence. Restorative justice plays with fire in organizing meetings between victims and perpetrators. Such confrontations will not lessen traumatic memory, and even if the perpetrators are not the same ones who violated the victims, there is a huge risk that the victims will be traumatized, dissociated, and thus more at risk for further acts of violence. As for perpetrators, they flare up when faced with victims and then seek to harm them or other victims in order to dissociate.

It might happen that traumatized victims surprised by the explosion of a traumatic memory that they did not anticipate and that did not provoke spontaneous disjunction resort to the dissociative "reflex" of violent behaviors toward someone close to them. If this is not a choice that they make and they do not consider their victim as inferior or worthless, they will be struck by terrible guilt, which is quite different from a seasoned perpetrator. They will not minimize the harm done and, on the contrary, will not stop trying to repair it. They don't consider it natural to act like nothing happened, will not force themselves on their victim, and will not use any emotional blackmail. They will put all their mental energy into trying to grasp what happened and understand why it did, torturing themselves with the consequences of their acts, controlling their every move, and/or seeking professional help.

A seasoned perpetrator is the opposite. He might apologize in bad faith when it is his only option, but he will quickly pick up his old habits. He tends to imply that the victim is responsible: "If you hadn't said that…, if you hadn't done that…, you are the only person who makes me act that way…, you should have calmed me down…, why didn't you leave…," and so on. He might also excuse himself: "I'm under too much stress… that's the way I am…, I'm just naturally jealous…, alcohol does that to me, or fatigue, conflict, lateness, frustration, changes of plan, disorder, criticism."

5.15 Pain and Failure: Legacies of Psycho-Trauma

All the psycho-traumatic mechanisms that we just described allow us to understand the symptoms that victims of violence present: Mental suffering, depressive disorders, suicidal tendencies, anxiety disorders (anxiety or panic attacks, phobias, OCDs), cognitive disorders (of memory, attention, concentration, spatio-temporal orientation…), dissociative disorders with frequent traumatic amnesia, personality disorders, issues with self-esteem and behavior (social withdrawal, addiction, problems with diet or sexuality…), and paradoxical behaviors (risk-taking, dependence on the abuser…).

Violence leads to premature death, accidents, depression, suicide attempts, alcoholism, drug-addiction, marginality, and prostitution. Studies have shown that 80% to over 90% of people who experience these were abused in the past. The health consequences for victims of abuse are severe, as numerous epidemiological studies have shown (Felitti and Anda, 2010), including cardiovascular, bronchopulmonary, endocrine, digestive, gynecological, obstetric, immune, neurological, rheumatological, ORL, and dermatological problems, in addition to chronic pain and fatigue.

Research on this can be understood in light of traumatic memory. The 2010 IPSOS-AIVI study has shown the dramatic consequences of incest in adult survivors, with 94% of them plagued by memories of the abuse (traumatic memory), 90% having recurring difficulties with falling or staying asleep, 86% having recurring nightmares, 77% finding it impossible to have sexual intercourse even if they want to, 68% not being able to concentrate for long periods of time or hold down a job, 41% regularly self-mutilating, and 12% prostituting themselves (over 70% of those in situations of prostitution having endured sexual violence in childhood). Compared with the overall population, 98% of incest survivors feel depressed, in contrast with 56% overall. As for fear of others and difficulty saying no to them, it is 93% of victims versus 29% of the overall population; suicidal thoughts or impulses: 86% versus 14% (with 53% of victims having attempted suicide); chronic pain: 85% versus 56%; eating disorders: 70% versus 9%; fear of having children and being bad parents: 64% versus 12%; and smoking, getting drunk, and taking drugs: Twice or three times more than average. Eight out of ten feel guilty, and victims wait for an average of 16 years before telling anyone about having been sexually abused. They are most likely to tell (in order) a friend, partner, relative, health professional, teacher, organization, social worker, and (lastly) police. Most adopt avoidance behaviors so as to not alert anyone to what happened.

A study on violence in Seine-Saint-Denis (Paris region) with 1,566 women ages 18–21 revealed that 23% endured severe violence in two-thirds of the cases repeatedly and by an adult in the family before they were 16 years old. Among these, 15% considered themselves in bad health (3% for the general population). They were three times more likely to declare a chronic illness and twice as likely to have unprotected sex.

In our large-scale study on the impact of childhood sexual violence on adult survivors (IVSEA, 2015), 96% of the 1,214 victims of sexual violence reported severe consequences on their mental health and 69% on their physical health. They were especially numerous (83%) to suffer a loss of self-esteem, and 71% considered themselves different from others. Almost 70% had dissociative disorders, with emotional anesthetization and traumatic amnesia for 40% of them. Sixty percent described significant mental suffering with recollections and intrusive images of the violence (flashbacks). Eighty percent had anxiety disorders, 60% had phobias and mood disorders, and half had attempted suicide. Half suffered from addictive behaviors and 36% from eating disorders, 15% had auditory, olfactory, visual, and tactile hallucinations, and 10% had episodes that qualify as delusional.

5.16 Pregnancy: A Catastrophic Consequence for Women

A large number of respondents in our study reported pregnancies resulting from rape, with 8.5% of rape victims becoming pregnant from the rape. Among these, 40% chose to have abortions, 25% gave birth, 14% miscarried, 5% had medically recommended abortions, and 3% took emergency contraception. In around 20% of the cases, pregnancies resulting from rape concerned minors between 9 and 17 years old when they became pregnant, the average age being 15. Only one of these, 15 years old when the rape/pregnancy occurred, carried the pregnancy to term. Sixty eight percent of victims could not bring themselves to mention the rape when they requested emergency contraception or abortion (78% for minors). It is important to systematically ask pregnant women and girls, including those seeking abortion or emergency contraception, questions about rape and abuse.

5.17 Mental Symptoms in the Body: Somatizations Resistant to Treatment

Somatic complaints (resulting from mental state but experienced in the body) are particularly multiform, chronic, recurring, and resistant to treatment. Our study of adult survivors of child abuse revealed that almost half suffer from somatic dermatological, gastroenterological, urinary, gynecological, cardiovascular, respiratory, and other problems (IVSEA, 2015). These complaints are often the reason they seek medical attention, treatment, tests, hospitalization, and surgery. In addition to direct consequences of physical violence, somatic complaints are a manifestation and expression of embodied traumatic memory and the stress that goes with it, as well as that of hypervigilant behaviors and anxious anticipation, all of which result in significant psychological and muscular-tendinous tensions. Such complaints might be the only psycho-traumatic symptoms that victims tell a doctor about, the other symptoms not being considered pathological by victims (they think they are "born that way" and it is their personality to always feel badly, anguished, phobic, depressive, suicidal, and estranged from the world). The other symptoms might also remain hidden because the victims are ashamed (especially of risk behaviors, scarification, and addiction). The most frequent somatic complaints emphasize tremendous fatigue and invalidating chronic pain. Some victims also find it difficult to evaluate pain due to traumatic anesthetization. Thirty six percent of respondents mentioned an elevated threshold of pain that sometimes meant not getting necessary treatment for serious problems.

Chronic fatigue is linked to enormous psychological tension and the permanent feelings of insecurity and danger felt by traumatized victims. Constant control of the environment means exhausting hypervigilance with sleep disorders aggravated by nightmares and being awakened frequently in the night by recollections. Chronic fatigue was reported in 56% of respondents for the pilot study in Hauts de Seine (2008) and in almost 60% of cases in our study of adult survivors (IVSEA, 2015).

Chronic pain is linked to the psychological and musculotendinous tension of hypervigilance, which is responsible for headaches, backaches, and pain in the jaw, muscles, joints, abdomen, and pelvis. These can also be manifestations of traumatic memory, with the victim reliving the exact same pains felt during the violence. These reminiscent pains are sometimes so overwhelming that the person can end up in the emergency room and subject to biological and radiological tests, hospitalizations, and even operations. Chronic pain is found in 40% of victims, and, on a scale of 1–10, is given a 6 by victims of interfamilial sexual violence, according to the pilot study in Hauts de Seine (2008), and it was found in nearly 60% of respondents in our IVSEA study (2015). Manifestations of stress and anxiety were reported by victims of sexual violence in 60% and 80% of respondents. These include sleep disorders for 82%, hypervigilance for 60%, and the feeling of permanent danger or impeding death for 40%. These manifestations of stress lead to numerous somatic symptoms that show a neuro-vegetative dysregulation. Since not recognized as such, these are the source of tremendous worry in victims or even hypochondria, with a long list of problems: Constriction in the throat, pressure in the chest, suffocation, palpitations, dizziness, congestion, skin irritation, hot flashes, excessive sweating, trembling, dryness of the mouth, nausea, intestinal problems, abdominal pain, and so on. Emotional reminiscences of fear and distress can provoke pressure and pain in the chest, which makes it seem like a heart attack, so that an ambulance is called.

As these specific psycho-traumatic problems are not identified by professionals, the range of associated pains are usually treated separately and never linked to the trauma that caused them. The treatments usually offered do not take the cause into account. They are therefore of little effect, since they only treat the symptoms; the problems become chronic, generating huge suffering and catastrophic personal, social, and professional loss. Untreated trauma is a marginalizing disability and causes premature death.

When victims get no help from those around them and receive no social, medical, and psychological treatment centered on the violence and its consequences, the negative impact of violence on the quality of life is considerable. Life becomes a dirty joke, as one of my patients put it, full of suffering, failure, and solitude, with no hope of improvement, to the point that, for many victims, death is awaited as a deliverance.

In our IVSEA study, mental suffering due to sexual violence is evaluated as highly influential by most victims (64% having felt it as highly influential at a certain time, 58% feeling it currently that way, and 44% feeling extreme solitude). Anxiety and ruminations invade them, and the simplest acts require enormous effort; victims' lives become hell. Fifty percent of victims experience poverty and social exclusion. Seventy one percent declared that the violence had a very large effect on their quality of life (a figure found to be the same in our study on the quality of life and safety (CVS ONDRP-INSEE 2012–2017)).

When violence has a psycho-traumatic impact, it ruptures the course of victims' lives. Nothing is as it was, and their view of the world, the confidence they had in themselves and who they were, what they thought and believed, their intelligence, the strength of their character, their ability to love and accomplish plans, and the confidence they had in life, the world, people, those around them, and what the future held for them… it is all swept away.

Victims do not recognize themselves. They are no longer the same in their eyes and often in the eyes of those around them, with the vital inner motor shut down. Even if they fight, as they all do, and develop huge reserves of energy, ingenuity, and creativity to advance bravely step by step, and even if they get by, even remarkably well according to everyone, with exemplary personal, professional, and artistic success, there is something deep down that does not function. This gives success a deeply bitter taste, a taste of strangeness, unreality, inauthenticity, and even imposture in the face of success and praise that are so well-deserved!

Whether their life is a total failure or an apparent success, it is not really their life; it is not the life that they would have wanted or that they were destined for and deserved: It is not their life. It's the life of the stranger they have become to themselves, a life of survival constructed from this and that, often with the energy of despair, on a terrain so full of mines that things had to be placed where they could be, without any sense of unity. This life is so fragmented that a large part of their available vital energy is used to give the impression of cohesion to a huge fragility, the rest to master and control the permanent feeling of insecurity. This is a life of automatization because I have to live, following others, doing as they do, watching them do it, and being envious of how well they do. It is a life where they have to try to do it all without problems or effort when everything is so difficult, complicated, and exhausting! It is a life that resembles an absurd play where they are just an extra, the central character having disappeared during the trauma. This is a life where everything is incomprehensible, and there is a total absence of meaning except in suffering again and again, a life of absolute emptiness, solitude, and despair.

It is also a life of shame, guilt, and catastrophic self-esteem: Shame about not being who they should be without understanding why in spite of all the efforts invested; shame of being incapable of doing what they should do, though that's all they want; and shame of being the prey to thoughts, mental images, emotions, and compulsions that are violent and that they don't want but that are there, that seem to belong to them but that they don't really recognize as their own but rather as imposed on them. Violent thoughts, mental images, emotions, and compulsions require torturously strict control. Sometimes an exhausting struggle wears down their will and they relieve the extreme tension by drinking, taking drugs, or scarring themselves or other self-harm, including unwanted, humiliating, or dangerous sexual practices. They feel shame about having been aggressive toward those they love most: children, partners, friends, and pets. The only solution to stop harming them might be to avoid them as much as possible—to leave, disappear, or kill themselves—and this can be a strong motivation to take the risk of consulting a psychiatrist.

5.17.1 Consequences for Emotional Intimacy

Half the victims in our IVSEA investigation reported that the impact of sexual violence on their love lives was significant, and 14% stated that it prevented them from having intimate relations throughout their lives. More than half (52%) consider that sexual violence had huge consequences on their relationships with their family and their children. Similarly, in one-third of cases, ties between victims and a part of their families were broken following acts of abuse or the telling of them. Additionally, one in ten victims state that they are unable to live in a couple relationship, and one in eight that they are unable to have children as a result of the abuse (IVSEA, 2015).

It is rare that victims of violence have the intimate lives that would have wanted. They often find themselves alone with avoidance behaviors that distance themselves from any situation of potential intimacy, which they perceive as threatening and unbearable because of violence committed against them by those close to them. They are afraid of couple relationships because of domestic violence they were exposed to in childhood or in a prior relationship, and they fear betrayal. If they were sexually abused, they are likely to be afraid of sexual relations, of pregnancy (something inside their body), of giving birth and experiencing pain (traumatic memory of rape), and of having children.

Traumatic memory and dissociative behaviors are part of victims' world, especially when abuse happened in childhood. This means that, paradoxically, it is "easier" for victims to live with someone perverse and abusive, who will "treat" their traumatic memory by provoking dissociation and anesthetization, than with a partner who is respectful and loving. The latter might also, through gestures, words, and behaviors, unintentionally spark the traumatized partner's traumatic memory, but he cannot be the catalyst for dissociation. This generates anxiety, behaviors of rejection, phobic avoidance, and a situation that might make it seem that the victim cannot stand to live with her partner, though in reality, she loves him very much. Similarly, sexual relations with a loving partner are often impossible, the field being too full of mines from prior sexual violence. Only sex in a state of dissociation is possible through getting drunk, high, or using "fantasies" and violent sexual practices. This is taxing and destabilizing for the couple's relationship.

Traumatic memory can also be at the origin of unfaithful behaviors that are actually compulsive dissociative risk behaviors that make victims wrongly feel they do not love their partners because they "desire" someone else. Linked to activation of traumatic memory, intrusive violent images jump out during sexual relations and can result in feelings of fear and rejection or incomprehensible blockages that threaten the relationship.

Traumatic memory of the perverted sexual excitement of the abuser colonizes the victim during sexual relations. This might also make victims think they are turned on by violent sex. They might accept this and even suggest it to their partner. Violence becomes part of their sexual relations, and sometimes there is an addiction to these destructive practices, heightened by the pseudo-orgasms that disjunction produces due to the production of morphine and ketamine-like neurotransmitters. This boost is mystifying, with its emotional anesthetization at the core. The return to reality is all the harder, with feelings of shame, disgust, and self-loathing. Soon no more relationship is possible, as confidence in the partner is lost.

In spite of all this, some victims are surrounded by family members, professionals, friends, and/or partners who are benevolent and understanding. Thanks to their patience and tenacity, victims can reassure themselves of their ability to love and be loved without being betrayed. Such loved ones give them security that can help them move forward and once again believe in the future and in happiness. It is necessary to support these loved ones and give them adequate information on the neurobiological mechanisms of psycho-trauma and the consequences of violence so that they can continue to offer support in the best possible ways.

5.17.2 Traumatic Memory's Effects on Sexuality

Forty three percent of victims consider that sexual violence has had a significant impact on their sex lives, and 8% state that it has led to them having no sex lives at all (IVSEA, 2015). For victims of sexual violence, especially in childhood, sexuality is a particularly mine-filled field. Traumatic memory is susceptible to explode with any gesture having sexual connotations, activating recollections and generating a state of unease, anxiety, and danger specific to the violence endured. If, for example, incest was committed within a manipulative context of caresses, any caress or foreplay in a loving sexual encounter could be unendurable. If the sexual aggression was extremely violent, perhaps loving sex with foreplay would be possible, but if a partner plays with putting his hands around her neck or wrists when she has previously survived an attempt at strangulation and a restraint, this could generate a panic attack.

Our study on the impact of childhood sexual violence among adult survivors has shown that one in two victims has sexual disorders such as phobias, frigidity, or vaginism, and one in three has problems with sexual behaviors such as sex addiction and unsafe sex. Avoidance behaviors are a solution, but when someone wants a normal love life, it is necessary to venture into the minefield of sexuality unless they have a partner who accepts and understands that sexual activity is not possible or must be reduced. This is a problem if the couple wants children. For incest victims, there is often a fear of pregnancy, birth, and raising children without being adequate as a parent.

This means that many victims' resort to dissociating behaviors to have access to any sexuality. This could involve drugs and alcohol that lead to a sufficiently dissociated state of emotional anesthetization. It could also involve extremely violent fantasies before and during sex, including scenes of rape and prostitution that are stressful enough to cause disjunction and create a state of dissociation and emotional anesthetization. This could lead to violent sexual practices, including sadomasochistic acts and unsafe sex (without protection and with risk of exposure to sexually transmitted infections or pregnancy, sex with strangers or violent partners, sex in dangerous places, in clubs, or in prostitution). Watching pornography can have the same stressful effect of disjunction and anesthetization (these dissociating behaviors were well illustrated in films such as Louis Buñuel's *Belle de Jour* and Michael Haneke's *The Pianist*). Such practices can become highly addictive and compulsive due to the dependence on morphine-like and ketamine-like dissociative substances secreted by the brain.

In addition to sex with a partner, victims of sexual violence might also practice dissociating sexual behaviors on themselves. This includes compulsive masturbation (small children might do this in public or at school), early sexual relations with a risk of teen pregnancy, pornography addiction, violent fantasies, and self-harm (reproducing the violence endured), including self- mutilation. This form of addiction to stress is deceiving, as it masquerades as a passion for sexual excitement. Disjunction, involving secretions from the brain, is confused with orgasm. Such behaviors, thoughts, and compulsions are usually troubling for the victim. They are not really what victims want, and this confuses them and heightens their feelings of guilt and shame.

Guilt and shame are ubiquitous in victims of sexual violence and contribute greatly to their difficulties in being able to speak out about the violence and denounce the abuser. The guilt and shame are above all imposed by the system of aggression in a particularly perverted reversal. The system of aggression includes the attacker, his accomplices (who might include friends, police, legal personnel, and everyone who should be helping the victim), stereotypes perpetuated by society, and finally, the traumatic memory of violence and of the attacker.

Perpetrators manipulate and violently twist reality through shrouding the victim their own attributes and then blaming the victim. He says that she is dirty, though it is he who dirties her; he says she is worthless, though it's he who chooses to treat her that way. He finds someone precious and covers her with his scum and then says that she's less than nothing, garbage... and that this justifies what he does to her! He takes a human being, treats her as a thing, and says that it's okay because she's just an object. He forcefully imposes sexual acts on the victim that he terrifies and tortures, then says that she not only consents but loves to play the martyr, cruelly attributing to her his own perverted pleasure. He premeditates his acts of violence and traps the victim to impose on her a demented scenario that has nothing to do with her, but he tells her it is she who fired him up, provoked him, and in any case was asking for abuse. Indecently, he crushes her truth and constantly substitutes its opposite. And a whole army of accomplices open the way, adhering to his perverse and pornographic view of reality, assisted by all the stereotypes upheld by society about women and sexuality.

Memories of the attacker's words and deeds heighten feelings of guilt and shame in the victim, colonizing her with killing phrases: "you like it," "you're nothing but a whore," and "you're just a liar." She might reexperience scenes of scorn and perverse pleasure of the attacker and wrongly attribute these feelings to herself. She then believes that she has nothing but loathing for herself and is horrified by the perverse pleasure she thinks she feels; that is false: "I am always worrying, doubting myself, my memories, and what I am... I tell myself atrocious things like 'I am a perverted, demonic liar' or 'you are a bad person, a mean person'... I am sick of constantly doubting myself and everything and of being afraid. I live in constant fear, and it exhausts me!" Lack of knowledge about the reality of sexual violence, strategy aggressors use, and how traumatic memory functions locks victims in horrific suffering, solitude, and abandonment.

5.18 Consequences on Schooling and Professional Life

The effects of psycho-trauma on children's and teens' performance in school and adults in the workplace are often considerable, especially when the violence began in early childhood. In our study, nearly half of victims interrupted their studies or careers as a result of violence (IVSEA, 2015).

Sexual violence and its psycho-traumatic consequences are often responsible for repeated failures in school, disruptions in the classroom, catastrophic life decisions, and professional failure. Traumatic memory and its consequences lead to cognitive disorders (trouble paying attention, concentrating, remembering, and lateralization), so that intellectual work and any kind of learning requiring focus and memorization become difficult and require much larger efforts from the victim than from someone having not endured violence. These difficulties have nothing to do with the real capacity of the victim, which is usually normal or even very high, but they lead to numerous failures.

Avoidance behaviors make many activities impractical and can be very prejudicial, preventing victims from taking exams, speaking in public, and going to job interviews. Such stressful occasions would risk lighting up traumatic memory and setting off tonic immobility of the psyche and a state of anguish with palpitations, shaking, sweating, dry and tight throat, hyperventilation with sensations of strangulation, tingling at the extremities, dizziness, and intestinal problems. Answering questions or giving an opinion can be felt as a great danger for victims who have known "instructional" violence where any wrong answer led to verbal or physical abuse, or when they have lived under the thumb of someone who degraded or discredited in everything they said or did. They find themselves blocked and unable to speak.

The feeling of insecurity and the sensation of danger might be responsible for phobias about school through separation anxiety and fear of certain people (students, teachers, colleagues, bosses). The fear of being closed in, stuck, and powerless can make it impossible to use public transportation and elevators, which can complicate, restrain, or prevent some professional choices. The flaring up of traumatic memory can involve inattention, motor ticks induced by intrusive reminiscences, or sudden loss of knowledge, all of which means greater risks in many jobs. This means that many fields are closed to untreated victims (for example, work with dangerous machines). Traumatized victims are fired for serious errors that they might have been helped to understand and overcome, through healing traumatic memory.

Hypervigilance, perfectionism, and conscientiousness, along with poor self-esteem, a search for connection, and an ability to dissociate when faced with malevolent intents make psycho-traumatized people choice victims in the workplace. They are chosen for their good qualities and their vulnerability and are transformed into perfect slaves. Not only do they find themselves overworked, but they are also required to respond to all the requirements and desires of their aggressors and serve their need for fuses or circuit-breakers. These situations often unjustly end with the victim quitting, being fired, or taking sick leave, and they can lead to suicide.

Hypersensitivity, irritability, and explosive anger due to emotional reminiscences and the impulsivity of some victims might also make their professional relations with customers, colleagues, and bosses very difficult and unstable. Studies conducted internationally have shown that nearly 50% of people having lived through trauma and chronic post-traumatic stress lose their jobs in the two years following trauma.

Child victims of violence often find themselves in situations of extreme vulnerability and are likely to be harassed or assaulted by classmates and adults. They become scapegoats for the class, the school, or the sports team. For abused children, everything is as if they are in a mountain-climbing competition with other children their age and must carry a backpack four times heavier than those of the other children, without knowing this is the case. They will have no chance of winning unless of miraculous endurance, and they are most likely to collapse from exhaustion as the others breeze past them. After a normal start, they will very soon be tired and out of breath and won't understand why it is so hard for them. They will compare themselves to their peers and conclude that they themselves are useless; they will be disgusted by this race and not want to continue or participate ever again. It's also likely that they will have to endure other children teasing them and adults shouting out humiliating and degrading remarks, due to ignorance or ill-will. The adults most often don't bother to ask the right questions: "What's going on? This isn't normal; that child should be able to get there as well as the others. There must be something holding him back."

Against all odds, some do keep up; this is at the price of physical overdrive, putting their entire reserve of energy into the competition, not taking any pleasure from observing the woods around them, chatting with friends, or taking little breaks to rest and relax. They might even win the race, but at the price of harm to their bodies due to an abnormal level of exertion and the total absence of social or emotional enjoyment. Their tremendous physical effort is a kind of risk-taking that, through physical stress, can create a dissociative state through disjunction. This dissociative state will dull physical warning signs (due to anesthetization) and allow for abnormal efforts that self-treat traumatic memory through emotional anesthetization. This is what happens with young, high-level athletes in endurance sports such as swimming or that require hard physical training such as dance or gymnastics. It also applies to intensive intellectual work among anorexics, often associated with physically exhausting exercise and with other learning that requires long, heavy, and difficult training, such as playing certain musical instruments. The "rewards" for all the suffering and sacrifice of a normal childhood or adolescence are considerable: Adults congratulate and are proud of them, and they are admired, which allows them to find meaning in a life that would otherwise seem for nothing. They find a socially accepted and even valued way to treat traumatic memory that also allows them to experience aesthetic pleasure (dance, acrobatics, music…). However, they often pay the heavy price of harm to their bodies, limits to human interaction, and having all their time and effort consumed by their activity. They might find themselves addicted to it and to the permanent recharging of traumatic memory that it provides. It is a ticking timebomb full of terrible suffering, ready to explode at any moment; traumatic memory is a threat hanging over their lives.

Sometimes, if the training is well-adapted and makes the victim feel validated and secure, it might be one of the rare settings where everything can function more or less normally. It can thus be a factor of resilience that helps with the restauration of self-esteem through offering a place for social identity to be built (school should play this role more often for children mistreated in their families). Other times, studies and work are overinvested in and function as escape routes that allow victims distance from any other reality and from reminders of traumatic memory. They function as dissociative behaviors if practiced in stress and until total exhaustion or if the work involves significant risks (such as in the army, police, firefighting, war correspondents, rescue workers, humanitarian doctors, etc.).

5.19 Consequences on Social Life

Psycho-trauma has serious consequences on social integration. Traumatic violence—especially when endured in childhood— often results in catastrophic life circumstances. Not given adapted care, many victims face years of suffering and struggle. They find themselves alone, worn out, unemployed, on long-term disability leave or welfare, and living in extreme poverty and uncertainty. They are often homeless, alcoholics, drug addicts, prostitutes, mental patients, convicts… In our 2015 study, we found that nearly half of victims go through periods of material instability and exclusion following violence. Ten percent had been homeless, and 7% had been prostituted (5% and 3% for overall population). We also found that having been a victim of violence is an important risk factor for revictimization and for perpetrating acts of violence. Seventy percent of victims reported having endured several types of violence throughout their lives—a long list for many of them (OMS, 2010, 2014; IVSEA, 2015; Fulu, 2017). Repeat victimization further compromises their life circumstances, and risky, delinquent behaviors are also more likely. Quality of life is deeply affected (as the astounding numbers of the 2018 Hauts-de-Seine study and our 2015 study have shown): 71% of victims declared that the trauma has had a very significant effect on their quality of life (IVSEA, 2015).

The consequences of psycho-trauma stay with victims sometimes to the end of their lives. And as they age, life events pile up: Loss, hospitalization, nursing homes… Such situations of insecurity and dependence put these people in great difficulty in managing their traumatic memory. Their usual survival strategies no longer work. The risk is of traumatic memory flaring up again—invasive, impossible to control—particularly when they require assistance to bathe, dress, or eat. They might experience many situations as aggressions and oppose these with panic attacks, agitated outbursts, loss of temporal and spatial awareness, and dissociative troubles such as visual, auditory, and kinesthetic hallucinations. To attempt to anesthetize this intolerable traumatic memory, the primary mechanism is the onset of new dissociative disorders. They might develop "illusions" of persecution and act out the violence they endured. They might also harm themselves or put themselves in danger, become violent toward others with aggressive and obscene words and possibly acts. These disorders can make caring for them very difficult and are also a risk factor for rejection and mistreatment by care workers.

6

See No Evil
Denial and Misrepresentation of Violence

The usual justifications for violence rely on myths. In reality, violence is not necessary. It does not stem from an original aggressive nature in humans (as Freud suggested) or innate cruelty (as Nietzsche believed). Studies on newborns have shown that humans are naturally empathetic. Historically and socially, violence against women and children is almost always presented as inherent to the human condition or the nature of desire in men, or it is justified for the sake of instruction, love, security, or economic productivity.

6.1 Totalitarian Semantics

Violence is confounded with instruction, and love, sex, and desire are confused with the eroticization of hatred. The words and concepts are so distorted that pure acts of violence can mysteriously be reversed into being considered acts of love: "I humiliate and mistreat you because I am your mother or father and I love you"—that's called disciplining a child for their own good. "I oppress you, hit you, and kill you because I am in love and terribly jealous,"—that is called passion or a crime of passion. "I put pressure on you so you will have sex with me and I say degrading things to you; I insult you and sexually abuse

DOI: 10.4324/9781003497516-7

you, I rape you, because I am crazy with desire for you"—that is called making love to a woman or having a sexual relation.

The reality of the violence of these acts is erased and replaced with a claim that they were intended for the victim's benefit, lifting any responsibility from the perpetrator. It is like in George Orwell's dystopian novel *1984*, in which slogans such as "war is peace, freedom is slavery, ignorance is strength" are constantly drilled into people's brains. We are persuaded that violence is love, sexuality is predation, and punishment is education. The victim aspires to be loved, and love is confounded with violence; therefore, she is portrayed as loving to be violated, or at least consenting to it. Thus, the victim is forced into scenarios in which "it's not so serious—this is what she wants." The deceptive reversal is achieved.

An adolescent girl who admires an adult in a powerful position and wants his recognition and appreciation should not complain if he sexually assaults or rapes her: She was looking for it; she provoked it. With this unreasonable reasoning, the desire for love, affection, appreciation, or simple recognition can prove very dangerous. This can extend to any behavior related to seduction. To be beautiful and seductive for a woman, through a perverted reversal, becomes in itself—according to some men—an invitation to commit a sexualized violent act of punishment, verbally or physically. One patient told me that after telling her grandmother that she was gang raped at 15, she was informed, "that's normal; for a man, you are like candy…" And if a woman rejects this and defends herself, she's considered irritating, incoherent, aggressive, and might be insulted: "What a bitch!" If due to tonic immobility, fear, abuse of authority, or economic necessity, she does not protest, it must be that she wanted it: "The bitch loves it."

Similarly, when raising children involves the idea of taming them through violence, a child who goes against this, makes a mistake, or acts out "was asking for it," and might be slapped, hit, spanked, or isolated and locked in a closet. The adult will say that the child made him do it: "Look what you make me do and the state you put me in!" Similar statements can apply to domestic violence: "If you keep making me angry and stay with me, you must like being degraded and beaten." Responsibility is thrust on the victim to be careful and censor herself, so as not to incur abuse that is presented as natural.

In this insane, totalitarian system, it becomes impossible to declare yourself a victim. Either you were asking for it, you consented, or you are turned on by it. Therefore, you are not a real victim. You lie for your own benefit, to get revenge, attention, or money. If you are recognized as a victim, it must be due to a moral flaw or weakness in you: You were complicit or locked into your victim status (I recently read such comments by a psychologist on her Facebook page about rape victims). The myth is that victims are submissive or gullible and could antici-pate an attack and defend themselves if they wanted to. Being a victim is disapproved of. Victims quickly learn that they have no right to complain and even less to be assisted and defended. They are condemned to silence and submission in the face of a tyrannical system, and this is additional torture inflicted amid general indifference.

6.2 Why Doesn't the Law Do Anything?

Why can't victims make use of the laws that technically should protect them? Perpetrators surely cannot pretend that they have the legal right to commit violent acts or ignore the law! The victim has not broken any laws. A woman has the full right to walk alone at night, wear a miniskirt or a low-cut dress, put on lots of makeup, drink alcohol, or have coffee at a male acquaintance's home, and none of this signifies that she is sexually available. Raping her is a crime.

The rapist's intentions are misrepresented. It is generally ignored that rapists intend to harm, destroy, oppress, and inflict as much suffering on the victim as possible, reducing her to an object dehumanized for their own interest and arousal. He scripts deceptive pretexts and deceitful staging to turn any guilt away from him, and society believes him (Sironi, 1999). Unfortunately, most people, including those who are supposed to uphold the law and defend victims, do not realize that violence is a violation of the rights of the victim and an assault on her physical and psychological integrity that is justifiable under no circumstances. They do not realize that the rapist is guilty and has everything to gain by misrepresenting his intentions.

Sexual violence is never natural, legitimate, logical, or coherent. Its perpetrators commit hate crimes on victims they consider inferior and worthless in a society that subscribes to the same sexist, racist, and exclusionary hierarchy. Perpetrators become violent because they were victims or witnesses of violence in the past. They use violence because they can get away with it and because it serves them as a drug and gives them the illusion of being all-powerful.

Victims are never responsible for the harm done to them. Nothing about her personality or her acts justifies it. She is always innocent. It is not her responsibility to make sure that the violence doesn't happen. It's not her responsibility to say no; it is the potential attacker's obligation to control and manage himself and to be absolutely sure of consent. To give in is not to consent and even less to desire. The absence of "no," or even a "yes," does not always mean consent; it is also necessary to make sure that there is no coercion involved. Victims are interchangeable members of a category (women, children, elderly, disabled, homosexual, Black, Jewish, Arab) chosen to play a role in a scenario that doesn't concern them, staged for the aggressor's own exclusive benefit.

Violence is never beneficial for the victim. "It's for your own good," "It's because I love you," "It's to better protect, educate, or take care of you…" Such reversals are common, as Alice Miller discussed in her book *For Your Own Good*. Miller broke new ground in opposing violent punishment as useful only to the person committing it. Abusive parents use violence to gain relief for themselves. Their goal is to impose on a chosen person the role of medication to treat their own traumatic memory. They instrumentalize and alienate victims, depriving them of rights and making them into soothing slaves/salves. Victims must be of service to abusers and develop vigilant strategies of management and avoidance to placate the abuser's traumatic memory. And if the explosion happens anyway, victims must be the ones harmed so that abusers can disjunct and gain anesthetization while inflicting no suffering on themselves.

6.3 Sexual Violence as a Tool for Domination

Violence is a privilege. It is symptomatic of an unequal society that distributes roles and attributes to each a value according to a fixed hierarchy. Violence is inherently necessary for any system of domination to last. Perpetrators allow themselves to break universal laws and impose any traditional law that works for their purpose or to create their own laws borrowing here and there, and chosen victims are forced to submit to these. Abusers declare themselves of another essence and adhere to a profoundly unequal view of the world wherein the law of might makes right can rule to their advantage. They often invoke their "freedom" to claim their "right" to commit violence. This freedom is presented as a superior value, and it means the freedom to do what they want in their families and relationships, and also "sexual freedom." Any limitations on such freedoms are deemed oppressive regression to reactionary values. With this reasoning in place, they can call those who stand up and speak out against violence prudish, backward, or even fascist.

In reality, everyone's freedom is subject to limitations that prevent it from trampling the freedom and rights of others. The law places restrictions on rights and especially on freedoms. The European Human Rights Convention makes this clear. The concept of freedom itself only makes sense in a just world wherein the equality and rights of everyone are respected. Freedom implies abiding by the law and must mean everyone's freedom, the weak as well as the strong. Freedom, law, and equality are indissociably linked. If this is not the case, it becomes the freedom of the fox in the chicken coop. This is reminiscent of Lacordaire's famous statement: "Between strong and weak, rich and poor, master and servant, freedom oppresses and the law sets free."

6.4 One Violation Leads to Another

Violence is not necessary, and humans are not violent by nature. People become violent because they were victims or witnesses in the past, usually in early childhood. They allow themselves to reproduce the violence using victims who are weaker, more vulnerable (or designated as such), in order to relieve their own angst.

Leaving victims alone to deal with their traumatic memory is irresponsible and feeds into an endless production of future violence. It is enough that a small minority of victims become aggressors and make new victims, a small number of whom will also switch roles someday. Abusers prefer victims who have already been abused because they are more isolated, less protected, and easier to terrorize and subdue. They play their roles better in violent scenarios due to their previous experience. Abusing someone who is already wounded and traumatized also allows abusers to enjoy even greater cruelty to unthinkable levels of transgression, feeding their sensation of omnipotence. Those who have already been abused are actively sought by new abusers and enlisted by force in a reality that only makes sense to the abuser.

Sexual violence is a scandal. It is violence, not the human condition, that generates violence; violence is not natural but social. Society allows for many forms of violence under the pretexts of being realistic or efficient: From child-rearing violence to war, and also repressive, economic, and sexist systems, are where future violence is forged. Violence is an assault on human dignity and human rights; it is dehumanization.

Newborns are not carrying future violence in their beings that must be controlled or contained through violent practices to "train" them. They have a large relational capacity that includes empathy, compassion, and the need for protection, respect, and benevolence to foster their physical, mental, and intellectual development. A child who never endured violence will have no reason to become a violent adolescent or adult. Men's sexual desire is not a vital need to be met at all costs or an uncontrollable impulse.

Specialized care immediately after violence occurs can prevent traumatic memory from developing or treat it if it is already present. Such care avoids tremendous suffering and revictimization and also prevents victims from becoming future perpetrators. In an unequal and sexist world, a boy who witnesses domestic violence or is a victim easily allows himself to become dominant later in life and treat his traumatic memory by becoming violent, which can easily be avoided if he receives specialized care early on.

6.5 Unspeakable Acts

In our society, everything about violence—frequency, serious-ness, causes, and consequences—is taboo. Victims are reduced to silence, their cries are not heard, and their suffering is ignored. They are isolated and separated from the world so that they do not contaminate it and so it remains livable for everyone else. When they do bravely speak out, they face a wall of indifference or systematic denial, discrediting, suspicion, and stigmatization. This often includes rejection from those, professionals included, who should be listening to them, believing them, caring for them, protecting them, and gaining justice for them. It is as if society is asking them to disappear, erase any trace of violence, and forget their trauma. Victims are annoying, very annoying...

6.6 The Illusion of Safety

The taboo that victims face is mainly built on the belief that vio-lence is inevitable in a world where not all people are given equal value. According to this belief, humans are fundamentally and innately violent predators hungry for power, domination, and sex. The law of might makes right is thought to be an inevitable part of the human condition.

But if this is all true, how can people stand to live in a world of insecurity where violence rules? Through reversal, so that they can still believe in a livable world and human goodness (love, the family, justice, and the future), they focus on the illusion of safe spaces where people are among "their own kind" and are civilized and sheltered from violence. These mythical safe spaces include the family, the couple, institutions, communities, schools, and workplaces wherein through a sort of magic, the wolf will transform into a shepherd, and where the sheep will be safe. All you need to do is belong to these herds and submit to their protectors, and you will not be subject to violence, but if you exclude yourself and step beyond these bounds, you might be—you'd have been asking for it (such as walking alone at night if you are a woman); violence is expected.

Everything about this belief is false. Violence can be prevented because all humans are born with empathy. Our inherent rights go against the law of might makes right, and respect for human dignity is at the heart of all democratic societies. The places that pretend to be the safest (family, couple, school, church…) are where there is the most violence. It is impossible that the "sheep"—meaning society's most vulnerable—can be protected by predators who think they are superior and that violence is their natural right. Society's most vulnerable are exposed to violence that is ignored because it is not supposed to exist in the places and ways it does. This violence is veiled as love, education, care, or sexuality. This is an enormous ideological lie that serves to fabricate social cohesion and the false sense of safety. Meanwhile, injustice and abuse of power can continue to favor the all-powerful masters. The false sense of security is a lure that destroys solidarity with victims, as they are considered necessarily responsible for their condition; victims are sacrificed to keep the myths intact. This is why when a woman is raped, so much effort is put into proving at all costs that she was irresponsible, provocative, taking risks, or even lying. This way, people can continue to think that women are safe in this unequal and profoundly sexist society (if they behave "correctly"). To recognize that an innocent woman was raped would be to recognize that all women are in danger under a system built on hatred of women. This avowal is out of the question, since it would reveal the extreme violence of the system.

6.7 The Violence of Denial

The fundamental human concepts of love, family, nation, work, education, and health are perverted to justify violence. There is confusion between the language of tenderness, protection, and care and that of "love" to justify possession or control. No spaces are safe in our society, except for predators.

Be quiet! Don't say the knight in shining armor raped the princess, the husband violated his wife, the mother mistreated her children, the father raped his daughter or son, the parents killed their children, or that the teacher, preacher, doctor, mayor, police officer, or judge is actually a perpetrator and that the government committed crimes. Everyone wants to believe that this is impossible or so exceptional that it could be in a novel or on the front page of a paper... an *exception* that confirms the rule and that will only ever happen to others. Because of this denial, victims are abandoned to their own devices. To see the truth is to endanger the illusion of safety or the almost total impunity that allows perpetrators to keep being violent.

Behind closed doors, violence is frequent and masquerades as love or discipline that many children endure from the beginning. This abuse is said to be for their safety or due to loss of temper, so that crimes are committed on victims who have no defense or recourse. This means the recharging of timebombs in perpetrators and many victims that will explode in future violence and create serious addictions to violence. This hidden abuse, unpunished and untreated, makes future victims necessary for the "effective" treatment of traumatic memory of those with the most power and means. This perpetuates an unequal and hierarchical society that assures the ongoing production of victims used as high-quality "medicine"—in total impunity.

This refusal to see violence perpetrated by those close to victims means that society's most vulnerable and dependent are in danger, including children, the elderly, the disabled, and the chronically ill. In the idealized institutions supposed to protect them, they have no rights and are subject to an epidemic of violence. As violence is not supposed to exist in spaces that societal myths deem safe, it is made over, and consequences on victims are never seen as such—they are not diagnosed, protected, or cared for. Awareness of the serious consequences of violence and the fear of being identified by perpetrators does nothing to stop it, as perpetrators benefit from near total impunity. They do not see themselves as responsible for the serious psycho-traumatic consequences of the violence they commit, since no connection is made between the abuse and the victim's psychological disorders.

When violence occurs outside, victims are more visible; however, they are also sacrificed to this system in a kind of catharsis. ("Too bad for them; that's the way it is.") Sometimes they are recognized, and justice is served on the condition that they were not asking for violence that they should have anticipated due to its known and predictable qualities, or because they chose the wrong side in terms of religion or community. Or maybe they are in a category that is supposed to receive this "inevitable" violence. It is necessary that the violence said to be innate in humans plays out visibly somewhere, on those who are not part of the interior world: The foreigner, the enemy, someone of another religion or skin color, the slave, someone worthless in society's eyes, designated as possible target for a cathartic discharge of violence. Prostitutes and pornography "actresses" play this role for sexual violence constructed as natural in males.

This longstanding system ignores violence using the adage: "Nothing to see here; everything is for the best in the best of worlds." This generates a huge number of victims not identified as such, with no recognition, especially children who develop tremendous suffering, traumatic memory, and dissociative behaviors that can result in new violence against themselves or others.

Lack of knowledge about the genealogy of violence— its causes and especially its mechanisms—and ignorance of coherent and logical explanations result in the belief that it is an intrinsic part of the human condition: Nothing can be done about it. It is "ordinary" violence to contain and hide. And victims, as they are the proof of the intolerable violence, put the system in danger if they are not invisible enough. The cohesion of society is fragilized by violence that has not been treated or stopped and that is cemented in through denial. In this system, it is the victims who must be erased to make the violence invisible; any urge on their part to identify as victims must be quelched.

Speaking out against violence and reporting it is very difficult. This is why fewer than 10% of family violence victims and under 8% of rape victims press charges (although rape is a crime). The nearly systematic suspicion that targets victims, their stigmatization, trivialization, and denial of their suffering are significant obstacles to reporting. This is reinforced by the downplaying of such violence and how perverted acts are turned into acts of love, desire, seduction, education, care, and so on. The perpetrator benefits from a slew of circumstances that are taken to be attenuating: "That's how he is: flirtatious, heavy, possessive, jealous, irritable, or under the influence of alcohol or irrepressible desire." It is rare that his premeditated intentions and cruelty are recognized.

It is possible to combat violence and decrease it effectively as long as this includes all forms of violence. It is necessary to find it everywhere it lurks, identify it, and denounce it. It is also necessary to punish it more effectively, and current laws that identify sexual violence as a criminal offense are still insufficient and must be amended. Courageous campaigns for awareness and political action must aim to protect the rights and dignity of all, especially children and women, and foster equality in society. It is necessary to fight all forms of domination: Misogynist, patriarchal, or parental, all sexist stereotypes, and all forms of discrimination. It is also necessary to diagnose and treat the mechanisms at work, particularly traumatic memory and behaviors of dissociation. This treatment requires above all an understanding of the mechanisms and the links between violence endured and resulting symptoms. Victims must be able to find their truth and dialogue with themselves with wholeness and dignity.

6.8 Violence Ignored by the Medical Establishment

At a time when everything is measured, dissected, analyzed, and where information is constantly poured out in real time with more and more efficient means of communication, we are still in a prehistoric age when it comes to knowledge about victims and psycho-trauma. The frequency and severity of violence, especially sexual violence and abuse within families, are for the most part seriously underestimated, even denied, and their catastrophic human consequences—disastrous for victims' health and costly to society—don't seem to interest anyone. What is going on, here?

Violence has always existed, at least in the versions of history that are typically known and discussed, and it is said to be necessary or just part of reality (wartime defense, political repression, torture, economic injustice). The most intolerable forms have been regulated or condemned (war crimes, genocide, homicide, infanticide, rape, torture). They have also been the subject of philosophical, theological, psychological, and sociological enquiry to understand the causes, though none have given satisfactory explanations. The question remains unanswered, though the need for answers is more urgent than ever, with the unprecedented genocide of the 20th century and the idea of absolute evil.

Medicine has been remarkably absent among the fields offering theories to explain atrocities. It is used only to treat the direct physical damage of violence. It made a timid appearance at the end of the 19th century with neurology, psychiatry, and psychoanalysis, which took some interest in the consequences of violence on mental health. Symptoms that follow traumatic violence—especially linked to war—were defined in terms of traumatic neuroses.

Following Charcot and Janet, Freud and his disciples made an effort to understand through psychoanalysis the origin and mechanisms of psychological trauma. However, psychoanalysis ended up tying the suffering to internal psychological conflicts rather than to the reality of violence itself. The internal conflicts were presented as dependent on violent desires repressed by the subconscious through the superego.

It was only in the 1970s that psycho-traumatic symptoms were described with precision and categorized as specific syndromes such as post-traumatic stress disorder (defined in the *Diagnostic and Statistical Manual of Mental Disorder, DSM III* in 1980), multiple personality disorders, and dissociative states. These past years, notably due to technological advances in neurological imagery, the knowledge of neurobiological mechanisms has improved with new data that coincides with psychiatric and psychotherapeutic research. Models have been elaborated to understand the origin of symptoms in violence, and much more effective treatments are now possible.

6.9 Psycho-Traumatic Disorders

Violence is serious and frequent. It colonizes victims and generates addiction in perpetrators. This is often contagious, transmitted from one person to the next and from one generation to another. The consequences on the quality of life, health, and physical integrity are devastating for victims' psyches. It is crucial that violence be identified, psycho-traumatic disorders detected, and psycho-traumatic consequences in victims treated. Such care will not only liberate traumatized people of their traumatic memory; it will also make avoidance and dissociating behaviors disappear and repair neurological damage through neurogenesis. It would be possible to address dissociative behaviors in abusers and prevent further violence, too. If we take into full account the seriousness of violence and its human cost, no longer thinking of it as inevitable, and if we stop justifying violence and give ourselves the political means to combat it through changing social norms and healthcare policies, it is possible to put an end to the horrific cycle of violence.

The severity of consequences remains unknown by most people, including professionals in the fields of health, social work, and law, in spite of the abundance of conclusive research conducted over the past decade. Today in France, there is no specific teaching on victimology and psycho-trauma in medical schools. In 2011, in the France's medical schools, only an hour and a half total of class time is set aside for the mistreatment of children, and this is only for post-university studies and continuing education for private practice. (Other countries are similar.) It is up to individual doctors to inform themselves if they want to, and offers of training are few and far between.

When they are diagnosed, which is rare, psycho-traumatic disorders are still too often seen as abnormal and due to something about the victim herself (her age, sex, "fragility," personality, personal history, or inherent psychological difficulties). However, these psycho-traumatic disorders are the normal and most frequent outcomes of violence, and the seriousness of them is in proportion to that of violence and the destructive intent of the perpetrator.

No one would find it abnormal or linked to individual pathology when a person bleeds and feels pain after being stabbed with a knife. All victims bleed and feel pain—an obvious fact no one would question. For psychological effects, it's another story—everyone has their own take on them. Denial of them is even considered a valid opinion and not what it actually is: The negation of a scientific, clinically proven, and universal reality.

Psycho-traumatic disorders are not only the normal consequences of violence; they are also pathognomonic, meaning that they constitute specific medical proof of trauma. They are a universal response found in all victims in the days and weeks that follow their trauma (McFarlane, 2000). The significance and seriousness of the consequences, as with the knife wound, depend on many factors concerning the violence itself, the conditions in which it happened, and the vulnerability of victims according to age, medical history, material resources, and quality of care and support.

The impact of violence on the nervous system is like that of a wound. It is a violation with neurobiological consequences that leave serious and lasting effects that must be treated to help the wound heal through becoming a scab, then a scar. A French neuroscientific team recently found that traumatic memory is like an open wound that cannot heal. It can only be covered up (avoidance behavior) or ignored/denied (dissociating behavior), but it can anytime be felt with the full suffering of when it was first inflicted (Desmedt, 2012).

6.10 Inappropriate Care

The impact of violence on victims' health is catastrophic, requiring long-term medical and psychiatric care, heavy treatments, and frequent hospitalizations, all of which increases their already high level of stress. The diagnosis of post-traumatic disorders is never offered, and no specific treatment is proposed.

The usual "treatments" are only of symptoms, without taking into consideration the origin of the condition. Victims are treated for anxiety, depression, eating disorders, addiction, or personality disorders. Worse, sensory recollections of traumatic memory are treated as auditory, visual, or kinesthetic hallucinations or even psychotic disorders (delusions, schizophrenia). Emotional recollections are (mis)treated as manifestations of manic depression or borderline personality. Victims are stamped with many labels (hysterical, borderline, addict, alcoholic, depressive, anorexic, bulimic, phobic, obsessional, asocial) that are supposed to describe their state. For victims, suffering becomes destiny, and they believe they were "born that way," chronically depressed, suicidal, phobic, "particularly fragile and ill-adapted to life," and they continue to survive only because they feel this is required of them.

When a victim is faced with agonizing suffering of traumatic origin, the psychiatric treatments thrust on them by mainstream medicine actually copy the survival strategies they habitually rely on, such as avoidance, control, and dissociating behaviors. Victims are locked up in medical institutions, isolated from those close to them, and have their activities controlled: They might be forbidden to leave, to make phone calls, or to be in any contact with the world beyond those walls. They are subjected to sedatives that anesthetize them (anxiolytics, antidepressants, and neuroleptics). The treatments may be even more aggressive: Locking them up by force, solitary confinement, and shock treatment (which short-circuits them to provoke disjunction and emotional anesthetization). Children are given amphetamines (which generate dissociative and therefore anesthetizing stress). There is often dissociative violence: Starting with shell-shocked soldiers in WWI, shock treatment, freezing baths, threats, blackmail, and constraint have been used on traumatized people. More definitively, lobotomies have been practiced, nullifying all emotional responses (these were still very frequent in the 1950s, though the discovery of neuroleptics in 1952 began their decline); they are forbidden in France but still practiced in many countries including the United States.

Psycho-traumatic disorders are almost never diagnosed as such. The violence at the root of the symptoms is not identified. Professionals rarely ask about causes. When they are aware of past trauma, they do not connect it to its symptoms. That is why only the symptoms are treated. There are direct physical consequences of wounds and fractures. When they result from violence, this often goes unrecognized because doctors are not taught about it and do not ask the right questions. Usually, victims and those around them are not forthcoming in denouncing violence, especially if the perpetrator is a family member and/or it is sexual violence. Doctors are not trained to ask routine questions that could uncover violence. It is difficult for them to ask parents or partners who appear to be very worried and concerned whether a child with wounds in the mouth, vulva, or anus was raped, whether a pregnant woman showing signs of miscarriage or premature birth was hit, and whether a fall down the stairs was provoked or burns from boiling water inflicted rather than accidental. Doctors also fail to ask about childhood abuse and sexual aggression endured by alcoholic, addicted, homeless, or prostituted patients.

Doctors must routinely ask all patients if they have been victims or witnesses of violence. This is the only way they can identify victims and give them appropriate care as early as possible. This routine questioning that we have been asking for was finally included in the recommendations of France's national plan to end sexist and sexual violence in 2018. When there is a suicide attempt, addictive behaviors, eating disorders, self-mutilation, or other risk behaviors, this routine questioning is absolutely necessary. It is also essential to ask pregnant women and women seeking abortions. Pregnancy can be the result of rape (25% of abortions are due to violence-related pregnancies), and this has catastrophic human consequences. A pregnant woman is at higher risk of domestic violence, which has serious effects on fetal development. Pregnant victims are more in danger of addiction, diabetes, arterial hypertension, and psychological disorders than pregnant non-victims. The only way to avoid missing the signs of psycho-traumatic disorders linked to violence is to ask all patients: "Are you being abused or have you been in the past?" Survival strategies can mask the violence so that it is often difficult to perceive otherwise.

In 2005 and 2006, doctors, midwives, and patients in Seine-Saint-Denis participated in a survey: During a general consultation, three questions were systematically asked about violence endured. The doctors found that, in spite of their apprehensions prior to the study, asking these questions was actually easy. And the patients found it easy to respond. The three questions were: Have you ever been a victim of verbal abuse? Physical abuse? Sexual abuse? The results were astonishing! Even Gilles Lazimi, the general practitioner in charge of the Medical Health Center of Romainville, who started the investigation and was already very involved in preventing abuse, was surprised by the results. For the first 100 patients—women 18–92 years old consulting about anything—54% said they had been victims of abuse (49% for verbal, 31% for physical, and 21% for sexual), and 90% were mentioning this to a doctor for the first time. Similar results were found in the 2006 study with 51 doctors and two midwives who systematically asked these same three questions of 557 patients consulting about anything: 63% declared having been victims of violence (62.8% verbal, 42.7% physical, and 17.8% sexual).

Once the abuse is recognized, it is easy to find connections between it and its physical manifestations, as physical harm implies concrete evidence such as wounds, bruises, burns, a broken arm or eardrum, and so on. Their impact and resulting disabilities can be discussed by experts. With psychological damage, however, the link is not as readily made even when the seriousness of psycho-traumatic consequences is clear.

What happened to several of my young patients who had been raped is a flagrant example: They presented striking symptoms in the months following the rape: Panic attacks, repeated suicide attempts, self-mutilation, serious eating disorders, and massive addictions. These symptoms led to their hospitalization in psychiatric institutions, often for several months. The hospital psychiatrists knew about the rapes but never took into account the significance of trauma or tried to find out more about what happened. They refused to make any connection between the symptoms and suffering of the victims/patients and the rapes. These women experienced the hospitalizations as additional violence that plunged them further into despair, and one even tried to kill herself while hospitalized.

Even when the existence of psycho-trauma is recognized, it is usually seen as only psychological, without any root or cause in the organism. Psychological harm is most often perceived as linked to personal interpretations that are theoretical, ideological, or even political, without any real scientific validity. They are seen as dependent on the personal opinions of doctors or psychiatrists and the "quality" of the victim, prior circumstances, her life history, her age, her sex, or her personality. This explains why doctors rarely acknowledge psychological damage as real neurological wounds with consequences characteristic of the type of violence.

The investigations that I led in the Hauts-de-Seine in 2008 and nationally in 2015 (IVSEA) revealed that victims of violence often present chronic physical symptoms for many years: Debilitating pain, intense fatigue, digestive, urinary, cardiovascular, pulmonary, endocrine, immune, dermatological, and especially serious and chronic psychological disorders: Post-traumatic stress, dissociative symptoms, overall anxiety, phobias, depression, suicide attempts, personality disorders, addictions, risk behaviors, sleep disorders, and eating disorders. All these symptoms involve intense suffering evaluated by victims at over 9 on average on a scale of 1–10.

The recognition of psychological damage is rare and most often depends on arbitrary criteria of individual doctors. Unfortunately, most of them are convinced that specific and scientifically validated symptoms do not exist. Traumatic memory is, however, proven to be the main psycho-traumatic symptom at the origin of victims' suffering and of violence itself. It is the common denominator of all violence—its consequences and causes. It only sets in long-term in the absence of support and adapted care. Therefore, not training doctors and psychologists in psycho-traumatology and creating specialized treatment centers means an unnecessary loss of physical and psychological health for victims.

Thankfully, since 2017, our demand for recognition of psycho-trauma as a public health crisis is finally being heard. Training for health professionals and access to free, specialized care for all victims are more common, with the creation of ten interdisciplinary centers for psycho-trauma in 2018 (out of the 100 that should eventually be created in France and its overseas territories). We see more and more health professionals committed to taking better care of victims, especially among midwives, ob-gyns, paramedics, and specialists in addiction and eating disorders. But there is still much to be done.

6.11 Contaminating and Colonizing Violence

We have now identified how violence produces more violence, as one person infects another, and abusers are made of former victims. If untreated, violence may treat itself through further violence committed by those in dominant positions and tied to anesthetizing and dissociative behaviors. These are self-treatment that acts as a drug, with the same horrific cycle of addiction, dependence, and tolerance, with a risk of violence increasing. It is absolutely necessary to protect children from all violence, especially very young children.

The World Health Organization (WHO), in its recommendations for domestic and sexual violence prevention presented on September 21, 2010, at the International Conference for Trauma Prevention and the Safety Promotion, highlighted for the first time that the main risk factor for being a perpetrator or victim of domestic or sexual violence is having been a victim in childhood.

Whether a person who has survived childhood violence and developed traumatic memory and resulting dissociative behaviors becomes a repeat victim or a perpetrator depends on several factors, and they become one or the other, not both. The ethical concerns and respect for others, the ability to get angry about injustice and express empathy, the absence of access to a dominant position, the quest for truth, and the development of thinking centered on coherence and universal rights... these are some of the basic factors that make it so the vast majority of victims never become perpetrators. The dominant position gleaned through unequal situations is the most significant risk factor for becoming a perpetrator. This is why the ideal approach to violence prevention involves fighting for a more equal society in which the respect and dignity of all, and the basic human right to never endure violence, are at the core. All victims must have access to everything that can help prevent traumatic memory and dissociative behaviors, including protection and support, detailed information on mechanisms of psycho-trauma, and access to effective specific treatment.

6.12 Traumatized for Life

Traumatic memory acts as a foreign body within victims. This foreign body contains not only the violence itself—the context and feelings of the victim—but also the perpetrators and all their lies, hatred, perverse arousal, and incoherent behaviors and statements. As long as it remains impossible for the victim to represent and verbalize this, the ghostly memory of violence endlessly haunts the psyche and submerges victims in deep confusion. They might ask, "Who am I really: a victim, the living dead, a worthless object, a criminal?" They might wonder what their real feelings are: Terror, anguish, emptiness, anger, hatred, aggressivity, or all-powerfulness.

Colonized by the terrorized victim that she was when the trauma happened and by the violence of the perpetrator, the victim has the feeling of being double, even triple, swinging constantly between the deepest depression and the desire to move mountains. Restrained by guilt and shame, she is anesthetized and indifferent. She is infected with emotions and acts that are not hers and that were imposed during the violence. And many situations seem "naturally" colonized by violence or even indissociable from it because it seems to have always been this way: Couple relationships, family life, and sexuality. The crime and farce of the perpetrator are stored in the cerebral amygdala of the victim in the raw state, with no representation or words to control or analyze it. Without treatment and understanding of mechanisms that fabricate traumatic memory, victims endure remembrances and usually adhere to them as psychological productions from their own thought process, which is particularly frightening.

Victims feel terrorized, in a panic state, or dying, when nothing is threatening them. They might suddenly believe that they are depressed, with no hope left, and suicide or disappearance is the only option, even when everything is going well and they love life. They might believe themselves to be guilty and ashamed, thinking themselves worthless, ugly, stupid, less than nothing, a piece of trash to throw away, though they are doing everything well. They might believe themselves to be monstrous, aggressive, perverted, and capable of doing harm when they only seek to love. They might believe that they desire violent and degrading sexual acts when they dream only of tenderness. All these beliefs and feelings are parasites; they belong to traumatic memory, not to the victim.

6.13 Anesthetization of Traumatic Memory

The parasitic feelings randomly play the roles of victim and perpetrator and what each did, said, and felt. Most victims extenuate themselves trying to avoid, anticipate, or control reminiscences while living in constant fear of harming themselves or, especially, harming others. The invasion of terror and tension is sometimes so strong that nothing can control it, and the harm is impossible to avoid. The ultimate recourse is to direct it against oneself to protect others, and this explains self-mutilation that often imitates the abuse previously endured. Doing this creates extreme stress, setting off the safety mechanism of disjunction and producing emotional and physical anesthetization that brutally calms the emotional storm of reminiscences.

This dissociative experience is powerful insofar as it offers the victim a way to escape anguish that is impossible to control, and she can reuse it. She will dread these dissociating behaviors and also pursue them. If the victim is young and without enough ethical reference points or identifies with the perpetrator's dominant position, dissociating behaviors might be directed at someone else.

Reproducing violence using a new victim forced into a scenario who has nothing to do with her, the former victim gives himself the less risky role of torturer—of the person who abused him in the past. Identification with the perpetrator is encouraged by those around him in a society that refuses to see, hear, or condemn violence against people in discriminatory situations of inferiority and dependence. The violent dissociating behaviors are unfortunately very effective for escaping the suffering generated by traumatic memory. This is how violence originating in trauma is at the origin of new traumatic violence, in a cycle that is endless if we do not put an end to it.

Disjunction involves "hard drugs" that the brain produces, and these quickly become addictive. Dissociative behaviors therefore become addictive, as does the violence itself—in increasingly high doses. Dissociative acts can even be used as "prevention" when any situation triggers reminiscences. Intentionally committing violent acts against another allows perpetrators to anesthetize themselves and therefore face situations that are frightening to them.

To be able to anesthetize traumatic memory by using another, the perpetrators need to have a standby pool of candidates to choose victims from. This requires force or manipulation. Just as directors choose extras available to use each time they need to film, there is a "film" of past violence recorded in the "black box" of traumatic memory, which victims and perpetrators both—though in different roles—replay. Unequal relations allow perpetrators to impose the victim roles on people arbitrarily labeled as inferior and who did not ask for any of this. For perpetrators to have access to potential victims, they must cultivate or piece together situations of discrimination. They decide which categories of people are worth less and can therefore be sacrificed to blow up in their place: Children and women, as well as disabled, marginalized, or discriminated people. Perpetrators do this without any coherence or justice, indecently and without having to prove anything, since the victims are cast as inter-changeable and worthless except for their more or less "cura-tive" value.

Such senseless violence relies on falsification and violations of human rights, which perpetrators justify through aberrant rationalizations in the name of love, desire, education, care, pro-tection, order, culture, religion, or the necessity for economic productivity, when these are nothing but dishonest stagings of what the perpetrators endured in the past—with the roles now distributed differently. As perpetrators position themselves as deserving privileges, they use the staging to escape traumatic memory and relieve themselves through emotional anesthetiza-tion at the expense of the most vulnerable, who can explode in their place on the minefield. Former trauma victims in a pos-ition to abuse their power, and choosing to use it, do not hesitate to betray the victim they were. They can treat their anguish by allowing themselves to exert new behaviors that will be trauma-tizing for victims.

Entire aspects of fundamental human functioning are instrumentalized to make them tools of violence, such as male-female relations, couples, child-rearing, parental love, sexuality, care, work, religion, and politics. Some of these become almost entirely fed by dissociative and violent behaviors, to the point where everyone has considered for a long time that violence is an inherent part of them. Violence, however, is not natural; empathy, benevolence, and solidarity are.

6.14 Domination: Symptom of an Unequal Society that Excuses Violence

Our society is based on male domination. Women, in spite of advances gained through intensive struggles of feminists, are subjected to sexist discrimination that implies violence both symbolic and real. This uses a script whose main point is their inferiority. Justifications for this have been pieced together over centuries through segregation, situations of powerlessness, and exclusion from leadership roles in society, economics, and politics. Women have been denied access to knowledge and artistic or intellectual creation. Restricted to roles of wife, mother, and sex object and condemned to unvalued and unpaid domestic tasks, subjected to (especially sexual) violence, women have been constructed by men in a mystifying image that many women have interiorized. Seeing themselves through the deforming lens of male domination, they fully underestimate their true abilities and see themselves as less valuable or worthy of rights than men.

After decades of social, political, and scientific progress, women should have obtained equality long ago. Women have shown themselves to be men's equals when they have access to the same educational, professional, and leadership opportunities. Scientific research has shown that women and men have the same brains, intelligence, abilities, and emotions, contrary to the false representations of essentialist stereotypes: The eternal feminine defined only as the negative of maleness, through lacking, weakness, and vulnerability. Why does sexist discrimination persist with such flagrant inequality?

The economist Esther Duflo, in the courses she gave at Collège de France in 2009, calls the unchanging discrimination that persists in spite of all evidence and social evolution "pure discrimination" that is "taken straight from history." She compares this with "statistical discrimination," which is based on the statement of facts to draw conclusions about a supposed natural and biological inferiority of women. For example, since there are few women in history who were great painters, philosophers, or literary geniuses, this signifies—according to statistical discrimination—that these are not in women's nature. Similarly, there are few women CEOs and political leaders, and this is taken as proof that women are not capable of such important functions.

Statistical discrimination is suspectable to evolve historically or even disappear as women gain more access to these roles and prove that they are perfectly capable of doing anything that men do, once the doors are open to them. With access to the best universities and positions of highest leadership, women are becoming accustomed to leadership, and their abilities are being recognized. Pure discrimination is pure deception-based on the desire to create and maintain profoundly unequal hierarchies such as in the old days; this is why it is resistant to evidence. Its purpose is to allow men to continue benefitting from exorbitant privilege and positioning themselves as superior and deserving more rights: The right to use, own, consume, scorn, and instrumentalize women and to commit any kind of violence against them: Psychological, physical, and sexual, including rape, torture, and murder.

Men have the right of life or death over all women, which women can feel in their family or couple relationship and in public places, parking lots, etc., where they are afraid to walk at night (a Canadian study reveals that over 60% of women are afraid at night in public places). Males have the right of life or death over females when Indian and Chinese families choose not to raise daughters and to eliminate female fetuses or kill females at birth: Millions of females are killed in these countries every year. Their potential lives are cut short due to the lesser value they are said to have and the cultural preference for sons. They have the right of life or death in couples, as a woman is killed by her partner every two and a half days (146 women were killed in 2010 in France). They have the right of life or death with all the little girls, teens, and women raped then killed, with all women in prostitution, among whom the primary cause of death is homicide. All this is femicide, a concept that was finally included in the penal code of Mexico and some South American countries in July 2011. The standard definition of "femicide" coined by Diane Russel is, "The killing of females by males because they are female."

This pure discrimination is also symbolic violence, well described by Pierre Bourdieu, which allows all other violence to go unpunished. It is like an authorization to instrumentalize women, who are trained from birth to be slaves and medication. This training is done through violence and sexist discrimination that is psychological, verbal, physical, sexual, and economic. Genital mutilation, incest, forced marriage, domestic violence, pornography, prostitution, and violence in public spaces or at work generate such control that they make it so any other violence can be committed without punishment, according to the whims of perpetrators.

6.15 The Grooming of Children

Raising children most often involves subduing them. Ordinary violence in the name of "teaching them a lesson" is accepted, normalized, or even considered necessary by most people (Maurel, 2009). In Europe and the United States, 60–90% of parents approve of corporal punishment to discipline children. Although this is now forbidden in schools, psychological violence, threats, hurtful words, and humiliation are still common. Within families, resorting to physical violence was legal in France until 2019 "as long as it is adapted and moderate," and it is still legal in all 50 United States states if it is "reasonably related to the purpose of safeguarding or promoting the welfare of the minor" and does not cause harm or severe distress (which ignores evidence of it being inherently harmful and against children's welfare). Currently, 58 countries have outlawed all physical punishment, including within families. Sweden was the first to do so, in 1966, and France is the most recent (2019).

The reasons cited for hitting or spanking children from a very early age are that they cry too much, don't want to eat, refuse to be dressed, cannot sleep, don't want to play or stop playing, don't want to return something or put it back, try to get what they want, disobey, say something they shouldn't, drop something, talk or move around too much, don't understand what someone is saying or what they are supposed to learn, and sometimes even because they got hurt, put themselves in danger, or strayed too far... Is any of this so serious or twisted as to justify corporal punishment? Yet these seem to be much more serious in the eyes of adults than the transgressions, neglect, or abuse that adults often commit. Children are forbidden to disobey, but adults can, in front of their children, disobey traffic laws, speed, drive drunk, and park anywhere, and no one will hit them; at worst, they will get a ticket if caught! Adults are allowed to not be hungry, not want to sleep, not sit up straight at the table, say mean things or swear, and not feel like concentrating… they have the right and good reasons—not so for the child!

Through the harmful magic of adult traumatic memory, which replays violence from childhood and the parents' words that went with it, the child is perceived as having bad intentions, annoying the adult, and ruining his or her life. The child is dramatically perceived as fundamentally bad, aggressive, provocative, and ready to "grow the wrong way" if not corrected in time.

Make no mistake: The first violence experienced and experiments with self-treatment, if not horrific enough to be immediately put in check, run a strong risk of opening the door to increasingly intense violence—including sexual violence. A child might first be attacked when a parent's traumatic memory flares up due to links with a past that does not concern the child: The parent's past. Secondly, through addictive mechanisms, the child is used as a scapegoat and readily available medication— and even a preventative treatment for anxiety, stress, or frustration that have nothing to do with the child but that flare up the traumatic memory of the parent-perpetrator. The system can get out of control and contaminate the child who is used as an interrupter at everyone's service with a total absence of compassion due to everyone being emotionally anesthetized (Salmona, 2016).

As "ordinary violence" is allowed against children, society holds a heavy responsibility, since this is the foundation for future violence, especially sexual violence. Society is especially hypocritical in showing surprise about the violence of young adolescents and their dissociative risk behaviors, which are severely condemned when they are actually direct results of violence endured. Violence and behavior disorders in adolescent behaviors are considered more serious than in adults, and most of the time, no questions are asked about family violence. It is even considered that these are golden children who haven't had any limits and haven't been punished enough!

Most dishonest of all, such adolescents are given the counterexample of perfect victims who do not rock the boat and who give the impression that they are doing well through not bothering anyone. These resilient "counterexamples" have supposedly even benefitted from violent disciplinary acts that "forged their character." The price they pay for this resilience is never discussed: Total sacrifice and enslavement to family loyalty mean that they carefully hide the consequences of abuse at all costs. They might be fully anesthetized emotionally through repeated and ongoing violence or dissociating risk behaviors. Very rarely, a victim is extraordinarily lucky, and the knife doesn't touch any vein or organ. These resilient victims reassure themselves through flaunting their well-adjustedness and non-victim status. They are used to "prove" that violence is not a big problem for everyone and that it might not have any consequences.

In the United States, children are the only people whom the law does not protect from physical violence—even incarcerated people are protected—what's wrong with this picture? The United States has signed the United Nations Convention on the Rights of the Child on November 20, 1989, and it asks nations "to explicitly forbid by law any corporal punishment against children in any setting, including family, school, institutions, and places of care and to promote awareness and values of raising children without violence." We now know that "ordinary childrearing violence" is a risk factor for serious mistreatment and produces psycho-traumatic syndromes that result in future violence.

Corporal punishment is a violation of children's rights and has no educational value. On the contrary, many studies have shown that it is ineffective, dangerous, and harmful to the health and development of the child. It increases the risk of behavior disorders and feeds lasting cycles of violence. The protection of children from all forms of violence is an absolute priority (Salmona, 2016).

6.16 Sexist Stereotypes and the Dismissal of Sexual Violence

Human sexuality is saturated with violence. Sexist stereotypes, male domination, and false ideas about men's sexuality mean that sexuality is confounded with aggressive dissociating behaviors such as prostitution, pornography, and violent sexual behaviors between adults said to be consenting. The confusion of sexuality and violence is maintained by degrading vocabulary and discourse on sexuality: The majority of insults have sexual connotations, as do many jokes, witticisms, and puns, and the lexical field of sexuality is based on war, crime, or hunting (Baldeck, 2010). This transmits a degrading image of women, reduced and chopped into pieces as sex objects. This is everywhere in the media, advertising, movies, and a large portion of publications. Male sexuality is constructed as predatory and impulsive, with caricatures of men and women. Most people adhere or conform to this misrepresentation of sexuality, and it infects male-female relations and love relationships. It degrades women and downplays many forms of sexual violence, which becomes for some men efficient dissociating behaviors to treat traumatic memory.

The confusion between violence and sexuality is at the root of serious addictions, prostitution, and pornography with a flourishing sex industry proposing increasingly violent practices, videos, and images. This results in an increase in trafficking and slavery of women and children, sex tourism, sex crimes, and violence against women, including in prostitution and pornography. This confusion also maintains inequality between men and women and deprives the majority of both men and women of access to their own sexuality and true love based on respect, exchange, and discovery of another.

The violence that saturates sexuality maintains confusion between true desire and addiction to stress, with painful arousal linked to sensorial traumatic memory that must be extinguished at all costs. It also fosters confusion between true, orgasmic sexual pleasure and the brutal orgasm-like release linked to disjunction and emotional anesthetization. There is also confusion between fantasies and actual visual and sensory reminiscences resulting from traumatic memory.

When someone's first sexual experiences were violent, sexuality may be entirely colonized by traumatic memory, and every sexual situation might carry violent images or humiliating words that impose themselves and seem inseparably linked to one's own sexuality (Maritée, 2012). Worse, the perverted pleasure of the abuser, which was exceedingly traumatic for the victim (pleasure in torturing, destroying, terrorizing, polluting, and degrading) might invade all experiences of pleasure and make it impossible to stand. Victims might give up all attempts at sexuality in order to avoid the false pleasure infected by violence that could make it seem that they enjoy their own humiliation and the pain inflicted. The "pleasure" is not real and is not their own, but traumatic memory makes this difficult to detect; it could seem very convincing (especially if they know nothing else). This confusion contributes to a catastrophic self-image and low self-esteem that makes victims even more vulnerable; it can lead to suicide.

Many women who were sexually abused find themselves having to manage severely traumatized sexuality infected with psycho-traumatic symptoms that are unidentified as such. They find themselves alone with this traumatized sexuality, with no tools to understand it or to communicate the violence endured in the past and separate what is sane and belongs to them from what is infected by violence and trauma. They have no choice but to integrate their sexuality as it is or to reject it altogether. Alone, they face a society of denial that gives them no clues to find their way and drags them further into alienating sexual representations. Society constantly transmits mystifying stereotypes about "female sexuality" that are in reality based on psycho-traumatic symptoms: The virgin, the frigid, the passive, the nymphomaniac, the uptight, the loose, the sex bomb, the skank, the slut, the whore... And all those who do not want to give up on a genuine loving encounter—and thankfully there are many of them—must fight to escape these reductive and imprisoning models. Women, and men too, have a lot to gain in repossessing non-traumatic sexuality in which they can finally be free to fully access their own desire and pleasure.

It is not enough to take care of trauma victims in identifying violence, linking it to their symptoms, and treating their traumatic memory. It is also necessary to combat all forms of violence, protect potential victims, and stand up against myths and misconceptions about violence, victims, and perpetrators.

It is essential to fight against sexism, inequality, and discrimination everywhere in society and do everything to make sure that perpetrators are brought to justice. This might allow them to get treatment and give up their addictive use of violence, and it is possible to thus prevent further abuse.

6.17 Which Violence Creates Traumatic Memory?

All forms of violence must be denounced and combatted, and all are traumatic when they occur. They do not all, however, result in long-term traumatic memory. The more destructive the violence is, the more likely it will result in chronic psycho-traumatic disorders. The most serious forms are violence that confronts the victim with possible death of self or other, including direct physical death and serious injury or indirect physical death through extreme stress generated by terror, distress, powerlessness, and incomprehension when faced with the incoherence of some forms of violence.

Some violence is destructive because it can cause physical death and some because it can cause psychological death. For the first, the risk of serious physical harm may result in psycho-trauma and traumatic memory with secondary psychological damage. For the second, the psychological harm results in psycho-trauma; physical harm is not always present, but when it is, it becomes an aggravating factor. Most often, physical and psychological assaults occur together, but psychological damage is always present and at the heart of psycho-traumatic mechanisms. Once traumatic memory has set in, how the traumatized victim is rescued, supported, and cared for is crucial for the outcome. Victims given appropriate treatment have every chance of disarming their traumatic memory and reintegrating the experience as autobiographical memory.

Psychological damage during violence manifests as tonic immobility of the thought process, which makes it impossible to modulate any emotional response. This generates a vital risk. Because of this, the brain disconnects the emotional circuitry, and traumatic memory sets in. Violence reduces the victim to physical or mental powerlessness through its unpredictable, incomprehensible, unthinkable, and monstrous qualities. This incoherent and intentional violence makes any mental representation of the event impossible and leaves nothing but a black hole—just as Medusa's head petrifies those who look at it. The most incomprehensible violence is that which makes no sense to the victim in its context and has nothing to do with who she is, what she did or didn't do, said or didn't say. This unthinkable violence is not about the victim! It is the reenactment of a scene from the perpetrator's own past. He forces the victim to play a role that is not hers in an unpredictable scene she knows nothing about, which the perpetrator is using to dissociate and anesthetize himself. He uses the victim to play the role he had, either of the victim he was or of the victim of violence that he witnessed in the past. He saves the perpetrator's role for himself, so that he is not himself exposed to danger and is instead all-powerful. The victim that he violates and terrorizes, through the horror of what happens to her and the extreme distress she experiences, is pushed onto the landmine and is sacrificed fuse (when it happens once) or interrupter (rechargeable for repeat violence) to short-circuit the emotional circuitry of perpetrators and give them a massive dose of hard drugs (endorphins and ketamine-like) that dissociate them and brutally and effectively relieve them for a certain time. Victims are also disjuncted, in an altered state, absent, and understanding nothing about the explosion of violence; they are deeply harmed psychologically, with the serious consequence of traumatic memory that can undermine their entire existence.

The most destructive violence comes from dissociating behaviors. It is endless, as each staging/disjunction recharges a traumatic memory that only gains strength. At the root of real addiction to violence, dissociating morphine- and ketamine-like drugs secreted during disjunctions lead to addiction, which is why violence is repeated and must become more and more severe to get the required dose.

Violence not linked to traumatic memory, on the other hand, is intentional and more predictable, logical, controlled, limited, and understandable, such as defensive violence.

If traumatic memory and desire for domination are not at work in people using violence (some military or police personnel, for example), they will have natural emotional limits that allow them to stop in time. Sufficient horror of the consequences of violence and natural empathy for victims are solid ethical barriers that prevent people from committing wrongful acts. But traumatic memory is so common that it can contaminate those in positions of power over others, so that they need to be attentively supervised.

Among those contaminated by traumatic violence, many manage it at their own expense, controlling it or using avoidance behaviors that only harm themselves, without ever finding themselves acting as perpetrators. Others are less brave and can easily switch to instrumentalizing others, especially when they have had a bad example from those above them in the hierarchy and/or benefit from social acceptance. Others still take advantage of power relations and use violence from their perverse stance of authorities/"superiors" who transgress.

6.18 Psychological Violence: How to Demolish Another's Identity

Psychological violence is present in all situations of violence and is used to immobilize victims. It is also a very efficient tool for making victims vulnerable and generating control over them that can appear to be consent, especially in situations of violence in the home or workplace.

Until recently, the only acts of psychological violence punished by the law were malicious phone calls, threats, or moral harassment at work, defined as "harassing another by repeated acts with the goal or effect of creating a work environment that transgresses their rights or dignity, alters their physical or mental health, or compromises their professional future." With the July 9, 2010, law, psychological violence within a couple is also a misdemeanor, defined as "acts that could take the form of words or deeds that worsen living conditions of the victim and alter their physical or mental health."

The goal of psychological violence is to dominate, subjugate, and instrumentalize victims, requiring them to play all kinds of roles. Domination through manipulation, intimidation, threat, terror, or unequal power can be exerted through a something as simple as a crazed glance and from the tonic immobility resulting from abnormal, incomprehensible, and totally unjustifiable behaviors. Those who constantly use this weapon in their relationships have been identified as narcissistic perverts (Racamier, 1995).

Psychological violence destroys victims' identities and conditions them to think that they are worthless, incompetent, unintelligent, guilty, and have the right to exist only for other's use. Abusers intentionally confuse victims and prevent them from seeing the truth; they are held in a state of incomprehension, fear, and guilt. Abusers destroy any possibility of opposing their demands and version of reality in victims. Made totally dependent, victims are slaves (often sex slaves) groomed to respond automatically to the master's every desire. The abuser can appear totally innocent, showing "proof" of his victim's consent. He can say that she willingly went on dates with him, answered calls or emails in which he proposed certain sexual acts, and even claimed to like it. In reality, she was playing an imposed role, dressing and acting according to the part he thrust on her. She repeated every word of the script he inflicted on her. Women find themselves participating in orgies, swingers/BDSM clubs, or prostituting themselves at partners' demands. They never want this. They are horrified by it and feel degraded, but they cannot get out of it except through death; such situations often end in suicide.

For this total takeover to work, abusers must hold victims in a state of terror. They consciously create a climate of physical and emotional insecurity for victims by fabricating all kinds of conflicts, intimidations, threats, emotional blackmail, or constant, subtle reminders, so that victims face permanent hostility, sudden outbursts, and intolerance of the least objection. It is a climate of constraint, control, and isolation involving constant surveillance (where she goes, who her friends are, what she spends money on, going anywhere, how she dresses, and so on).

Strict rules are imposed along with constant harassment, disregard for privacy, and sometimes sequestration. Neglect, refusal of care, and disrespect for fundamental needs are also common. The abuser makes sure that the victim feels inferior and ashamed by humiliating her and criticizing how she looks, talks, thinks, works, raises children, keeps house, and behaves romantically and sexually. He makes her feel guilty and incompetent through constant complaints and criticism. He further ensures that she won't protest through instilling feelings of loyalty and debt. He presents himself as necessary for her and sacrificing himself for everyone's good: "You couldn't survive without me," "Without me, you'd be in the street," and so on. He uses constant emotional blackmail: "If you don't want to do that for me, that means you don't love me." His incoherence functions to make the victim constantly doubt her own perceptions, feelings, and thoughts. This further reduces her self-confidence and increases his control.

Psychological violence relies on complete falsification: Everything the abuser says or does is a lie, abuse of power, or tool to manipulate and inflict suffering on the victim. Psychological violence is always intentional. It veils its lies and harm in pretexts such as love, education, need, responsibility, or professional, economic, or security obligations. The perpetrator always blames the victim's attitude: "You drive me crazy; you are insufferable, dangerous, and do everything to push me to the limit." These are pure inventions scripted by perpetrators for their own purposes. They feel free to use such lies because of how well they correspond to stereotypes of the family, love, sexuality, education, work, obedience, hierarchy, and security. Perpetrators know that it is dishonest and morally reprehensible to transgress the rights and dignity of others. They do so anyway because they know that they can get away with it, especially behind closed doors.

Psychological violence is often present from the beginning of a relationship but masked by a climate of seduction in which the abuser is hot and cold, pretending to want to protect the victim. Very often, the victim is aware that this is abnormal, unjust, or incoherent but lacks confidence in her judgment and emotions. The abuser succeeds in explaining things in a way that shows his total reversal: He insists that he is right. He acts out the total conviction that he believes everything he says. It's totally false. The abuser knows this. He knows that he is shamelessly lying, and he has premeditated this.

Stereotypes prevent the victim from defending herself or realizing she is right: "Parents always love their children." "Men are just like that: awkward, needly, not very tuned in, and they have huge sexual needs." "Women are more intuitive, sensitive, romantic, and generous." "It's normal to make sacrifices for love and to serve the man you love." "At work, you have to obey orders," and so on. For the victim, it is impossible to think that the abuser's behavior is intentional—and that is a trap: "He doesn't realize what he's doing." "He's just like that; it's not his fault." "I'll have to explain it to him." "He has suffered; I'll change him through my love…"

The abuse then intensifies, progressively and irrevocably, in proportion to how committed the victim is to the relationship or job and how much she adapts to the violence in developing an uncanny ability to understand the abuser. The victim is aware of the abuse and the hell she is living, but she is trapped, since her analysis and emotions are constantly disqualified or denied by the abuser: "It's no big deal; you're exaggerating; can't you take a joke…" Such remarks prevent the victim from realizing that the abuser has no right to behave this way and to see that he does so intentionally.

The psycho-traumatic disorders engendered by repeated violence also create a dissociative state and emotional anesthetization that make it so the victim cannot understand her reactions and emotions. She knows that the violence is serious and unjustifiable, but she doubts her own judgment. Buried in the incoherent emotions of the abuser, who explodes all the time, she thinks she might be crazy. This state of uncertainty and confusion in victims allows abusers to be sure of their control and to manipulate, dictate, and restrain victims' emotions, thoughts, and roles.

Victims quickly find themselves colonized by the traumatic memory of abuse. This will increase their feelings of incompetence, as the degrading insults of the abuser invade her psyche. She mistakes these for her own views of self and disastrous judgments that she has made: "You're a loser, my poor daughter!" "You're not capable of anything!" "You always get it wrong!" "You're worthless!" "You don't deserve to live!" "No one can stand you; all you do is complain!" "You'll never love or be loved!" These are inventions of the abuser and part of his script of guilt, shame, and absence of self-esteem that are to be interiorized by the victim even when she is no longer in contact with him.

Such psychological violence is destructive and leads to serious psychological consequences that frequently end in suicide. But they can be difficult to prove, all the more so in that the abuser is often successful at manipulating police and justice personnel who have had no training in identifying the mechanisms and effects of control over another. It is an essential right to be able to gain justice, and much evidence is usually available to prove abuse (writings, strategies, testimonies, recordings, medical certificates, etc.). Victims must be given the tools to recognize the mechanisms of control and set themselves free. They also need appropriate care to treat psycho-traumatic disorders, decolonize themselves from the abuser, and regain confidence in their perception and self-image.

The five usual strategies of abusers (according to Marie-France Casalis of the Feminist Collective Against Rape (CFCV) are as follows: Isolate the victim, deprive her of resources and contact with friends and family; devalue and destabilize her; reverse the guilt; create a climate of terror; present yourself as all-powerful; and be sure of impunity by cultivating allies. To oppose such strategies, it is necessary to do the opposite: Support the victim, emphasize her worth, recognize her courage and abilities, help her to be safe, use the law, hold the abuser accountable, and do everything possible to end all forms of violence.

7

The Lives of Victims

7.1 In a Victim's Own Words

"When leaving a party, I was raped in my city by a stranger who threatened to kill me. After a month, someone finally got me to talk about it. I'd lost 10 kilos. That day, I completely fell apart, and the following days were worse and worse. First, I went to see a general practitioner, then a psychologist, and they first told me that I had nothing to be ashamed of and that I had ten years to press charges. I was put on anti-anxiety medication and then on antidepressants, neuroleptics, and sleeping pills. These only made it worse, as I felt doped and couldn't get out of bed in the morning. No matter; I was pushed to go to work anyway in this state. Empathy gave way to, 'You've got to take responsibility; what were you doing outside that night; stop thinking about it!' I felt more and more guilty… and when I'd talk about pressing charges, I'd hear, 'What good would it do to put him behind bars?' or 'He saw you again and didn't bother you, so you don't need to worry anymore.'

I saw him several times while dropping off or picking up my child from school. I told my psychologist and my employers, but no one reacted… Clearly, in others' eyes, this rapist was only dangerous to me… and I felt more and more guilty for having been raped and for my suffering in a way everyone found disproportionate.

DOI: 10.4324/9781003497516-8

Sometimes, I'd go outside in the middle of the night. Other times, I would cut my arm, and shortly thereafter, I tried to commit suicide with an overdose of medication. I felt like the living dead, who just needed to work and keep quiet about what had happened. My sick days piled up, and I felt very guilty, with an increasing urge to throw myself under a train.

I saw him again in the city. He smiled perversely. I went home with my child, completely terrorized. I feel I'm being followed and am in danger. I talk about it again; no response. I start asking myself if I am crazy… a week later, in the afternoon, I am face to face with my rapist! I'm with children, right next to a school… he hits me in the face and ribs just to remind me! Second death threat! The police, sirens blaring, take me away for questioning, pressing charges, making a computer-generated portrait of the rapist, and they tell me they'll do everything they can to find him. They end it by telling me to get some pepper spray so I can feel safer…

I then got a psychiatric evaluation, which was awful. I had to answer many questions about my childhood, my schooling, my parents, and a series of 'whys': Why did I move out of my parent's house, why I wasn't with someone… I was also made to talk with this male psychologist about my current sex life, if I had a sex partner, if not, did I masturbate, and so on. It was not only abhorrent, but they made it worse by adding: 'Is that really such a hard question?' I really wanted to explode in that office, and when I asked whether I was required to answer a certain question (about my childhood), the psychologist answered, 'It's to help with your case.' I walked out of there alone wanting to die. It was hard to get back, especially since I was expected to go to work! I talked with my therapist about this awful experience, but she saw nothing wrong with it…

I moved after that, but to a neighboring area so I could keep my job, though I was not at all fit to work, and I was in danger in my former city, but apparently that was nothing! For everyone else, my well-being, health, and security were secondary.

Four months after I pressed charges, the police called me in. When I asked how long it would take, so I could organize child-care, they said, 'That's totally up to you'!

I went there alone, and an officer said to me: 'We think you are not telling the full truth. We think you know him.' That killed me! He was basing this on my psychiatric evaluation. He continued: 'We're going to have you look at some photos and ask you more detailed questions. I repeated that I absolutely did not know the rapist. He showed me photos of people I knew, and I felt a pressure that made no sense unless the goal was to make me feel even more freaked out. He then asked me who I talked to at the party on the night of the rape, what we talked about, how I was feeling, how many drinks I had, etc. They asked if I saw other people around me during and after the rape. I couldn't take it anymore! They ended it by telling me the next time I saw the rapist, I should take a picture and call them immediately.

From then on, I stopped everything: Medication, therapy, and work. I went several times to the police station to see whether they had made any progress. They'd say, 'We're going to need you to run into him again and get a picture this time, or we'll have to wait for a fresh victim.' So it was up to me to stop my rapist! No matter how dangerous such an attempt would be; I had the horrible feeling of being responsible for him going free and thinking about other potential victims. Meanwhile, those around me said, 'Why aren't you working? You have to live a normal life for your child's sake.'

I felt tremendous distress and could not go outside without having an anxiety attack. The only time I went out at all was to drop off and pick up my child from school or do groceries very far from home, with a feeling of constant danger. In parallel, my traumatic memory flared up violently with flashbacks to my childhood, during which I was sexually abused, tortured, and almost killed.

Today, I am no longer alone. I finally have appropriate care for my trauma with a specialized psychiatrist, and this is what's keeping me alive and moving forward.

A week ago, I ran into my rapist again, and he saw me. I was in a car with my child a few meters from the police station and alerted them within 2 minutes. After saying what he was wearing, I was required to describe his face again, though they already had the computer-generated image. They searched for half an hour, and it was over: 'We didn't find him. We even went as far as the city.' Did they get out of their car? No. Did they ask anyone in the places where I'd seen him instead of going to the neighboring city? No.

They finally realized something: He must know people nearby.' I'd been telling them that for eight months, but what are a victim's words worth?

Then they told me that I should have stayed close to my rapist and followed him from the safety of my car to see where he went while calling them! 'Do that next time you see him,' they said. They didn't understand that I wanted above all not to have a next time. They were then very 'reassuring' and 'concerned,' telling me to stay home that evening and not be alone.

Today, I am constantly afraid. I have anxiety attacks every time I leave home, even if far from the city where the rape happened. I haven't been out of the house in four days. I'm the one who lost my job, had to move, and will have to move again. It's my job, the victim, to protect myself. It's my child who had to stop school all of a sudden and can't go to the park with her friends. During all this, the unpunished rapist can easily walk down the street with a feeling of all-powerfulness."

7.2 Serial Injustice

The above testimony is unfortunately not an isolated miscarriage of justice. As long as there is no proper training and awareness, impunity of perpetrators and accumulated suffering of victims are the norm. More often than not, institutions that are supposed to help victims actually increase their hardship and despair. Victims are left alone with their suffering or blamed for it, either due to an overall ignorance or malicious intent toward them including in the criminal justice system.

In addition, victims battling with psycho-traumatic symptoms that no one understands find themselves constantly asked by those around them to explain or justify themselves. They are constantly made to feel guilty and subjected to lectures, socially stigmatized, and said to complain too much; they are judged as annoying, vindicative, incoherent, weak, lazy, stupid, or crazy.

These projections target victims and not perpetrators. People bombard victims with questions: "Why were you at that place, dressed like that, doing that?" "Why did you provoke, arouse, or anger him?" "Why did you let him do that to you?" "Why didn't you defend yourself/say no/scream?" or, "Why didn't you let him do it? Why did you take the risk of defending yourself?" "Why didn't you report it earlier? Why don't you remember all the details more precisely and the order of events?"

These questions imply that the violence is somehow the victim's fault and that her behavior is to blame. She is cast as irresponsible, allowing or encouraging violence, or somehow able to have avoided it. All this is entirely false. Such questions totally ignore the fact that whatever she did, no one had the right to assault her, period! Such questions are symptomatic of unquestioned male domination, insofar as almost all attackers are male and victims are female.

The victim tries desperately to understand, and all of a sudden, she feels terribly guilty as traumatic memory scrambles all certitude and self-awareness: The feeling of unreality and traumatic dissociation and the destabilizing and anguishing experience of emotional anesthesia make her feel detached, not herself, a fake. Temporal-spatial distortion and memory disorders linked to disjunction make her words imprecise and generate doubt. The perpetrator, on the other hand, does not seek to understand but to shed any guilt and to rationalize his behavior. Having intentionally committed and usually premeditated the violence, he feels no guilt, and he scorns the victim because he believes that his superior position gives him the privilege to use her. He also benefits from the psycho-traumatic consequences of the violence he commits, particularly the emotional anesthetization that he seeks to relieve his tension. This allows him to be unaffected and feel no anguish about his acts and their consequences. He can lie without any shame and easily play his role of the innocent: He didn't mean to hurt her; she didn't understand; he couldn't control it; he was victim of his impulses, rage, jealousy, passion, or what he pretends are the lies of the victim.

The life of a traumatized victim becomes a hell of suffering and solitude, made worse by the fact that everyone views her through a lens of ignorance and sometimes malevolence, unfairly pinning the fault on her. There is huge pressure on her to be quiet, constantly censor herself, hide her suffering and symptoms, and only show the façade of someone perfect and extremely well-adjusted. The vast majority of victims are extremely courageous, coherent, and rigorous. Though they may not seem this way, they are strong and solid in the face of anything. They didn't wait for anyone's permission to develop their treasures of intelligence, reflection, analysis, observation, and ingenuity to survive anything and, in spite of it all, to move forward in life without ever giving up on love, truth, justice, and respect for others.

7.3 Lies About Victims

A small percentage of traumatized victims give up on their ideals and treat their traumatic memory through identifying with their abuser and adhering to the law of might makes right, abusing others to anesthetize themselves. But this small percentage of victims who become torturers is enough to feed the cycle of violence through creating new traumatized victims. These torturers—former victims—are at the root of false discourse about all victims. To put themselves on the side of the privileged and escape the constraints of traumatic memory, they must erase having been victims from their own story and erase or deny the trauma of their victims to be sure of their own impunity. They also have to deny the truth of all victims who might remind them of their own story. They construct a myth of all-powerfulness in which the victim they once were has no place and is intolerable; they must silence that victim forever. From this stems the mystifying discourse about victims, which constantly doubts and silences them.

7.4 Reversing the Guilt

False, reductive discourse about victims allows perpetrators to deny responsibility and to avoid identifying as victims themselves, which would mean admitting their inferior status according to the value system they adhere to. They like to claim that victims are too passive and need to take responsibility for their role in the violence as active players in the events of their lives. The only other kind of victims mentioned are those who supposedly derived significant benefits from their status. These two types of discourse should exclude each other, but they coexist in unquestioned incoherence, just as the Jews in Nazi Germany were said to be, at the same time, scornfully inferior and all-powerfully dangerous.

In both cases, the focus is on the victim and on reversing who is guilty: The victim is not so innocent; she is dangerous because she provokes temptation and therefore violence. The assumption is that if she hadn't been there, as she was, there never would have been an aggression—she should have been more responsible. This is a favorite line of perpetrators: "I just don't understand; I've never been violent before…" Victims are also often blamed for not taking charge of their lives and for staying stuck in their "pathetic victimization;" the assumption is that they should be ashamed of being victims and that their inability to move on as if nothing happened is proof of weakness. Sometimes it is said that victims are cruel: The poor perpetrator will lose everything and go to prison because of her, "for some stupid little thing, a fleeting loss of control"—shouldn't she be more understanding and less bitter? Human rights or laws appear nowhere in such discussions.

These usual deceptions sweep under the rug the seriousness of violence, its criminal status, and the intentional, premeditated quality involved in almost all acts of violence. The destruction of a victim's life is nothing—it is downplayed, contrary to possible consequences for perpetrators. We know that victims are interchangeable for perpetrators, chosen for how well they may be instrumentalized to gain anesthetization and represent little risk of getting caught—this is considerably lower if the victim is a child or someone isolated, vulnerable, dependent, and/or used to staying quiet due to previous experiences of victimization.

7.5 Making Victims Disappear

Telling a victim to take responsibility, stop complaining, and forget what happened only serves to ensure impunity for perpetrators. Contrary to common beliefs, society rarely mentions victims or lets them speak. The media habitually gives voice to those (less numerous) in dominant positions; most victims are not famous and thus are of no interest. Although it is easy to identify and dismantle sexist and reactionary discourse of privileged men, the discourse of women in dominant positions is more difficult to denounce. The common denominator of all these mystifying discourses, formulated by women (and men) higher on society's ladder, is the refusal to position oneself as a victim of the dominants (since the dominants are always right). They can, however, complain about being victims of the dominated (cruel victims who endanger the entire hierarchy). Such discourse can be very confusing, for example, when it is used by the rare prostitutes who claim to be proud to prostitute themselves and campaign for prostitution to be recognized as a job like any other.

Overall, victims are told to be quiet, and everything is done to prevent them from recognizing their status of victim. As long as society remains contaminated by unjust hierarchies and might makes right, being a victim and saying it puts someone on the side of the inferiors. It is necessary to fight against this manipulation by calling violence what it is and clearly stating who is responsible by reminding others of the fundamental rights and laws that everyone has, and also demolishing the mystifying discourse of perpetrators. Guilt and shame should no longer be thrown onto the victim's side. For victims, it is equally necessary to understand that nothing they did could ever justify the violence; they were forced or manipulated into playing a role in a scene that had nothing to do with them and only served the abuser's own anesthetizing escape from traumatic memory. The hatred and scorn he scripted are not really for her but for the victim he once was and now hates and wants to destroy and erase, because having been a victim means he cannot be on the dominant side.

It is absolutely necessary for victims to know about the psycho-traumatic consequences of violence and that these are normal when no adequate treatment is given. They explain tonic immobility and paralysis during violence, the state of dissociation and emotional anesthesia when facing the perpetrator, and the avoidance and hypervigilant behaviors along with depression, anxiety, and danger-seeking. If not, these only increase the guilt and bewilderment of victims. At least knowing what is happening can allow them to find themselves again, though they also deserve adapted care. This is hard to find since most professionals do not have the knowledge or tools.

7.6 Instrumentalized and Sacrificed

One is not born victim, just as one is not born perpetrator; we become these essentially through manipulation, discrimination, and injustice. Inequality allows victims-turned-perpetrators to instrumentalize those who will become their victims and trap them in a story that is not their own and force them to play traumatizing roles in violent scenes. Victims are made to pay for violence that they did not commit and repair damage that they are not responsible for; they care for wounds whose origin they do not know and absorb horrors that have nothing to do with them. They are stuck with the blistering abscess of horrors injected into them that can burst anytime. They are expected to make the violence disappear so that those around them, and society as a whole, don't have to see it. No one wants to see the violence. If victims don't get rid of the violence by forcing it on another (becoming perpetrators), they unjustly become pariahs, annoyances, lunatics…

Victims are condemned to either be scapegoats (as prostitutes often are) on which society pins all its horrors to get rid of them, excluding them from the world of the living—if she doesn't disappear, someone will make her—or they have to take care of the corpses of violence and clean them up so well that they are presentable; she must constantly makeup them over or hide them. In any case, it is always the victim who has to hide, sacrifice herself, and be estranged from the world. Perpetrators, through getting rid of their traumatic memory by thrusting it on others, are perfectly integrated into society.

Victims are always innocent of the violence that is unleashed on them, whether they are babies, children, teens, women, men, or the elderly. To the biting questions: "Why me? What did I do to deserve this? Am I responsible for any of it? Did I make a mistake? Why didn't I see it coming," no answer can be given except that violence is by nature blind, unjust, unthinkable, and incoherent. Everything the victim is in her reality, humanity, or vulnerability that normally should elicit compassion does nothing, and nor do her weaknesses or mistakes. Nothing means anything, since violence exists in the realm of the absurd. All that counts, unfortunately, is to live with someone (through obligation or choice) or to come across someone in the street (which can be totally by chance) who has an explosive traumatic memory that will kick in at that particular time (perhaps because of a symbolic association) and that can, due to precise circumstances (power, domination, impunity) transform him into a perpetrator who uses violence to treat his traumatic memory.

7.7 How Victims Are Chosen

1. The traumatic memory of the perpetrator might flare up due to something about the victim. It could be something simple and harmless that is not linked to her at all but to a situation in which she finds herself, her age, appearance, the way she looks at him, her emotional state or well-being, which reminds the perpetrator through subconscious associations of abuse he was subject to sometime in his past, usually in childhood. Or, it might remind him of violence that he committed that also contributed to his traumatic memory. The flaring up of his amygdala generates tension, anxiety, and distress with partial reminiscences such as images, words, feelings, and violent urges. To escape this state, he allows himself to commit violence in a situation that seems incongruous but is actually much like the violence he previously experienced, which is at the origin of his traumatic memory. This provokes the disconnection of emotional circuitry and relieves his tension through anesthetizing him emotionally. This is very dangerous. The victim's apparent indifference makes it difficult for others to perceive the seriousness of the situation.

2. Victims are chosen for their vulnerability, dependence, isolation, and absence of protection, which means that the abuser does not risk being held accountable. This vulnerability should naturally solicit benevolence and protection, but it is twisted to enable violent behavior. Emotional anesthetization and dissociation in victims aggravate the risk of further mistreatment from those around them, as the mirror neurons do not function. There is no feedback, and others cannot detect the emotions of dissociated victims or relate to them. Others can mistreat them without remorse, because anesthetized victims emit no signals of distress; their security, integrity, and rights can easily be disregarded. This explains the extreme abuse many victims continue to suffer from.

3. Through malicious reversal, victims are chosen because of their strengths (attentiveness, kindness, helpfulness, ethics, and even the ability to question and attempt to understand circumstances, especially of others). These make such victims the perfect slaves in service of treating the abuser's traumatic memory, especially for a parent or partner. The victim puts in place for the abuser avoidance behaviors that require strict observation and constant vigilance, as well as totally exhausting mental effort to understand, identify, and analyze all stimuli susceptible to set off a violent outburst; victims must anticipate and prevent this. If avoidance behaviors fail, the victim will be subject to violence, as this will be her failure, her fault, and her mistake. The abuse will anesthetize the perpetrator. To make sure he is placated, she must forget herself and only be at the service of his traumatic memory: A ticking timebomb to handle with care. The perpetrator's suffering due to traumatic memory is considered much more important than the victim's terror and anguish. No matter what the victim does—no matter how hard she tries or how well she accomplishes the task thrust upon her—the results will always be that she loses.

4. The perpetrator realizes that the victim has a catastrophically low level of self-esteem, most often due to an

absence of love and kindness in childhood and a traumatic memory charged with disparaging remarks ("you
are stupid, worthless, ugly, incapable, mean, guilty, and
only good for one thing..."). This makes it easier for the
abuser to gain control over the victim and to manipulate and transform her into a slave who can be used for
everything, ready to sacrifice herself for the well-being of
her master. (To those unfamiliar with the mechanisms of
trauma, she appears to consent to the abuse.)

5. The victim's own traumatic memory (linked to the terror
    of past violence) makes her easy to control through a
    simple gaze, phrase, or gesture. This will fill her with the
    terror she felt as an abused child. This helps the abuser
    in two ways. Firstly, it economizes the effort he needs to
    control her. Secondly, it makes her reaction more intense
    and thus more "satisfying" (anesthetizing).

Someone previously abused is less likely to defend herself,
oppose any action, or report any crime. She is often alone in the
world, defenseless, and seeking protection (which the abuser
will pretend to offer). She has been brainwashed to think that she
is incapable of getting by on her own. The law of silence is easy
to implement in someone who often doubts what happened,
doesn't remember very well, or doesn't understand and therefore asks herself: "What did I do?" Emotional anesthetization
and dissociation also abstract her from the seriousness of abuse.

The supplementary terror of someone who has already been
a victim means that it is easier to get strong, extreme responses
from her, setting a scene so stress-imbued that it is very effective
for relief of the abuser's traumatic memory. The victim is his
drug, always available to be sacrificed for his comfort, so that
after an outburst of violence, he becomes (and this is a huge
problem) more calm and more kind. And, pinnacle of incoherence, he might even console and care for his victim after: "Look
what you made me do, when I love you and want so much for
everything to work out between us," "If you didn't provoke me,
everything would be so good," "If you didn't frustrate me so
much, we could have avoided all this." For the victim, this is

taken as proof that she must be responsible for the abuse; she sees herself through his eyes as incompetent, clumsy, and frustrating because he has instrumentalized her so much she cannot perceive reality.

7.8 Powerlessness, Anguish, and Suffering

Faced with such abuse, the victim is powerless. The toolbox that she had put together until then to understand, survive, and defend herself in the world no longer works—no matter how effective it is. Nothing could have prepared her for this situation in her past, her knowledge, her ability to analyze, and her self-confidence. Everything is taken from her in the unintelligible world the abuser has thrown her in. If she doesn't know the perpetrator, the victim will ask: "Why me? Why has someone who didn't know me become obsessed with me? What did I do, so that he pins on me intentions, behaviors, a personality, and a functioning that I don't have?" But if she does know him, she asks: "What happened to him? Why is he suddenly unrecognizable and transformed by hatred, with a voice, a look, words, and gestures that don't resemble him at all? Why did he do that to me, when we were so close? Why such anger and hatred all of a sudden directed at me? Why does he want to destroy me? What did I do? Why is he so indifferent to my suffering? Why is he attributing thoughts and intentions to me that I don't have… yet he must be right, since he is so sure of it; could I maybe convince him he is wrong?" In reality, no convincing is possible, because the abuser knows exactly what he's doing and is in flagrant bad faith; it is all a lie!

Child or adult, the victim cannot find any coherence in what happens, because there is none to be found. A child has little experience and acquaintance with the world of adults, and it is normal for a child not to understand certain gestures, words, or behaviors (such as sexual molestation); children blame themselves due to their lack of knowledge. They need help from caring adults to "translate" the experience, but usually no adult does this—of course not the perpetrator, who is a total fraud and uses incoherent and mystifying statements and prefers to ignore irksome realities. Other adults surrounding the child might be dissociated and living their own traumatic memory, preventing them from taking effective action.

For abused children, the adult world definitively loses its protective power and explanatory filter, and they are cast into terrifying solitude with no way to find their way in a world perceived as hostile and agonizing. They are condemned to facing questions with no answers and figuring out how to protect themselves with very limited means, putting in place a significant psychological retreat, avoidance, and dissociating behaviors to face anxiety, terrible distress, and solitude that no one understands. Adults and children around abused children constantly criticize them for their survival behaviors and try to get them to act like everyone else. They exclude and shame such children, using moralizing discourse and guilt-provoking stigmatization: "Wake up! Show a little willpower for once! You have everything needed to be happy! You're ruining everything! Aren't you ashamed, after all we've done for you? It would be better if you got a job or joined a sports team, went to bed earlier, stopped listening to music or playing on your computer all day, stopped smoking, drinking, taking drugs, eating so much, or hanging out with those people..."

Traumatic memory causes anguish, fear, panic, phobia, suicidal fantasies, pain, and strange sensations "not really your own." Victims are blamed for all this: "Stop exaggerating and complaining! Many people are in worse situations than you are! Forget it and move on! We protected you too much and were too indulgent—time to change that!" Traumatic memory has dramatic effects: Pain-remembrances can lead a person to the emergency room, often with invasive examinations and surgery (useless, of course). There are sensorial phenomena that can result in getting locked in a mental hospital, as the hallucinations are not correctly identified as reminiscences, and traumatic memory is very rarely understood or taken into account even by professionals who should be most concerned. Traumatic memory is often misdiagnosed as schizophrenia and patients given heavy neuroleptic treatments. Teens are often labeled delinquent when they show signs of trauma that include addiction, risk, and danger-seeking. When children show cognitive disorders of confusion linked to dissociative symptoms or when they avoid thinking and are afraid of school, they are judged intellectually deficient, a label that is hard to shed.

For adult victims, the discourse may be a little less "educational" but at least as shaming and moralizing. They are quickly labeled fragile, not very resilient, overly sensitive to pain, depressive, exhausting, apathetic, masochistic, and who "like to think themselves the most unhappy people in the world."

7.9 The Mind Becomes a Minefield

It is extremely difficult for victims to defend themselves against the myths and not internalize them. They usually end up believing that they are worthless, boring, stupid, incapable, and inconsiderate, a weight for those around them to bear, tolerate, or reject—they are unloved and brutally alone.

In addition to suffering immensely, victims find themselves asking many questions with no answers about the violence, the perpetrator, and what really happened. These take possession of their minds and grow like tumors. Victims cannot integrate them or get rid of them. No one and nothing allow them to really understand the abuser, since his reasons are usually even unknown to him. If the victim or legal professionals ask him, he usually says he has no idea why he did it or gives such a poor and absurd explanation that it seems ridiculous. During the abuse, this fundamental incomprehension explains the tonic immobility of the victim and paralysis of her thoughts. Meeting the traumatic memory of the abuser, like the head of Medusa, petrifies the psyche of the victim and digs a gap between the experience and all mental activity; the mind is no longer free and no longer her own.

The mind becomes a minefield in which there are no more answers, and the surrounding world doesn't make sense anymore. Everything the victim once believed in disappears, and nothing seems reliably clear anymore. An overwhelming insecurity invades everything, with a loss of confidence in her capability, plunging the victim into a feeling of permanent danger, constant mental exertion, and exhausting vigilance. All the victim's thoughts are occupied by events that are inconceivable and terrorizing, which continue to threaten her well after the violence ends, often at a distance after she has broken off all contact. Sometimes the distance is so great that she no longer perceives a connection between her fears and the original abuse. Little by little, the invasion of her mind makes her a stranger to herself and to others. Everything happens as if the victim has left the world of the living—those who live in peaceful certitude in a world they perceive as intelligible. Non-victims have no need to question each moment, situation, or reaction or to feel perpetually in danger. They don't feel incapable of doing what others do easily. The exhausting efforts victims deploy to micro-analyze what they and others do aggravate the feeling of incapacity, total solitude, and terrible injustice, as all these efforts serve no purpose.

If the victim consults a professional, she might at least feel supported, advised, and helped, though the vast majority of victims don't even get this. Those who do almost never receive answers to the question of their persistent feeling of solitude. They can get to know other victims who endured similar violence or read testimonies, watch programs on television about violence, participate in group therapy, and realize that they are not the only ones who feels foreign to this world, rejected, and not understood. They might realize that other victims also understand nothing about the violence of their perpetrators and could not stop them or escape, and that they are not believed by those around them. They might still try to persuade themselves that they were unlucky, that's the way it is, some people are evil monsters. This might help victims feel less guilty and not so worthless, realizing that no one has miracle solutions, but it will not provide answers and is not enough.

Victims can become aware that the violence is not as society portrays it. What the perpetrator did was totally wrong, and he had no right to do it no matter what. He should be held accountable by society and the justice system, be judged, condemned, and go to prison. But all this doesn't answer the "why." Why so much violence, sometimes from a person that the victim loved, thought she knew, found to be kind, helpful, or even just normal during a long or short time, and who remained this way toward others, for example, other colleagues or friends. Or maybe he was someone she felt moved by because of his story and his suffering, and she wanted to help him. Perhaps it was an unknown perpetrator who is described by those around him as pleasant, kind, a good neighbor or colleague. All this makes it difficult to see the perpetrator as the monster he is. The violence really did happen, though, and during that time, there was no doubt in the victim about him being a total monster. But before? After?

The perpetrator who ignited in his victim an unnamable terror often appears as someone pathetic, manipulating, lying, and incapable of saying anything convincing. In vain, the victim tries to find the monster she saw during the attack, and it is destabilizing to have doubts about what she experienced and perceived. The perpetrator plays at being someone no one could imagine would ever commit such violent acts when faced with the justice system or others around him. Everything seems unreal to the victim, and with good reason: She was not only confronted with someone in a specific context but also with the reality of his extremely violent past. This has nothing to do with her, but his traumatic memory is thrust on her. He allows himself to use her to play the victim role so that his traumatic memory can transform him into the incomprehensible and unpredictable monster he previously faced, using a look, a voice, behaviors, and a personality that have nothing to do with anything she does or is, anything she previously knew about him, or anything that was happening even moments before. He uses her to gain relief/anesthetization to escape from his traumatic memory, inflicting it on her.

7.10 Incredible Injustice: When Institutions Fail Victims

Only 14% of domestic violence victims and under 9% of rape victims report the crimes. This is not only due to threats and the law of silence but also because they have little confidence in the police and the justice system. These have a history of casting suspicion on victims and condoning perpetrators. The criminal justice system mirrors the dysfunction in society as a whole and its denial of sexual and family violence. Catastrophic stereotypes persist about women, men, children, families, couples, and sexuality. The vast majority of abused children are not known by child protective services and are left at the mercy of their torturers. Reporting crimes is a terrible struggle for victims. In police departments, if those handling violence were better trained and psychologists were readily available, the risk of facing a police officer ignorant of victims' rights would be less. We found that 82% of victims had a negative experience when they did report abuse or violence (IVSEA, 2015). Some French departments have made tremendous efforts to receive victims better through putting in place committees that bring together everyone concerned as well as representatives from organizations that specialize in defending victims. These committees have also led trainings, made awareness posters, and held conferences.

Still, many victims find themselves faced with officers who refuse to investigate. They may offer only to record the charges in the police log or require a medical certificate when one is not necessary. For undocumented, homeless, and prostituted victims, their rights are even less respected. Undocumented victims are sometimes put in jail, even though the law states that they are protected when they report crimes. The risks taken by victims in reporting domestic and family violence are rarely taken into account. Sufficient information about the justice system, necessary care and support, and useful organizations is rarely given to victims. Worse, filing a complaint or attending a hearing is sometimes an occasion for further violence to victims, with psychological pressure to "admit" that they are lying, threats, verbal violence with humiliating, sexist, or racist remarks, and all kinds of assertions and judgments. The conditions of hearings are very destabilizing for victims, in open offices with constant comings and goings. Many police officers choose to consider as mitigating many circumstances that the law actually considers as aggravating, such as the abuser being intoxicated.

7.11 The Denial of Justice

Rarely do charges pressed result in an inquiry. Usually, the charges are dropped and cases dismissed; rape charges are changed to the lesser offense of sexual aggression. Seventy percent of all rape charges (60% for rapes of minors) are dropped by the prosecutor, who can require proceedings with or without a preliminary investigation (Le Goaziou, 2016). This is why convictions are rare, and criminal justice proceedings for domestic and sexual violence are most dysfunctional of any.

For domestic violence, the dangerousness of the violent partner is rarely taken into account, and intimate partner rape, which is often present, is almost never recognized. Victims rarely mention it unless asked, and if they do speak about it, the rapes are rarely qualified as such. In France, a woman is killed every two and a half days by her intimate partner, and yet when she reports death threats or murder attempts to the police, they usually ignore her. In the United States, 20 people per minute are abused by intimate partners, and 94% of those killed by an intimate partner are female (ncadv.org/STATISTICS). This is, unfortunately, a worldwide problem. A man who is violent with his wife is often still considered a good father, ignoring the terror of children present, who have even sometimes been witnesses of rape, and the huge psycho-traumatic impact of growing up in a violent household. These children are often left in the perpetrator's care; he usually at least has visiting rights, since family court judges have no regard for the reactivation of trauma in children forced into the hands of the man who almost killed their mother. Judges also irresponsibly disregard the opportunity this gives the father to use the children to continue exercising violence and threats on the mother. Thus, even if the father is not violent with his children themselves, his violence toward their mother harms them in several ways, and children should not be required to see him. When making custody arrangements, the judge is often not even aware of the charges filed or even the convictions (this should no longer be the case since the July 9, 2010, law, which requires judges to issue protection orders, but this still rarely happens in practice). Even when the perpetrator abuses the children, particularly with sexual abuse, and the mother separates from him and reports the abuse, she is systematically suspected of lying and of having Parental Alienation Syndrome (trying to turn children away from an innocent father). This accusation is used to prevent her from obtaining suspension of visitation rights. The courts put children in great danger in the name of "father's rights," a movement that is part of the overall backlash against women. It is why many mothers have broken the law and fled with their children in order to protect them from abuse, sometimes hiding in foreign countries. Sometimes they have been found, arrested, and sent to prison, and their children were given to the abuser, without any investigation or precautions taken for the children's safety. (He is believed, she isn't.)

Under 10% of rapes are reported, 3% are heard in court, and under 1% of rapists are convicted (2012–2017 French government statistics). Compare this with homicides, in which there is almost always an investigation and in 50% of cases, a condemnation. Rape and attempted rape are crimes with an impunity unlike any other.

When there are judicial proceedings for rape charges, these are dropped in over half the cases. Rape is also often charged as a misdemeanor, although it is a crime according to law; it is judged by a lesser court (Schmitt, 2012; Le Goaziou, 2016). Forty percent of "sexual aggression" cases heard in court are actually rapes. The pretext is that the lesser courts are faster and less costly. It is, however, a violation of victims' rights that is against the law (France's March 10, 2004, law states that crimes, which include rape, must be judged by the higher court). France's penal code considers rape a crime, and not judging it as such in court should not ever be admissible. In the United States, rape is considered a felony. However, for every 1,000 rapes, 384 are reported to police, 57 result in an arrest, 11 are referred for prosecution, 7 result in a felony conviction, and 6 result in incarceration (RAINN). So where are all these rapists—isn't anyone concerned about that?

Are the rare rape victims who manage to press charges in spite of all the hurdles mostly liars? Are those they accuse innocent? What would make anyone want to lodge false accusations, when they know they won't be taken seriously by the police or criminal justice system? There must instead be a systemic problem, when between pressing charges and conviction, 90% of victims are rejected through the silencing of cases closed, dismissed, or dropped. How can society call itself democratic, and what justice system can pretend to protect people, when over half the population is so poorly defending against the worst kind of violence, defined as a crime?

7.12 No Punishment for Rapists

Raping a woman, man, or child poses almost no risk for the rapist. Pressing charges against someone for rape and hoping that the rapist will be found guilty is, on the other hand, extremely stressful and almost never succeeds. After multiple hurdles and stresses for victims, most cases are dismissed. There is also the risk of the charges being turned against the victim, accused of defamation. If in spite of the numerous, serious risks, the victim does press charges, it is certainly not to get revenge or so the rapist will rot in prison. It is above all to protect potential victims by preventing the rapist from raping other women (which he most likely would, due to traumatic memory's addiction-to-violence mechanism).

In 20 years of experience as a psychiatrist for rape victims, I can testify that almost all my patients endured serious mistreatment from police, the legal system, medical personnel, and social workers. Our 2015 study quantified this, with 70% of victims reporting that police and the justice system ignored their pleas. Sixty seven percent of sexual violence victims did not receive any protection, 82% of those who pressed charges had a negative experience when they did so, 89% who had a trial reported the conditions as disturbing, and 81% considered that the justice system failed them. Additionally, victims not acknowledged by police and the justice system were more likely to commit suicide than the average rate for victims (IVSEA, 2015).

This institutionalized or systemic violence is so extreme that some of my patients regret having pressed charges, even though they are convinced that they deserve justice: "It's just so hard," they say. Sixty two percent of those who did press charges say that they would do it again. Their main motivations are to protect other women who would be in danger if the rapist is not brought to justice and their need to have the wrongness of what happened to them recognized (IVSEA, 2015).

Why is it that when victims press charges for rape, there are so few trials and when they do take place, rapists are rarely found guilty? "Lack of evidence," people say: "It's her word against his." Except in the case of murder, DNA samples and other traces of rape are not sufficient to prove non-consent, we are told. Violence that is classified as sexual is presumed to be consensual and therefore not condemnable, the victim is assumed to be a masochist. There is no search for serious, scientifically valid clues, such as taking into account psycho-traumatic consequences, which could lead to a trial and conviction.

A woman or even an adolescent girl is considered a priori as consenting to a sexual act

> even when it is with a stranger who doesn't use a condom and it lasts a few minutes,
>
> even when it is with several men or a man in a position of authority,
>
> even when it is in a place that is supposedly safe such as the family, school, sports ground, church, hospital, or workplace,
>
> even when it includes violence such as degrading acts that violate human dignity and do harm,
>
> even when it is in a situation of dependence or significant economic constraint,
>
> even when the victim's judgment is altered or she is vulnerable: Alcohol, drug use, psychotropic medication, mental disability, exclusion…

7.13 The Constant Questioning of Victims

Why is it the behavior of victims, rife with psycho-traumatic symptoms that the international medical community considers pathognomonic (therefore medical proof of the existence of trauma), is not considered as evidence? Why do courts not recognize tonic immobility (the inability to scream or fight back, the normative neurological mechanism in rape), emotional shock, peritraumatic dissociation (confusion, doubt, feeling of strangeness, spatio-temporal disorientation, memory disorders, and so on)?

Why are aggravating circumstances (according to the law) most often turned against victims, as if they cast doubt on their credibility: Being a child, married to the perpetrator, under the influence, mentally disabled, or having psychiatric disorders? Why are events from the victim's past that have nothing to do with the rape used to question her credibility, such as promiscuity, addiction, prostitution, incarceration, or psychiatric treatment?

The plaintiff who says she is a victim of rape must be perfect, pure, virginal, not too young or too disabled (a child or mentally ill/handicapped person tells all kinds of lies, right?), not too old or too ugly (who would want to rape her?), not too poor (maybe she's seeking financial compensation), not too pretty (ah, that would explain it—he couldn't help himself!), not with "too free" a lifestyle (asking for it!), not foreign and undocumented, and, of course, not in prostitution (that wouldn't be rape but disagreement about payment). She also shouldn't know the perpetrator very well and not be his wife or partner, or else her word will have no weight unless she gets killed.

She must be ideal according to the dictates of a sexist society wherein women are above all sex objects consenting a priori and submitting to the definitions men give them. If she couldn't avoid his desire, which she must have aroused, she must assume the consequences. If she says she didn't consent, she is lying to get attention, revenge, or money from the man. If women don't want to be sex objects, they should censor themselves in how they dress, where they go, who they date, where they work, how they act, speak, and so on. But if they self-censor effectively, they are not quite women, no longer "a good fuck" and won't interest most men; they might even not really be considered human beings that count and instead are invisible or transparent... and that's the price to pay for not being raped.

Girls, become sexy as soon as possible and be a desirable object to look at and flirt with, but don't complain if you are harassed, attacked, or raped. Or you can censor yourself and disappear from the realm of seduction, but don't complain if no one sees you anymore and no man has any interest in you. Forget about true love and Prince Charming. Make your choice! Women are expected to artfully navigate between these two and learn to tolerate harassment and be hypervigilant to avoid the worst. And if it happens, too bad for you. You didn't pay enough attention and you took careless risks. The game is set up so women can't win.

That women want to be full human beings respected in their rights and dignity, that sexual desire not be reduced to consumption or predation, and that sexual relations require mutual trust and consent and must never involve pressure, deceit, force, or payment should be obvious to everyone. But that is far from being the case.

In addition to being the perfect woman before the rape, the plaintiff is required to have the perfect behavior during the rape. She must be able to explain all her responses and reactions. A psychological examination is routinely required. The good victim must present herself as extremely coherent, remember everything precisely, and have reacted in an ideal manner: No question of having not said no clearly, not having screamed, fought back, or tried to escape. Tonic immobility during the rape—a normal and usual psychological survival mechanism through which the victim is paralyzed due to the extreme terror of the situation—along with feelings of powerlessness and incomprehension—should be proof that something very serious happened; instead, it is used to discredit the victim. It's not acceptable to be dissociated and emotionally anesthetized or to have taken some time to realize the reality and seriousness of the situation. This dissociation and emotional anesthetization for the traumatized person carries paradoxical and automatic attitudes. Someone who didn't say no during the rape, didn't scream, fight, or run away, is seen as consenting if judges are not aware of the mechanisms of tonic immobility and dissociation. Thus, the penetration even of 11-year-old children is not considered rape, as we saw in 2017 with two little girls, since there was no legal age of consent in France under which any sexual acts are automatically considered non-consensual no matter what.

In spite of the traumatizing situation, the victim may appear indifferent, behave apparently normally for a certain time, say that everything is alright, and continue to be in contact with the perpetrator. This is because she is in a state of dissociation and emotional anesthetization that can last for several days or even weeks or months. This neurologically rooted mechanism is well-described in international scientific research as characteristic of rape victims. It explains perfectly why victims may not be aware of the seriousness of what happened, since they feel nothing about it. The neurotransmitters responsible for peritraumatic dissociation (morphine- and ketamine-like) can give her the feeling of indifference, disconnection, and even of everything going well. Life goes on as if the victim knows something serious happened to her, but it doesn't really seem to concern her. If confronted with the perpetrator, the process is reactivated due to the traumatic memory and dissociation for self-preservation. Awareness comes later—quicker if she has adequate support, assistance, and protection. She collapses emotionally. Dissociation and peritraumatic emotional anesthetization are scientific proof of how severe the trauma is but are most often misinterpreted and used to cast doubt on the victim's words. If the victim didn't speak out right away, seek help, or press charges, and if she for an instant minimized what happened to her (if she stayed with the perpetrator or in contact with him for a time, answered his phone calls), she is blamed for it. To make things worse, when professionals are faced with dissociated victims, the anesthetized absence of emotion makes it difficult to feel any empathy, benevolence, or concern. It makes them disbelieve victims even more and often mistreat them. The more unpleasant or violent they are, the more the victim will dissociate, and the more doubt others will have, in this vicious cycle. Confrontations with the perpetrator also increase dissociation and massively retraumatize victims until they lose reasoning and are invaded by doubt and unreality; they are often easily put under the abuser's control again, and everything they previously said is doubted.

Victims are not allowed to have memory disorders or problems with spatiotemporal orientation, which often happens: Lacunary amnesia due to neurological damage (black holes) is common. In addition, dissociative survival strategies can lead to traumatic amnesia for the moments of most severe suffering. This is very frequent: Up to 60% of victims experience partial amnesia and 40% experience complete amnesia. This is more common in very young victims and with incest involving penetration (Brière, 1993; Williams, 1995; IVSEA, 2015). Spatiotemporal disorders are also frequent due to how disjunction puts the hippocampus temporarily out of service. This organ is necessary to analyze spatial and temporal information. The victim might experience huge distortions about placement and chronology of events; it is difficult to determine the exact time or date. Such distortions are unfortunately interpreted as incoherence or lies that discredit the victim's words; they are actually pathognomonic systems (medical proof of trauma). They might make the investigation and the establishment of evidence more challenging but are in no case proof that the victim is lying. The perfect victim—the only one listened to—cannot have been totally under the perpetrator's control, manipulated, cheated, or dependent on him emotionally or financially. The victim is not allowed to have her discernment altered through alcohol or drug used, though this is legally an aggravating circumstance. In practice, the victim is blamed for it, and it is considered risk-taking behavior that she is responsible for. These requirements, that hinge on misogynistic social norms, are integral to the perpetrator's strategy, which is rarely decoded during the investigation.

The perfect victim (the only one listened to) is not allowed to fall into depression after the rape or use dissociating behaviors to survive the trauma, such as drinking, drug use, risk-taking, and promiscuity. These are attempts to self-treat aimed at emotional anesthetization through creating significant stress that sets off safety mechanisms again in order to shut down the emotional suffering linked to traumatic memory. These dissociating behaviors are most often held against the victim, and frequent dissociative states in victims, especially hallucinations, are misdiagnosed as psychoses by psychiatrists not trained in psycho-traumatology. Victims are put in mental hospitals and treated with neuroleptics. Such diagnoses strongly discredit the words of victims.

7.14 Society's Complicity in Rapists Walking Free

It is statistically evident that rapists get special treatment among criminals. Their crimes are not considered as such under the pretext that the acts were consensual, with no consideration of universal human rights and dignity (consenting to be killed or tortured doesn't justify these crimes). It is easy to understand why the accused would want to deny the crime, question the victim, and take advantage of presumed innocence. (Presumed innocence would be fine if the victim benefitted from presumed credibility.) What about those who accuse the victim, downplay the rape, deny the violence and its consequences, and use the victim status to denigrate the victim? Why do they do this, when common knowledge is that rape is serious and that rape victims are traumatized? Why are victims constantly made to give explanations and justify their words and behaviors? It would be revealing to save speculations for the rapist's character and spare the victim!

This is mostly due to avoidance and cowardice. All those who are in a conflict of interest due to their loyalty to the perpetrator seek to preserve their advantages (financial, security, employment). Avoidance benefits those who do not want to question their convictions and beliefs and who cannot stand to be confronted with horrific violence that agonizes them too much. Denial is a strategy to escape the discomfort that they don't want to face. Sexist collaboration is another explanation, revealing adhesion to stereotypes from a pornographic view of women and sexuality. Its consequences for women's safety—whether actual or potential victims—are catastrophic. Unrecognized perpetrators are another reason, though the reality of male violence is rarely mentioned (Romito, 2006). Among the anonymous masses who accuse the victim, there is a non-negligible number of perpetrators—this is statistically certain and is not often enough taken into account. They have a direct interest in confusing the situation and disguising other's crimes as well as their own to avoid detection and punishment. They know that they are lying and that their reasoning is totally false! Their arguments of neoliberal modernity and sexual liberation are only alibis of zealous collaborators and criminals. Their outbursts silence victims and intimidate those who want to protect and support victims. It is time that reprobation and suspicion are cast on them as soon as they open their mouths. It is they who have done wrong; they are the criminals.

A significant number of professionals (in police, courts, social work, care, the media) spend much of their time watching pornography and getting aroused by seeing women scream during violent and degrading sex acts. Many of these professionals also use prostitutes and are accustomed to imposing their sexual fantasies on women who do not desire them, through the coercion of money. How can we hope that they behave ethically and appropriately when faced with rape victims? Why does society have blind confidence in them?

Few can imagine how much institutionalized sexist violence victims face. A young woman of 18 consulted me: She had never had sex and was a victim of armed rape and beatings. I saw the official transcription of her complaint. The police officer had no shame in asking, with no fear of reproach from his superiors, the prosecutor, or judges, what the rapist's erection was like, if she "got wet" during penetration, and if she experienced pleasure! How can we interpret the extreme brutality of this officer? Another example: An adolescent girl of 13 years old was raped by three adults having authority over her, who made her watch a pornographic film and did to her everything they saw on the screen. The male and female police commissioners who took her deposition (this was filmed because she was a minor) started laughing when the victim described the rape scenes. Worse, they told the victim that she was a libertine… They asked if she liked being sodomized… they even dared to ask: "Do you really think a girl who is raped behaves like you did?" What to think of these laughs and commentaries? It is difficult to imagine that such reactions can come from professionals who are supposed to be impartial and serve justice when charges are pressed for rape. Not surprisingly, these officials took eight months to process the charges.

Another patient, an adolescent girl of 15 years old, was raped by a former classmate. She had also never had sex. The rapist admitted that the victim had said no and that he'd firmly held her two arms. Why then did the prosecutor dismiss the case? Is it because the victim forgot to tell them about the messages they'd exchanged before the rape? Before being raped, a victim is expected to know she will be raped and thus avoid the potential rapist; otherwise, it is her fault. The smallest detail she forgets is worth more than everything she remembers and tells. The prosecutor did not only dismiss the case. He also followed up on the charges pressed by the rapist for defamation and locked up the victim! While detained, she was insulted by the police and called a liar, told that what she did was very serious and risked ten years of jail time.

A 14-year-old girl who is also one of my patients was sequestered and raped by two men for ten days. The police tried in vain to get her to say she was lying. She explained again that she screamed many times. He replied: "Yes, but out of pleasure." When she warned him that she was getting nauseous and was about to vomit (she was taking a preventative treatment for HIV), he said, "Don't do that, or I'll give it right back to you!" The same officer told her that she had better tell the truth because everything was filmed and the judge wouldn't be happy… She had the courage to answer: "I don't think the judge will be happy to see how you are mistreating me."

Another patient, a young woman of 25, pressed charges for sexual violence in her workplace. The officer told her: "Given how you reacted, I could rape you right now, here, on this desk"… unthinkable brutality and explicit complicity. But that's not all: He kept her very late for her deposition—so late that there was no public transportation. Driving her home, he tried to force her to kiss him and threatened her so she wouldn't tell anyone about this aggression.

Yet another patient, a little boy of ten, was raped with anal penetration by a 17-year-old cousin. The prosecutor dropped the rape charges, saying that the little boy wanted this, and therefore it was not rape. She didn't consider that it was automatically sexual abuse because the victim was a minor.

A woman under my medical care was raped at work and subject to a psychiatric evaluation during the preliminary inquiry. She was subjected to the usual sexual allusions that destroy victims: The psychiatrist asked if she likes being sodomized and if the rapist was attractive to her. Not stopping there, he asked if he himself was attractive to her and said that she would be to him if she lost a few kilos. This harassment increased: He called her many times to try to get a date and used his institutional power to erase the traces of these transgressions; he wrote in her report that she was seductive and histrionic.

These are just a few recent examples of what I've encountered in my clinical practice. A huge number of professionals who are supposed to support and protect victims are actually abusers themselves, or at the very least collaborators of sexism. As many examples have shown, they are pure products of pornography: Everything is false, and their perception of rape victims' testimonies mirrors their view of women in general. The reenactment of pornographic scenes and the accumulation of aggravating circumstances, along with the tears of victims, only lead to police laughing at or even abusing victims. What do they hear when the teenage girl says she screamed when being raped? They hear a scene from pornography with one of the million women depicted as screaming with pleasure while being violated. What do they feel when playing out "their film" when listening to victims? Far from empathy, the therapists get aroused. Far from listening attentively, the police get aroused. Far from impartiality, the judges get aroused. Pornography is increasingly pedo-criminal. What do they see when a young victim presses charges? They see a Lolita (see Sokhna Fall's article, "L'éternel détournement de Dolorès Haze," 2010). What justice can they give victims when their complicity with perpetrators is automatic? A large sector of society is colonized by this catastrophic vision of sexuality, predation, and violence, including journalists. This explains the lack of appropriate care for sexual violence victims and why justice is denied to them.

It is also frightening to see how frequently victims receive death threats and are not protected. In France, there is no truly effective legal protection program for victims and witnesses. I see many domestic violence and rape victims in danger, threatened by perpetrators and their allies (sometimes even in hearings without the judge taking any action). This includes victims of attempted murder, who are forced to hide and protect themselves with their own means; some even get cosmetic surgery so as to not be recognized. Training for police and judges is absolutely necessary so that they can protect victims, many of whom are killed after leaving an abuser, reporting a crime, or pressing charges.

8

Who Are the Perpetrators?

VIOLENT DISSOCIATING BEHAVIORS, WHEN COMBINED with a dominant position and adhesion to the law of might makes right, are at the heart of how a perpetrator is made. Such behaviors provide an escape from perpetrators' own traumatic memories of abuse they endured, usually in childhood, and also of previous violence they committed.

8.1 Violent Dissociating Behaviors

Previously, violent dissociating behaviors seemed incoherent, especially when they involved compulsive, self-destructive acts (addiction, risk, self-mutilation), dependence on the perpetrator, and risk behaviors that reproduce the original violence either against oneself or against another. Currently, these behaviors are perfectly understandable as behaviors provoking a calming and anesthetizing effect. They are used to escape the anguish of traumatic memory when avoidance behaviors are not working to prevent it from flaring up.

When traumatic memory sets in, to relieve the insufferable tension, a traumatized victim might find the only solution to be self-harm (banging head against wall, tearing out hair, burning, biting, or scarring). Victims might also expose themselves to risks such as a deadly fall, crossing the road without looking, driving very fast, or following a stranger who looks dangerous. This is

DOI: 10.4324/9781003497516-9

effective in gaining temporary relief from traumatic memory, but it also reinforces it for more severe long-term effects.

This "senseless" violence directed at oneself recreates a psychological effraction with tonic immobility and an extreme state of stress, which provokes an "overload" and disjunction of the emotional circuitry, just as during the initial violence. This disjunction entails the secretion of morphine- and ketamine-like neurotransmitters. Emotional anesthetization and dissociation set in. The same thing happens if the violence is directed at someone else instead of at oneself, and this is especially effective if it is explosive, incoherent, and unjust. It then has the bonus of being paralyzing then anesthetizing and dissociating through the disjunction that it generates. Many people have experienced this when hitting a child or screaming at someone to relieve tension.

8.2 Violence at Another's Expense: A Cruel Cycle

The immediate advantage of violence against another instead of against oneself is unfortunately quite obvious: Abusers thus gain relief and anesthetization without exposing themselves to harm. Someone designated to play the victim is used instead. Betraying the victims they were, casting aside their victim status and all ethical concerns, some traumatized victims transform into perpetrators through power dynamics that work in their favor. The violence generates traumatic memory in new victims, and some of them will choose to use others: A vicious cycle. This is a major reason we need to uproot violence through prevention and specialized treatment of trauma while fighting against all forms of violence, especially those most likely to uphold the cycle: Abuse of very young children.

As we have seen, violence does not stop shortly after an attack. It generates suffering that can last years or a whole lifetime. A small number of traumatized victims self-treat through harming others whenever society tacitly allows them to do so because of their dominant position in the sexist, racist, and exclusionary hierarchy based on social myths about love and the family.

Victims-turned-perpetrators trade in their ethics, coherence, and intelligence in a sort of pact with the devil, flipping to the side of evil and choosing to identify with perpetrators rather than with victims. Adhering to the law of might makes right; they allow themselves to do to others what was done to them. Each new perpetrator produces several new victims, which is largely enough for the violence to persist.

Many of my patients who were sexually abused as children already committed many sexual aggressions on children younger than themselves. Treating these young abusers and getting them to stop using dissociating behaviors that harm others has been very effective. First, it is necessary to get them to stop these violent behaviors and substitute other ways of treating traumatic memory. I help them put in place avoidance behaviors that can prevent new explosions. We work on their story and its links to the symptoms and violence they were subjected to. We decolonize their psychological space through playing out how perpetrators function, dismantling their traumatic memory little by little, and liberating them from colonizing violence. Violent dissociative behaviors then disappear since they no longer need to emotionally anesthetize themselves once their traumatic memory is disarmed.

Once emotional anesthetization wears off, new perpetrators are faced with the brutal reality of what they have done, and this is difficult to face. They are invaded (and this is normal) with regret, guilt, and sometimes even suicidal thoughts. This emotional collapse under the weight of guilt is a coherent human response. It allows them to begin an authentic therapeutic process that involves denouncing all violence (as victims and former abusers). It includes recognition of all victims and their rights. They also need to gain a decent understanding of psychotraumatic mechanisms and stereotypes about victims, as well as lies and rationalizations that dominant people use to commit violent acts and get away with it.

8.3 The Added Torture of Impulsive Phobias

Think about young parents who were severely abused in childhood by their own mother or father, a nanny, or any other person supposed to care for them. Most will be very careful not to inflict the same detested violence on their children. However, due to their traumatic memory, they will need to take special precautions such as avoidance behaviors to not get angry and to eliminate all situations of tension, which can be very taxing. They might even torture themselves, wrongly interpreting explosions of their traumatic memory as impulsive desires to commit the violence they are reliving. We refer to this as "impulsive phobias."

When caring for their children, such mothers or fathers are suddenly invaded by mental images of violence or by anger, hatred, or sexual excitement. These terrify them and stop them in their tracks. They might see themselves drowning or burning their baby when giving the baby a bath, dropping the baby, cutting the baby when scissors are nearby, or sexually abusing the baby when changing a diaper. They seem to be experiencing unexplainable anger or sexual aggression, and cruel phrases run through their minds. These are actually reminiscences of violence that a parent or other adult inflicted on them, usually in very early childhood, and the memories of anger, hate, or scorn of these adults. It includes their abuser's perverse excitement or murderous phrases—but the victim who became a parent doesn't identify these as such. They make no connection between these violent mental images from the past they have tried to forget or that they don't remember due to psychological amnesia of survival or psychological amnesia when the abuse happened before the age of three (due to the immaturity of brain circuitry).

Caring for a child whose sex, age, vulnerability, crying, and behaviors remind them of their own history and victimization flares up their traumatic memory with flashbacks that may include hallucinations. They are in danger of confusing these memories of violence that really happened in their childhoods with fantasies of violence pieced together from the fragments running through their minds. They might wrongly believe that these mental images are the fruit of their own imaginations fed by monstrous subconscious desires. They are horrified with themselves and terrified by the idea of committing violence against their children. They might even fear having committed and forgotten the violence, though they know they would never want to do so and that they loathe such abuse.

These fears can become a ubiquitous part of their dissociating behaviors, meaning the paradoxical compulsion to terrify oneself with what is most feared to gain anesthetization and destroy oneself with constant questioning. Such parents live in a state of mental torture and think themselves monstrous. A patient who was severely abused from birth onward, including sexually, was able to escape the colonizing effects of traumatic memory and impulsive phobias by raising her children in an entirely different culture and speaking a different language.

Such parents are not at risk of committing acts of violence, as they have no intention of harming their children or using them to gain relief, as do abusers. On the contrary, their children being abused is what they most fear in life and would do anything to prevent it. They are absolutely not taking the abuser's stance of rationalizing violence by blaming the victim and relinquishing their own responsibility for self-control. The thought process of young parents suffering from impulsive phobias is radically different from the neurosis that psychoanalysts might diagnose since they never blame the child; on the contrary, they entirely blame themselves. They do not realize that they do not subscribe in any way to the violence, and they think they must have some kind of terrifying shadow side. Their self-image is catastrophic. Such impulsive phobias mean that many people decide not to have children at all or to do any job in which they would be in contact with children.

It is very difficult to reassure these parents when they seek help. They don't stop torturing themselves and living under draconian and exhausting control and self-censorship. Instead of accusing the adult who abused them in the past, they accuse themselves due to a lack of access to the explanations that would make it clear what they are going through. If the therapist doesn't understand the mechanisms of impulsive phobias either (which is likely the case), such victims are told that they have subconscious desires or fantasies. They might commit suicide out of extreme despair. They can only feel at peace when the mental images, sensations, and phrases that torture them have been understood and identified as raw, incontrollable reminiscences of the abuse they endured from a very young age.

8.4 Abusive and Incestuous Parents

Most young parents who were abused as children would do anything to protect their own children; however, a minority of them inflict the same suffering by not putting in place effective avoidance or control behaviors. Adhering to the incoherent system of might makes right, they accept the idea that it is normal to have angry outbursts, as they often saw in their own mother or father, to hit with adult force a small child, claiming it is the child's fault, or to use a child as a sex object.

For them, as for the abusers in their past, their position of superiority lets them pretend that it's children's responsibility to control themselves and that the child must adapt to them. The child must submit to their desire and their mood, just as they had to as children. And to gain relief from a state of unbearable tension, they recreate violence very similar to what they endured: Same outbursts, insults, gestures, and scenarios. As they are now playing the role of their past abuser (their child having the role of the child they were), they will often use the same voice as their mother, father, or other adults who abused them. They'll take on the expressions and attitudes of their own former abuser and become unrecognizable. This will make the abuse all the more terrifying for the child, who will no longer recognize the parent transformed into a monster (fairytales show this very well when women become witches and men become ogres).

These parents rationalize their violent behavior by blaming the child: "He's out of control. Only a good thrashing will calm him down," or "I had no choice. I had to prevent him from... force him to..." They will claim they are sorry they couldn't do things differently. They might even cry and have the child console them for putting them in such a state. Nonetheless, they know very well that this is not acceptable and that nothing the child did could justify the violence, whose only purpose was to gain them relief.

What the child experiences and feels during the rage or sexual abuse and the injustice of the trampling of her rights or the serious lifelong consequences of this mean nothing to abusers.

They only want to erase any remains of the victim that they were. The unspeakable hatred that explodes during the violence is not really directed at the child. The victim that they hate is themselves, and they will make the child they were disappear by substituting another victim—their child—forced to replay their own story so they can better deny and erase it; the victim is always wrong. It is out of the question to become that victim again—and that's what traumatic memory forces on them—and be submerged again in the dreaded past. Better to betray oneself and become the abuser now that they have the privilege of being on the other side of the fence. Emotional anesthetization set off by the violence is used by abusers to claim their innocence since they and the child feel nothing (so, they say, it must not be very serious); the child knows something deeply wrong happened but is anesthetized. Nothing the child did or didn't do can justify the violence, and it is really about the need to destroy the child-victim that the perpetrator was (which resurges as traumatic memory) through using the child. If abusers become aware of psycho-traumatic symptoms linked to traumatic memory of the abused children that they were and the children they mistreated, that they have no right to relieve themselves in this way as their parents did, and that they are not worth more than their child, they can stop this vicious cycle of transgenerational abuse and treat their trauma otherwise.

8.5 Children Traumatized by Scenes of Domestic Violence

Children who were powerless witnesses of domestic violence committed by a parent are likely to do the same to their partners someday. In the meantime, they might "practice" on siblings or a parent, enacting verbal, psychological, physical, or sexual abuse, tyrannical behavior, or scenes of jealousy. Recent infomercials from the French government's department for the family and solidarity have shown this well.

The first infomercial shows a couple. The woman puts the dishes in the dishwasher and the man is at the table, visibly angry. A fork falls noisily. The man gets up and hits the woman, calling her incapable. She falls to the ground and whimpers. A little boy, seven or eight years old, enters. The viewer expects him to rush crying into the arms of his mother to console her or be consoled by her. Instead, he kicks her in the side. In the next scene, we see two children playing house, pretending to be a mother and father. Only their feet are filmed under the table, wearing adult socks and a pair of white high heels for the girl and black slippers for the boy. The little girl serves the tea and suddenly the little boy attacks her: You spilled the tea! You are useless! The girl terrorized, tries to apologize as we watch her feet nervously twisting in the heels, but to no avail; the tension rises. We see his slippers moving around the table, approaching the heels. A slap and the little girl falls to the ground. It's not a game anymore. The following message appears on the screen: "Children learn a lot from their parents, including domestic violence."

8.6 The Need for Adapted Care

Child patients of mine who have witnessed domestic and interfamily violence can be violent toward siblings, their mother, and at school toward other children and adults. As in the infomercials, they reproduce the tyrannical law of might makes right by identifying with the violent parent. Little girls are often martyrized by elder brothers. This was the case of a young patient named Aurélie, abused from ages 5 to 12 by her brother, until finally separated from him. She was threatened, terrorized, and beaten up by this brother four years her senior when in her father's custody. She was kicked and hit hard in the head along with other dangerous acts such as causing her to have biking accidents, trying to drown her, throw her out a window, strangle her, and "play mom and dad" at night with sexual violence. The father, who clearly preferred the son, walked in on them one night. Considering it child's play, he punished both by making them write 1,000 times, "I must not play that game with my brother/ sister." The son got out of it, and only the little girl was punished.

Thankfully the mother, worried about the many symptoms her daughter had such as anxiety and nightmares, succeeded in making her feel safe enough to talk, which meant the mother could protect her and take action. Aurélie was relieved to be able to talk about it and be understood, and that others were enraged by what was done to her, saying that her brother had no right to do this, that it was very serious, and that he needed to be held accountable. She understood the psycho-traumatic mechanisms very well. Understanding her traumatic memory and analyzing what set it off and the extreme distress that followed allowed her to better control it. From our first meetings, she succeeded all by herself in finding the origin of flashbacks she didn't understand before. She understood her own distress when she saw a family in the waiting room with a big brother and little sister or why, when she came across a photo with her brother in it while cleaning her room, she got a headache (subconsciously reminding her of the blows to her head). She immediately understood dissociating behaviors and identified them in herself in the form of scenes full of violence and horror that she imagined and played out in her mind as soon as she started feeling bad. These scenarios, of which she was ashamed, disappeared under my care.

Maxime, a boy of ten, witnessed dramatic scenes of domestic violence until he was four. After that, his parents separated and he only saw his father rarely. On one of those occasions, he was molested by a 17-year-old half-brother in the father's home. His mother pressed charges of sexual aggression, but these were dropped. Maxime said during the hearing that he had consented and also that he had inflicted sexual acts on other children of his own age. The justice system considered that this was not sexual aggression but molestation, d'atteintes sexuelles, and as the perpetrator was a minor when this happened, he could not be held guilty of even that.

The complaint lodged by his mother and that he was able to talk about the sexual violence allowed Maxime to stop harming other children, in spite of the judge's decision. During therapy, Maxime felt guilty and ashamed. He explained that he could not think about people around him (school friends, girls or boys, teachers, family members) without being invaded by violent and degrading sexual images. When we examined together where these were coming from, after I explained how traumatic memory works, Maxime spoke for the first time of the many pornographic films he'd watched at his father's house from the age of six onward, after flipping through channels when he was left home alone. He is relieved to know that these images don't come from him but from the films that traumatized him and to know that pornography is not representative of adult sexuality. In a few sessions, he was completely freed of these images.

At the beginning, Maxime also had significant phobias: He couldn't stand to see a kitchen knife and would start screaming, running away, and demanding that his mother stop everything to put it away. He was always checking that the windows and shutters of the apartment were closed and couldn't sleep before checking many times, making his mother do the same. Quickly, with his mother's help, we made the connection between his symptoms and the scenes of domestic violence that he had witnessed before four years old, the father having chased the mother with a knife and threatening to throw her out the window. Maxime had no recollections of these scenes. I explained that his fears came from what he experienced as a young child and that he was terrorized and traumatized by his father's violence. This improved the situation, though the phobias remained to a lesser degree. His mother told me that she'd forgotten to mention that her son came into her bedroom almost every night. He'd stand there by the bed looking at her until she'd wake up, which made her very uncomfortable. When I talked with Maxime about this, I could tell he felt very bad. He said he had something to tell me, but he was too ashamed of it, and he cried for the first time. He asked to be alone with me, and he desperately explained that he was making sure his mother was still alive because he was afraid he'd killed her. That is why he was afraid of knives and open windows: Fear of cutting her or throwing her into the void. "But I love her," he told me, sobbing, "and I don't want her to die." When I asked him to elaborate what went on in his head those moments, he told me that he "said to himself," "I'm going to kill you!" "I'm going to stab you!" "I'll throw you out the window, you whore!" He thought this came from him, even though it was absolutely not what he wanted. In analyzing these phrases that were in his head, I helped him become aware that it wasn't the voice of a little boy that he heard but of a screaming man. I explained that these were not his phrases but those of his father that he had heard when little: Traumatizing phrases that became the expression of the traumatic memory colonizing him. Maxime was tremendously relieved to understand this. He'd thought of himself as a monster and was so afraid of this that he'd considered suicide. We worked together to understand at what moment these phrases appeared (certain times of day, meals or bedtime, or when his mother yelled). Quickly, he gained control over these phrases and made them disappear, along with phobias and obsessional behaviors. Maxime finally felt free of an enormous weight.

Similarly, Damien, a four-year-old boy, was brought to me by his mother after he'd set a closet on fire at home (thankfully put out in time). When I asked him why he did it, he spontaneously mentioned a phrase that he heard constantly in his head: "I'm going to burn this fucking house down! I'm going to burn this fucking house down!" The year before, Damien had witnessed domestic violence, with his father threatening to kill his mother and start a fire by pouring gas at the entrance. It was after an argument between his mother and his stepfather, which flared up his traumatic memory, that Damien lit the fire. In spite of Damien's very young age, it was possible to treat his psycho-traumatic symptoms through explaining to him where the phrase (which he didn't remember hearing) was coming from. He understood that it wasn't him speaking but words coming back to him from his father, and that he should not obey that voice.

Another little boy of five years, victim of mistreatment and sexual violence in his family, was brought to me by Child Protective Services to treat his trauma and violent sexual behaviors inflicted on other children in his foster family. He was so stressed by this first meeting that he "switched" right in front of me and yelled, "I don't give a fuck" with a threatening air! But I offered him some candy, and that was enough for him to come back to himself and his reality of a child who was cheerful, curious, and aware. Even very small children understand well, when it is explained to them, the origin of images and violent scenarios that invade them. They are usually very interested, and using drawings, they can visualize what is going on in their minds. This helps them control the flaring up of their traumatic memory and eventually put an end to it. In just a few sessions, this little boy stopped committing sexual violence against other children and was able to go back to school.

Adrien was 13 years old when his mother, in despair, told me about the severe abuse (scarring and burning) that his son inflicted for several weeks on a first-grade boy in the boarding school they were attending. In my consultation with him, Adrien showed no emotions or remorse, and his coldness was striking. The school had not reported the incidents and had only suspended Adrien for three days. It was rapidly silenced to avoid a scandal about this prestigious school. This forced the little boy who was the victim to be in contact with his torturer. Adrien was incapable of explaining his acts to me or linking them to any prior violence he was victim or witness of. Finally, his mother told me what had happened when he was two years old and was in his grandparents' care for two months. After talking to him on the phone with him crying and distraught, she quickly went to her parent's house and found him with marks of violence all over his body (wounds, burns, and bruises). The grandfather admitted to having hurt his grandson many times. The mother did not press charges. After not speaking to her parents for several months and after her father apologized, she was in contact with her parents again and never told her son about this violence. As if nothing had happened, Adrien continued to see his grandparents regularly and got along with them.

At 13 years old, when Adrien was separated from his mother to attend boarding school, this set off his traumatic memory of violence endured as a small child and that of the sadistic pleasures of his grandfather. That he had no conscious memory did not prevent him from being colonized by the sadistic scenes and abuse. To dissociate and anesthetize himself, he imposed these on a little first-grade boy that he had total power over. The absence of charges and the silence about serious violence—the protection that his grandfather benefitted from—meant denial of the trauma the child endured and denial of the severe transgression of his rights. This sent the child the message that violence was not serious and taught him the law of might makes right.

The school's administration, covering over serious violence and not getting the law involved or doing anything to protect the victim, were also accomplices in the denial, injustice, and feeding the cycle of violence. Psychotherapy allowed Adrien to treat his traumatic memory, decolonize his psyche from the violence, and escape from his emotional anesthetization. We established connections between what happened to him when he was an abuser and what happened to him as a victim and he learned about how the law is supposed to restore rights so that victims can reclaim their dignity and find coherence in life again.

This was also the case for a little girl named Lisa, who had been severely mistreated and raped by her father, who was also very violent with her mother. As soon as Lisa felt threatened, she would switch to speaking in a violent and humiliation way toward her mother and other people. She said obscene things that were in no way part of her normal speech. Her mother telling her how wrong this was only made her more violent. Becoming aware that she was colonized at these moments by the violence of her father and that these statements were totally incoherent with what she wanted to be made it so she no longer switched.

8.7 Vengeance and Rage Mechanisms

There is another process through which children become violent, which involves revolt and vengeful rage against those who represent their fathers. They target boys or adult men who resemble their fathers in behavior, expressions, and violent or incoherent statements and make them pay for what their fathers did.

Franck, an adolescent who was witness to his father's violence against his mother as a small child, was kicked out of several schools for hitting a P.E. teacher and some class monitors. But with his friends or at home with his mother, he was described as calm and kind. When asked why he'd been so violent, he explained his acts as reactions to what he considered injustices. He described himself at those moments as being in a state of extreme stress and boil "like a pressure cooker," with the feeling that his heart and head would explode if he didn't let loose his rage. Only after a precise analysis of these violent situations did he become aware that these men who enraged him so much had behaviors similar to his father's. He understood that he was invaded by feelings of distress from the little child of his past, terrorized and convinced that his mother was going to be killed before his eyes. He felt rage and hatred toward anyone he subconsciously associated with his extremely violent father. Making this link with his childhood while talking about and analyzing the violent scenes he had witnessed allowed him to control himself better and begin a reasonable dialogue with himself so that he could calm down. This enabled him to go back to school, and everything was going well.

Anna, a little girl of nine years old, witnessed a terrifying outburst during which her father tried to crush her mother by crashing his car into the little grocery store where she lived and worked. Anna panicked and jumped through the first-story window and was found worn out and running down the national highway through the traffic. Shortly thereafter, she lost most of her hair and almost never slept, woken by nightmares that her mother was going to die. Her father was accused and convicted but did not actually end up in prison because there was no committal order. To hide from him, the mother and daughter had to move and leave no address. At school, Anna became very irritable and fought with fury against any boys likely to tease or bother her. Talking about the scene of violence and, describing in front of her mother her fears and nightmares and learning about psycho-traumatic mechanisms allowed her to understand herself and not feel so alone. She learned to control her anxiety and aggressivity. Anna wants to become a judge.

8.8 When Victims Become Torturers

Some children spend their entire childhoods under the tyranny of violence from one or both parents, under which no stress, frustration, or questioning were allowed. The parent would scream, and the children would stay very still, not daring to laugh, play, or speak. Some children are required by violent fathers to not speak to their mother or show her any affection; they stop doing so as soon as he puts his key in the lock. These children could reproduce the tyrannical behaviors with younger siblings, pets, schoolmates, and later at work or in their own families. Once again, children would be forbidden any manifestation of joy, enthusiasm, or tenderness toward their mothers. This would annoy the father (former victim), and that's inexcusable! The father will allow himself to terrorize his family so he doesn't have to face traumatic memory of his own childhood. When they become adults, victims of child abuse are submerged again in a family universe, and their own children's behaviors will reignite their states of stress. A yell or laughter will remind them of traumatizing situations with their own father or mother. Allowing themselves and being in a position to do so, they will require their family members to avoid any situations likely to make their traumatic memory explode, even if this means living a totally abnormal life. If a family member fails to avoid provoking an explosion of his traumatic memory, he makes her suffer in his place through screams, threats, and violence.

In the childhood of a man who was strangling his partner to death in front of their seven-year-old girl (who saved her mother's life by calling the police), there was unspeakable violence that he witnessed, horrified and powerless, from ages 7 to 8: His own father, violent to the whole family, hanged his 17-year-old daughter because she was pregnant... a crime "of honor" that was not brought to justice. This man-become-monster was replaying the atrocious crime of his father. He was fired up with the impulse to kill his wife by strangling her and became totally unrecognizable. His wife and daughter had never seen that crazy expression and or heard that terrifying voice. It was the voice, expression, and impulse to kill his father. He replayed the crime he had witnessed in order to disjunct and anesthetize himself. From being a witness and victim, the son became a torturer, and his wife was forced to play the imposed role of the assassinated sister, their little girl playing the role of the victim-witness that he himself had been.

This is like a terribly dangerous terrain rife with landmines that could explode at any moment. Perpetrators choose slaves to walk ahead of them and step on the mines so they can stay safe. They sacrifice others, their slaves, just as they were sacrificed as children. The perpetrators know this is horribly and deeply unjust, all the more since they lived through it, but, "Oh well, it's someone else's turn now... too bad for the weak. I went through it, so why shouldn't they have to?" Through the violence they commit, the perpetrators develop emotional anesthetization that makes it easier—since they feel no emotions—to proceed unencumbered by the natural empathy people feel when faced with the suffering of victims. This makes them more and more dangerous. They want to feel no guilt, as guilt could be a source of anguish, and do everything so their victim feels guilty in their place. This includes lying shamelessly and planning mystifying situations. There is a total scorn for life, which is perceived as a jungle where might makes right and its everyone for themselves; the only goal is to be on the right side: the side of the perpetrators. To move forward on the minefield, abusers need slaves, which they choose for their intelligence and humanity. They need brave, skilled people to walk that minefield for them, and they need to have experience and devotion. Victims are also chosen for their vulnerability and dependence (easier to dominate them) and their isolation (no one there to defend them). Abusers might also train new slaves in subjecting them to destructive psychological control, as happens in cults, sometimes from birth onward if it is their own children.

8.9 How to Fight Violence

Specialized psychotherapy helps traumatized victims not only to understand themselves but also to understand what the perpetrator did to them and why. Once they see what he is acting out, they are no longer trapped in his script and the role he wants them to play. They can see what an imposture he is. The scene is from his past and has nothing to do with them—they are not really in the same play. The scenes have nothing to do with actual reality or with their reality. Once they see this, confusion disappears, and they are no longer petrified by the violence. The violence that was totally inconceivable can be understood by relating it to the traumatized past of the perpetrator, and victims can refuse to participate in the scenes, no longer prey to manipulations that guilt or shame them into staying. From the moment they understand what is going on, they can identify the scene and roles and no longer be trapped. They can be free, no longer the frozen prey that the perpetrator needs for his scenes to be convincing and effective for him. The play no longer works when the victim steps out of her imposed role leaving the perpetrator no longer able to play his. He is forced to face himself in the mirror's reversal and his original role: The role of victim that he absolutely doesn't want to be. There is no more sense or interest to the play, and he has to learn to dissociate and calm himself in other ways.

Violence can be highly contaminating due to direct psychotraumatic consequences and traumatic memory. Combatting violence is above all about protecting victims. It is essential to give them adapted care as early as possible to avoid lives lost, tremendous suffering, and also new violence. Every non-identified trauma victim who receives no care or protection is forced to survive through using disabling avoidance behaviors or dissociating (risk) behaviors. These often involve violence toward self and sometimes toward others, as some switch the side of perpetrators. Often they have several victims, some of whom choose to become torturers: A vicious cycle of violence. To eradicate violence, it is necessary to prioritize the following:

Protection of potential victims. This means people in situations of vulnerability and implies informing them and educating the public to change mentalities. We also need policies that guarantee that everyone's rights be respected and specific laws to promote non-violence in education, care, work, families, romantic relations, and sexuality.

Protection of traumatized victims. No victim should be left without care or protection. Making sure they are safe, giving them adapted treatment, and gaining justice for them are absolute imperatives. Perpetrators must be punished by laws that it is necessary to apply. They need to receive treatment from the first violence they commit and taught about the mechanisms of traumatic memory. Treating a perpetrator in time means avoiding an addiction to more and more serious acts of violence and creating new victims; it makes for a better future.

8.10 Violence as Antidote to Anxiety

It is not normal to commit violence. Every human from birth aspires to a worthy life with authentic connections of friendship and love. A newborn is nourished by connection, attention, and tenderness. If deprived of these, the newborn will not thrive. A child growing up seeks to be in relation with the surrounding world to discover it and herself and be recognized by others. Committing violence means giving up any possibility for authentic exchange, emotional relations, and legitimacy; it is alienation from one's own dignity. In exchange for all-powerfulness, perpetrators give up real bonds with the world and people around them. It is an empty existence based on illusion. It means isolating and excluding oneself. On the surface, he might appear to have many friends and relationships, but he knows this is a lie, and he is alone. No one can really want to be alone surrounded by ghosts, anesthetized, and drugged forever on the violence committed with no hope of true love.

For a man, being violent with women, dominating them, and keeping them in domestic and sexual slavery means depriving themselves of exchanges, discovery, and love, with nothing left but power over. For parents, being violent with their children, training and controlling them, means giving up the treasures of shared tenderness and mutual enrichment since seeing the world through a child's eyes is to rediscover it and find unsuspected truths that were covered by abhorrent rationalizations that adults produce to justify the unjustifiable.

To be locked as a perpetrator in a world of alienating violence, there must be terrifying reasons. These are never tied to the victim but to the traumatic memory of violence the perpetrator endured in his past or witnessed: The traumatic memory that he doesn't want to deal with and will thrust on others at all costs, even the cost of his soul. He perceives this traumatic memory as a threat that will drive him crazy, and it's scary because it is stigmatized by irresponsible social norms, according to which violence is always preferred over anxiety, which is seen as destructive.

8.11 Violence as Instrument of Inequality

This same society offers no solution except recycling the same violence to maintain an illusion of social stability and avoid self-destruction. There are only two options, and both are based on power play. On one side are the privileged, who have the right to live, as in Huxley's *Brave New World*. They have the right to not self-destruct but to destroy others in their place. On the other side are the non-privileged, the inferiors who have the "right" to self-destroy or be destroyed by the privileged. For them, being part of those to be destroyed is "recommended" in order to feed the army of slaves necessary for the privileged to anesthetize themselves. To destroy themselves instead is looked down on, as they are considered marginal or mentally ill if they don't want to play society's game and are "irredeemable."

Violence is an effective mask for the troubling psycho-traumatic symptoms that no one wants to acknowledge. It is an imposture that creates a state of emotional anesthetization, allowing perpetrators to escape stressful situations while brainwashing and silencing victims.

Violence is a privilege that survived the transition to democratic societies and recognition of universal human rights. It requires the inequality that it both feeds and feeds on. It's a poor privilege, a drug, a masking of misery that only allows for an artificial life that admits powerlessness. Though it is lamentable, it is also destructive and capable of reproducing trauma from generation to generation. Brute physical force was a tool put in place for this domination reinforced by lack of rights. Women pay the price throughout their lives; from birth to death, they are an endless reservoir that represents half of humanity. Children also pay heavily (but when they are male, many of them can flip to the side of the privileged as adults). Let's not forget the disabled, ill, elderly, and everyone who suffers discrimination based on origins, religion, politics, or sexual orientation. This ubiquitous privilege blocks attempts at true equality. Violence is very effective for domination and submission because it involves dissociation and emotional anesthetization that transform victims into slaves and emotional anesthetization of perpetrators that transform them into machines of destruction.

We have everything to gain from protecting victims as soon as violence happens. We need to make sure it won't happen again and that they are safe. Respecting victims' rights in gaining access to justice and compensation as well as measures to make sure it doesn't happen again are essential. We also need to end the impunity of perpetrators and give them care early on to overcome their addiction to violence. Treating victims with early, adapted care will prevent psycho-traumatic disorders and decrease the number of future victims and perpetrators. This includes avoiding that dissociating behaviors are used and thus preventing future contamination, to finally reach our goal of a more equal and violence-free society. Protection of victims means making sure violence won't reoccur and that new violence doesn't happen.

8.12 Why Do People Commit Violence and Abuse?

Just as one isn't born a victim, one is not born an aggressor; one becomes an aggressor after being a victim or witness of violence. Contrary to the victim struggling with traumatic memory at the price of tremendous suffering, debilitating avoidance behaviors, and dangerous, self-risking dissociative behaviors, the aggressor is confident of the power relations and uses someone else to treat his traumatic memory at less risk or harm to himself.

8.13   Violence Is Always Intentional

The perpetrator always intents to harm the victim, even if the violence is compulsive; it is only done to someone in an inferior position and is a power play of domination and control. The intentional quality of violence doesn't mean that the perpetrator intended all the consequences. Nonetheless, the emotional anesthetization that the violence entails makes the perpetrator totally insensitive and indifferent to the victim's distress signals. In addition, when faced with the consequences of violence, he might trust his own perceptions, which are totally falsified by the emotional anesthetization, a safety mechanism he's used since early childhood: "The same violence happened to me, and I didn't die from it; I'm even stronger because of it, so I can do it this child, I can go ahead, it's not very serious," or "My parents were right to hit me and humiliate me because I was a troublemaker, and if they hadn't done that, I never would have straightened out."

With this catastrophic reasoning, an infant can be left to cry with distress for hours or hit: "It won't kill him!" The natural anguish that would make such situations unbearable is not only absent; it is transformed into anesthetization. When sober reality barges in with its terrible consequences, some people collapse in horror at their prior indifference or feel extremely guilty and question their twisted position. Others continue to rationalize ("too bad for them") or blame the victim's fragility to avoid questioning themselves or feeling any guilt. These perpetrators are especially dangerous: They think they are above reality and of another essence. Harming others doesn't bother them, as their defensive system is a solid wall. Their addiction to violence is so important to them that it would be difficult or impossible to give it up.

8.14   Types of Abusers and Perpetrators

Those who commit destructive acts of violence come from every walk of life with no exceptions. Each has a unique traumatic history and specific way of operating depending on the violence endured and committed. These create traumatic memory, which flares up due to sensory, emotional, and contextual cues that are usually subconscious and belong specifically to the abuser. However, we can distinguish two major types of aggressors according to how often they use violence to dissociate, and between these two extremes, there are many intermediary positions.

First, there are occasional aggressors. Perhaps they seem respectful, but when overwhelmed by an unexpected explosion of traumatic memory, they do not realize their anguish is due to subconscious reminiscences, and they don't identify their actions as unjust, excessive, and incoherent. They will feel so attacked that they unleash uncontrolled violence and benefit from their dominant position. When it's over, the return to reality is catastrophic. They are horrified by what they did and won't stop apologizing, trying to make up for it, and taking responsibility without trying to falsify what happened. They will be wary of themselves and put in place a system of control, limits, and assistance so that it doesn't happen again. They try to understand and often want to start therapy.

On the other side are "professional" aggressors. They are self-centered narcissists who believe themselves superior to others and are highly addicted to serious violence, predation, and manipulation; they have no conscience or scruples. They constantly search for new victims to use as drugs or transform into slaves, inflicting terrible violence while numbed by total emotional anesthetization. They take no responsibility and never question themselves or their behavior, and they never feel guilty. They see himself of another essence with rights for them alone, beyond all laws (they believe themselves above the law). They are incapable of any compassion for victims. They are, therefore, extremely dangerous.

This category includes serial killers and serial rapists who constantly plan detailed scenes of horror. This preparation is already in itself a dissociative drug that creates dependence and ascending horror that climaxes with the violence itself (the killing or rape), which provides extreme disjunction. Each disjunction further recharges an increasingly explosive traumatic memory and creates the conditions for another crime, sometimes endlessly or until arrested. This can be a man or woman, a sexual aggressor of children and women, a pimp, a domestic tyrant, a business tyrant, or even a nonprofit tyrant in a medical or social field who uses this as a disguise and to lure new victims. These perpetrators might also play the roles of protector, honest man, ideal mother, or devoted professional.

8.15 Pretending that Victims Consent

The perpetrator uses a very effective dissociation strategy to create extreme dependence in victims, with behaviors that swing between a perfectly normal attitude (even a kind, attentive, and tender one) that seems to indicate real concern for the victim, who feels flattered, loved, appreciated, and finally understood by someone who presents himself as very important. But then he says and does things that are incoherent, worrying, totally inappropriate, and terribly perverse, and these are incomprehensible and terrorizing. This is perfect for generating surprise, tonic immobility, and tremendous anguish in his victims, most often awakening the traumatic memory of their ruined childhood. With the flaring up of this traumatic memory, a fire that he intentionally lit, the perpetrator can (like a pyromaniac firefighter) offer to quickly put it out. This involves a radical dissociative "treatment" with a panoply of serious (often sexual) violence that causes disjunction and anesthetization in the victim.

By procuration and running no risk to himself, the perpetrator can dissociate at the victim's expense. She's the one exposed to the consequences and will paradoxically seem to ask for this again, which hides the criminal intentions of the perpetrator. As the same scenarios take place, the victim finds herself with an increasingly recharged and hypersensitive traumatic memory, ready to explode at the least situation that seems threatening or stressful. As the perpetrator holds the most effective treatment— the violence he inflicts that inundates her with dissociating hard drugs (morphine-like and ketamine-like), she becomes dependent on these drugs and thus on the violence/provider of violence (the abuser). This is the same phenomenon of habitu-ation and tolerance that we find in drug addicts. It can lead to an escalation of violence since disjunction is only possible with higher and higher doses of the drug.

The perpetrator is both poison and antidote. In a malicious inversion, the poison is not detected—as it is encapsulated in talk of love, care, and help. The antidote/abuser, whose abnormal and violent qualities should be obvious, might be considered by the victim as saving her, or at least as necessary. He gives her brutal, orgasm-like relief when she's faced with extreme tension. She confuses this with desire, need, fulfillment, and maybe even love. It is a huge scam. Anguish and discomfort are perfectly logical feelings when faced with a narcissist who transmuted vio-lence into (false) desire—or even love—by using the mechanisms of traumatic memory. The mystification of love can take the form of, "I've got him under my skin" (when it's really in the cere-bral amygdala that she has him). Victims feel they cannot live without their abusers and would follow them "to Hell and back." Violence, rape, and serious physical and psychological damage are transmuted into an illusion of pleasure that is the effect of a dissociating hard drug. The degrading treatment and distress set off by traumatic memory recharges it endlessly. It creates dis-sociation and dependence that the perpetrator can use without any fear of punishment: The victim considers herself consenting, although she is not freely choosing but under constraint. The mys-tification can operate even more effectively since the perpetrator benefits from a catastrophic and ubiquitous discourse about "sex play" that integrates many violent and perverse behaviors into what's considered normal sexuality. This consumeristic falsifica-tion is seen in ads, mass media, magazines, and academia. When the victim becomes aware of the aggression, manipulation, and perversity of what she endured and wants to report the violence or the rapes, the perpetrator denies his guilt and shows proof that the relationship was consensual and that it was a passionate love story (messages, dates, love letters, witnesses).

With his all-powerful certainty that he will not be punished, he even brags about his control and violence: "you like it," "it's good for you," and "you can prostitute yourself for me."

He usually tells her how things are going to be early on after gaining some control over her, just to shock/immobilize her. He will tell her that loving him is dangerous; that she will suffer; if she wants to be loved, she'll have to give more than others; that he needs her to prove her love in accepting to please him and be his slave; that they need to "spice up" their relationship with "exciting experiences": Sodomy, sadomasochism, swingers' clubs, etc. He will enjoy telling her: "I am your drug." He might even—height of deception—tell his victim, if she says she's not doing well and wants to get psychotherapy: "You'll see, your psychiatrist is going to prescribe ME as your medicine to take morning, noon, and night!" And if she complains too much, he will make her feel guilty by telling her he is disappointed, that she is incapable of loving him, or "I warned you, you knew, you wanted to be with me, you don't know what you want" and then reassure her with soothing words: "I love you!," "You're every-thing to me," and "I can't live without you."

The more vulnerable the victim is due to her violent past and the more isolated she is with a catastrophic sense of self, the better it is for the perpetrator. He can more easily play many roles. He'll play at being someone of great value, power, kindness, and intelligence who miraculously, as in a fairytale, is interested in "this poor, ugly, boring, isolated girl," which is how the victim sees herself. But there's a price to pay for being with someone so superior to oneself: A few bad points are the other side of the coin. These worrisome elements, presented "artistically" by the abuser, would easily make anyone flee who was not constructed by a past of trauma. The traumatized person is also aware that this is not normal—she has at least as much awareness as a non-traumatized person—but the anxiety flares up her traumatic memory and immobilizes her so that she cannot flee. She is in a state of waiting for the worst and has a need to finish quickly to no longer suffer (meaning reach the summit of violence so that she can disjunct). She will interpret this need to finish quickly to no longer suffer as a kind of desire, which is crazy and incom-prehensible to her, but that she has anyway: "That's the way I am, love makes me stupid, I need sex." The perpetrator's act, playing Prince Charming or Amazing Lover, allows the victim to rationalize the paradoxical and absurd situation: "Yes, but he is so handsome, smart, kind… he's a good lover, so powerful, so manly… that's why I love him anyway, even though I shouldn't; I can't help it."

8.16 Addictive Violence

The aggressor in between these two extremes will quickly find that an explosion of violence is effective in calming anxiety and smoothing out tensions. They usually discover this in adolescence, when rapid changes make traumatic memory flare up. At first, it might involve self-harm (banging their head against a wall or biting/hitting themselves), damaging objects, or watching violence over and over (movies, video games, pornography). They might also imagine scenes of violence in which they play a role. In parallel, they develop other dissociative behaviors: Addictions (alcohol, drugs, video games), risk behaviors, danger-seeking, and anything that has an anesthetizing effect on their anxieties. If they avoid questioning their own behavior or violence in general, if they do not put in place powerful prevention measures, and if society doesn't help them enough, they can allow themselves to enact the violence in real life when their traumatic memories flare up. This is usually when they are faced with someone in a relation of unequal power; they draw from the examples enacted in their own family or those that are tolerated in society.

They'll enact one of the (often sexual) violent scenes in imposing a role on someone. They will taste this violence, which is very effective and quickly becomes addictive and needed in higher doses. For disjunction to happen, more and more (self-produced) dissociative drugs are required, meaning a higher level of stress (violence) is needed.

Violence relies on confusion between the victim's reality and the ghost-reality of the aggressor's traumatic memory. For example, an abusive parent confuses the baby that cries because of normal needs with recollections of violence that endured as a baby or already inflicted on other children. Crying can ignite traumatic memory of living through insufferable stress associated with the violent parent's self-hatred or loathing of the child. This creates the illusion of being aggressed by the baby and attributes to the baby the intention of destroying the adult. This pushes adults to inflict the hatred coming from all the aggressors that colonize them on the baby. Lies and manipulation come to the rescue to combat the obvious reality (the fragility and lack of development of the baby), which normally would make violence impossible (it is normally unthinkable to hit, brutalize, or shake someone so small). Victims are instrumentalized, and perpetrators rid themselves of anxiety, helped by catastrophic theories about childrearing that advocate the use of violent measures to prevent children from becoming spoiled or unruly. Reality is of no interest to aggressors, as they seek to impose their own traumatic past (without criticizing what happened) just as their own parents did. What they falsely declare to escape their own anxiety becomes truth to which the victim must adhere. Society allows this violence so that their word can replace obvious truths with unreal, fabricated illusions. For them to use violence continuously against the most vulnerable, there needs to be a lot of complicity from society and those around them. There needs to be an intergenerational system of violence that the victim cannot denounce or recognize as unjust or wrong. For this, abusers must train victims to find it normal and their own fault. The victim is guilty because she is worthless, good for nothing, and this is her destiny. The abuser succeeds in taking up the victim's entire being, invading all her mental space, and making her give up her own certitudes and question her reasoning until she is incapable of reacting or understanding. She is petrified, immobile, shocked, and invaded by constant questions: "Why did he say that? What does he think of me? Why is he acting that way?"

8.17 The Privilege of Violence

The perpetrator knows he is in bad faith and that he lies to and manipulates the victim. He also knows that the victim is not guilty. He might at best feel some remorse later on and be upset, apologize, and try to get help so it doesn't happen again. Even in this rare case, he will probably find that those around him and professionals he consults will minimize the violence and not help him: "She really asked for it; parenting is hard sometimes," "Women are like that, frustrating, annoying, insufferable." Most often, the perpetrator prefers to shift all responsibility to the victim: "Look at the state you put me in!"

It doesn't matter that these rationalizations are totally false, incoherent, and indecent. He has the right and the privilege that he has given himself to be totally unjust and not feel any responsibility for others or any guilt about the violence. He has the right and privilege to not be contradicted, anguished, or frustrated, contrary to the victim, who doesn't have these rights because she doesn't have the same worth in the unjust and unequal system of the perpetrator. This dogmatic system doesn't make any sense and could easily be denounced, but it persists with the support of society as something obvious that no one should question. The perpetrator has the right and privilege to not make the deep human effort to put himself in the victim's place and not ask himself any questions or use his intelligence to objectively analyze the situation. He has the power to deny reality and not pursue and logical or coherent conclusions. He has the right and privilege to recreate and rename reality however he feels like and to do harm, insult, humiliate, and require, in spite of it all, love, desire, and appreciation. He has these rights and privileges, just like those who abused him when he was a child, and he finds it much more "comfortable" to identify with them in betraying, scorning, and silencing the child that he was.

The other, who has the victim role, must accept this and consider that she is there to serve him and endure his unilateral decision because it has always been that way, generation after generation. This is a ready-made discourse that continues without questioning and with perpetual guilt in the victim, who finds herself at fault, in failure, worthless, incapable, and tormented by the feeling of constantly deceiving and receiving reproach no matter her efforts. It is necessary for the abuser to place judgments and reproaches on the victim to reinforce the hold over her that makes her a robot. He uses violence to dissociate at the expense of the victim and not of himself.

The discourse about who's to blame is necessary to keep the victim ensnared. There is a demand for perfection that is unrealistic and impossible, and needs that are completely removed from the situation, which the abuser would never have for himself or others he doesn't have control over. At work, he would never hit an adult who bothered him, but he does this to his little, defenseless child! He asks the impossible so that the other will necessarily be at fault and he can use the pretext of anger, when necessary, to take it out on them. He pretends to believe the child is at fault and to be angry so that he can abuse the child without any blame and without appearing to be guilty. Victims feel this when they realize that it's "going to blow up soon."

The abuser needs to be indifferent to consequences of violence to continue using it. He is assisted in this by an array of effects and emotional anesthetization through the neurobiological mechanism of disjunction. But to justify himself, he must manipulate denial, derision, and scorn, minimizing harm by saying that the victim always exaggerates or seeks to inflict guilt on her. He has to not care about the symptoms and disconnect them from the violence, using them to say: "See, you are crazy, worthless, mean, incapable, too fragile and precious, always playing the victim." In this totalitarian system, the victim doesn't even have the option of reacting naturally: No right to respond, to cry, complain, or get angry. She only has the right to endure.

8.18 New Perpetrators in Reserve

As long as violence is blindly thrust on society's most vulnerable with total indifference and lack of punishment for perpetrators, there will always be a reserve of potential future abusers. Children will become teens and adults with incomprehensible traumatic memory likely to flare up in any new situation that might overpower their avoidance behaviors. Traumatic memory colonizes the mind and is a disabling and uncontrollable burden that it is necessary to get rid of at any price. Young people having little experience and self-knowledge are in danger, responding with violent impulses to the feelings traumatic memory imposes, even if they want to be decent and kind.

In couple relationships, a conflict or frustration might reactivate scenes of violence in a climate of anguish and suffering, for example, in scenes of domestic violence witnessed as a child or prior violence toward a former partner. Not identifying these as reminiscences, the young person might believe that he really cannot stand being contradicted and that it is an aggression or frustration that is totally unacceptable, that he was not respected (respect meaning honoring the power relations of might makes right), made easier by his dominant position and the myth that women need to be subjugated.

If babysitting children, traumatic memory might flare up with violent, sexual images, and flashbacks. The young adult might try to stomp out these painful and agonizing sexual sensations wrongly identified as desire or act on them in spite of the horror they represent. The violence inflicted on a person in a vulnerable position subdues the perpetrator's state of extreme tension. The sexual violence and the child's terror lead to disjunction and emotional anesthetization in the perpetrator, which make it easy for him to commit violence again.

When dominant in an unequal situation, the perpetrator feels all-powerful and believes he can act unjustly, indecently, and in total bad faith. Victims' views or feelings do not count because they are inferior. Abusers allow themselves to ask no questions and to be totally incoherent. They are not worried about precision, rigor, or truth. The law of might makes right become an ideological absolute and imposed absolute truth: The strongest is always right and is allowed to do anything. Whatever he does, he must be respected and obeyed. The exercise of this all-powerfulness allows him to be at peace, without shame or guilt, always right because he said so, no matter how absurd. It is the one who endures the violence who must try to understand, analyze, and question herself endlessly.

The violence inflicted is like a puss-filled boil, tumor, or bag of trash that is gotten rid of by making someone else take it. It's the hot potato that gets passed to someone who is not able to refuse it or pass it on, doesn't understand, is immobilized, or doesn't want to pass it on. The main problem is that no one has any clue what is going on. Explanations depend on a person's status, coherence, and self-awareness. Someone dominant in the social hierarchy due to a history of discrimination can, unfortunately, very easily not question himself when anguish and violence surge in him as his traumatic memory flares up. If he feels authorized to do so, he can easily use someone at his disposition due to unjust power relations or who unintentionally sets off his traumatic memory (a crying child, for example). He will not criticize the absurdity, injustice, incoherence, or seriousness of being violent toward another. It's inconceivable that *he* has to suffer this anguish, and he can make it not so: "I'm worth more than they are," "They put me in that state," or "I had no choice"… Just as was seen in childhood.

At that moment, the victim's suffering means nothing to the perpetrator. It is denied or at least minimized, as his own pain was, all the more so because dissociation prevents him from remembering that he endured the same thing. His self-awareness is distorted (he tells himself, for example, that it was no big deal when he was hit as a child). Dissociation has become chronic, but he doesn't realize this. When given by a child, the same slaps that "didn't hurt when he was a kid" are intolerable for the adult he has become. He should realize the contradiction of this and try to understand what's really going on. The total incoherence is invisible to him, and he has no keys to understand, yet he never stops and says, "This isn't okay, it makes no sense!" How can he not be seized by the absurdity of the situation? The usual dishonest alibi is lack of respect (of the strongest), but the bad faith of this explodes when he can hit a child who hit another child, saying it is wrong and bad to hit someone smaller. What incoherence! That should help him realize this is what his mother or father did, and that it is totally incoherent to hit a child, when we don't allow a child to hit another child or even a much larger and stronger adult, even though it would barely hurt them, it is not tolerated. Nonetheless, adults allow themselves to do what was done to them, though they would never hit another adult, for example, at work.

The perpetrator takes only into account his own interests, and the many forms of violence he commits attest to this: Sexual, child-rearing, domestic, or toward employees. The social construct of authority, hierarchy, and sex inequality, with power relations considered natural and inevitable, make violence between humans appear normal: That men are more violent than women and are sexual predators, the violent discourse about raising children, that there is war, and so on. This serves to deny the serious consequences of violence on psychological and physical health. If perpetrators could see the consequences of their acts, those who don't seek to fully destroy or kill someone and are only trying to escape traumatic memory would restrain themselves. For the more cynical who care absolutely nothing for anyone, a society better trained to identify violence and its consequences would make them more afraid of being identified and debunked. They would lose their status of people who are seen as good no matter what, and they place great stock in this. Knowledge of consequences would throw a wrench in their well-oiled system through showing the absurdity of their imposed rationalizations.

With better recognition of mechanisms that explain violence, victims can be less destabilized and more able to point out the deceitful acts of aggressors. Through identifying traumatic memory at the origin of violence, they can refuse to be trapped by a "ghost story" that is not theirs or to play the demanded role. If they cannot find victims, aggressors will have to confront their own violent pasts. The spell of traumatic memory is then broken, the curtain falls, and the "all-powerful monster" is shown to be what he really is: A pitiful actor. Instead of questioning and doubting themselves, trapped in their reactions of terror, victims can observe and deconstruct the aggressor's acts. They can look at him without the lens of his control, a look that allows the falseness of the scene to be perceived. The mirror-gaze sends the perpetrator back to his own story in which he is in both roles: The monster and the terrified child he was. Then, he will either have to harm himself or calm down. This mirror-gaze has the power of the shield offered to Perseus by Athena (goddess of wisdom and reason), and it can petrify the head of Medusa by turning her own powers of petrification against herself (making her see herself in the mirror).

It is essential to recognize that perpetrators play out scenes from their own traumatic memory. They force victims to play the most vulnerable roles that have nothing to do with who they are. The new victim is forced to play the victim that the perpetrator once was, while this time, the perpetrator has the "lead part" of the one with the power. This serves to anesthetize him so he can avoid confronting the realities of his traumatic memory. If the victim refuses to play her part, the scene cannot go on, especially if she exposes the falseness of this virtual reality! The hatred, rage, and destruction have no meaning except for the perpetrator to disconnect. If the scene fails, he has to find another way, through self-harm or through facing his traumatic memory and getting help. The scene is based on no real reasoning, no real anger, and no real sexual desire. The "inhuman monster" is a fake monster who is really just a person. The terror the scene produces is a high-end drug. Everything is like a bad horror movie in which the perpetrator does anything to elicit terror in victims, using cliched tricks.

Once it is all shown to be an act, the violence no longer has a terrifying effect and is of no interest to the perpetrator because he can no longer gain disjunction through instrumentalizing the victim. The perpetrator is faced with himself alone and must find another way to calm his anxiety… He might choose to terrify himself in a closed circuit to gain the calm of disjunction. But if this isn't sufficient—if it seems too ridiculous—he will need to use other strategies of dissociation, including self-harm or other risk behaviors. It is sometimes shocking to see how a perpetrator deprived of his usual drug (violence against his chosen victim) can find other solutions to calm himself.

Some perpetrators, even if they aren't of total bad faith, are troubled by their behavior (especially if those around them and society as a whole disapprove), and they want to avoid it, not have it happen again and have coherent tools to understand. In this case, explanations about the mechanisms at work can help them to contain themselves, find other solutions to "treat" their anxiety, or use solutions they've developed in other situations in which they were not in positions of domination.

8.19 In a Victim's Own Words

The following was presented at the Conference on Sexual Violence hosted by the organization Traumatic Memory and Victimology on November 10, 2010

"To you, my son, I want to speak,
For you, my son, I want to scream.

You were 8 years old. I had to leave you for the whole month of August. You were going to explore Corsica with your father. I had no way to get in touch with you. I was petrified.

Your father had shown such an aggressive attitude toward you that he was deprived of visiting rights for 2 years. He appealed this judgment and won by forging your writing. Every time I left you with him on weekends, I feared you would be killed. It was 30 hours of horrible, interminable waiting.

When I was required to leave you with him for a whole month, I thought I would die. I have never been so sick and heavy-hearted. I was dying of sadness.

The psychological evaluation stated that your father was a bit unusual and your mother too worried, but that was actually with good reason.

You were 8 years old, your eyes were blue as an angel's, and when you came back, they were sad, faraway, and vacant.

Your father committed incest, 'the worst form of incest,' you told me 10 years later. Your father forbid you to tell me, saying he would kill me if you did. You said nothing.

You were brilliant, yet all your schooling was torture. You loved the Scouts, but you found yourself in terror every night. You were a champion athlete, but you missed all chances to prove it.

You became deeply depressed. Throughout your adolescence, I thanked God every night that you were still alive. I supported you without fail, however I could, without ever understanding what was happening. You were so unhappy.

I didn't know about the heinous crime your father committed on you until I read a letter you left on your desk. You were 19 and still didn't want to tell me anything. I would have screamed it to the whole world.

Among those close to us, my family and friends, so few wanted to listen to, support, or even tolerate us. We stayed alone in my apartment, you with your insurmountable suffering, your immense difficulty in picturing life as a college student, an adult, an employee, and me battling breast cancer.

You phoned your father and spat at him all the truths of what he did, his atrocities, everything he destroyed and murdered in you, and you told him you never wanted to see him again.

I loved you as much as I could. I helped you with your plans, forcing myself to stay as positive as possible, but you went through some ugly things, some places of very high risk, friends who were unbalanced and mistreated you. I was terrified sometimes.

You struggled so much. You met with many twisted people in your path, and it was so hard.

You even had to leave jobs you'd worked hard to get.

It's not over yet. You are full of courage, energy, strength, and fragility before the threat that terrorizes you. The strength of love was not extinguished in you, but there's a huge price to pay for that.

We have in common this deep love of life, even though your father has destroyed so much of it. He won't have the last word: I will always be there when you need me to reassure you and help you on your way, your own way that you make for yourself.

But will that be enough for your happiness? Will it help you find that vivacious laugh you once had and that clarity and presence in your gaze?"

9

Surviving Unspeakable and Unspoken Violence

9.1 Handling Traumatic Memory Without Specific Treatment

For a victim to escape the most serious consequences of violence (traumatic memory and dissociating behaviors), she needs to analyze the violence she endured to avoid being trapped and colonized by the perpetrator's scenarios. She needs to identify the violence in terms of dissociating behaviors engendered by prior violence and find the origin in the traumatic memory of the perpetrator.

Nothing in society prepares anyone to do this work. Violence is seen as a necessary evil inherent to the human condition and part of every person's past since humanity began (Cain and Abel). Worse, knowledge of good and evil given by the forbidden fruit is taken to be at the origin of human suffering. Original Sin is not committing the first violence. It is seeking to know the origins of it, seizing unauthorized knowledge and questioning an extremely hierarchical system. Only superiors are allowed knowledge, along with the privilege of deciding who is worthy or not. We are surrounded by denial of violence behind closed doors (idealization of marriage, families, workplaces), the banalization and tolerance of most forms of violence (especially

DOI: 10.4324/9781003497516-10

sexual and childrearing), and misinformation about violence, its severity, and its consequences.

Violence is a paradox insofar as it is both too much (incompatible with the right to live in safety) and indispensable (as a dissociative behavior to, in spite of it all, survive in a society that tolerates it). It is simultaneously hidden and used. For this, it can be enough to disguise it so it doesn't appear to be violence: As love (sexual and childrearing violence) or as necessary for public good and defense of the nation and for order and security.

But violence disguised is still too much due to its consequences. It is either reused against another, in the game of hot potatoes, tossed from the powerful to the more vulnerable, or it marginalizes the victim, who is the receptacle (or scapegoat) of it. This exclusion erases the consequences (dissociative behaviors used by the victim) or does away with the victim herself (suicide, early death, isolating, exile). This means terrifying injustice for most rape victims in the world who, for reasons of family or marital "honor" can be condemned to exile, repudiation, prison, or, worse, death by stoning. In this crazy system, a raped woman casts disapproval over all the community, dishonoring her family and husband. The violence and immorality of rape have stained the community and cast doubt on its perfection.

9.2 An Unequal System of Values

In a hierarchical system that heavily discriminates against women, their inferior status makes them merchandise that has no value except what it brings the legitimate owner (father, brother, or husband). Women serve men's comforts, and any violence is allowed. The invisibility of serious violence and trampling of dignity is accomplished through a false value attributed to women as trophies through their virginity, faithfulness, sexual morality, and motherhood. This fake value is an emotional farce: It is only at this price that they can be loved. They are loved only if they are virgins, have undergone genital mutilation, are good objects, are fertile, and are protected from any male gaze except that of their owner. At this price, in spite of their absence of worth, they can be protected in the perfect universe of the family, couple, and community. But it is really about men protecting their goods, their precious drug that is faithful and always available, through making sure the woman doesn't revolt or free herself. She is made to submit under the pretext of love to family and religious values.

When such a woman is raped, and it is impossible to disguise it because her virginity was destroyed or because the rapist was accused, the whole system is in danger: The victim is sacrificed even if she is valued. She isn't any longer, and she can have no place in the system; the trick doesn't work anymore. She could very well continue to be an excellent drug—that's not the issue—rather, it's the continuance of the system itself that is threatened. If a man keeps a woman who has no more value and loves in spite of it all, a woman who was raped, or not mutilated, or sterile, or emancipated, that means the community's values are not the only ones possible for a woman. It means that women do not only exist for a few specific functions and that their inferiority is not so obvious! And if they aren't inferior, if they are equal to men, it is impossible to keep using them as domestic slaves and as drugs, and men are too attached to this enormous privilege.

Such a system—and this is highly effective—excludes women from gaining knowledge and education in many countries. It is easy then to show that they are less intelligent than men! The inferior status of women allows men privileges that are essential to their continued inflicting of violence they were victims of as children against their wives and children in an endless cycle that deprives almost everyone of access to authentic and mutual love.

This is why hierarchical and unequal societies value dissociating behaviors that correspond with social status. Everything is done so that violence used by someone in a superior position is never identified as such. But when violence is used by someone designated as inferior on a person self-defined as superior, it is denounced as very serious. For example, it is "normal" for a parent to hit a small child if the child "misbehaved," often unintentionally and due to physiological immaturity, such as spilling milk. But it is seen as serious and abnormal if the same child hits a parent for doing something similar. In many countries, it is also normal for men to have extramarital relations, but for a woman, this is a crime. In France, a man who has many "conquests" is known as a Don Juan, whereas a woman who does is pejoratively qualified as a nymphomaniac. Maintaining this unequal system explains why adults are intolerant of adolescents violence and of female sexuality that resembles that of men.

9.3 Empirical Management of Traumatic Memory

For victims of violence, there are several possibilities. Some can find those even more "inferior" and inflict dissociating violence on them, which is accepted by society (for example, women on children). Others, because they are at the end of the line or because they do not want to harm others for reasons of ethics and coherence, can only use costly and dangerous avoidance or dissociative behaviors toward themselves in order to survive on the minefield.

Avoidance behaviors are those of renouncing and self-censoring. They consist of reducing as much as possible the landscape on which one lives to avoid anything that could at all resemble violence; it means limiting contact with the outside world. It is as if, on the minefield of traumatic memory, only a small piece of it has been de-mined, and it is safe to stay within that space.

Dissociating behaviors are dangerous and addictive. They make the victim venture farther on the minefield. They provide emotional anesthetization that ensures that they do not feel the terror and distress that would otherwise surge. The same strategy has been used by national armies during particularly bloody battles, such as the first waves of embarkment at Omaha Beach. The intoxication of soldiers allowed them to run between bullets, just as during the Vietnam war, drugs were frequently consumed by GIs.

When they need to confront a situation that might set off their traumatic memory, many victims try to dissociate by taking alcohol or drugs or by having risk behaviors that can be paradoxical. For example, a victim who was raped as a child might find having sexual relations in a normal, loving situation impossible because it risks setting off traumatic memory. On the other hand, it is possible to have unsafe and violent sex with strangers because that generates dissociation. Dissociative behaviors lead to disjunction, which allows them to walk on the minefield, but at the cost of recharging their traumatic memory constantly and aggravating psycho-traumatic consequences (contrary to avoidance behaviors). (The mines are still there and the harm is still done.)

Avoidance and dissociative behaviors do have some overlap. Victims alternate between these depending on how dangerous, navigable, or inevitable the minefield becomes. The risk is great when traumatic memory is set off in adolescence since young people are traditionally asked to become autonomous, gain freedom, face many new situations, and formulate plans for the future. They also discover their sexuality. Traumatic memory allows them almost none of this. The environment they were able to demine and the avoidance behaviors they've put in place become useless, and they constantly feel in great danger. They can try to fully retreat, but that is difficult, and they will feel different from others and painfully isolated. Most often, this is not even possible for them: Everyone around them is pushing for them to move forward. Their peers push them, and adults cannot stand to see them as passive and reclusive. They are forced to move forward on dangerous terrain, and their traumatic memory quickly explodes, exposing them to distress and intolerable panic attacks. The only option of escape, except for depression or suicide attempts (when all else fails), is to put in place dissociative risk behaviors. They quickly find out from experience that when they feel really bad, they can hurt themselves (hit, burn, strangle, self-mutilate) or put themselves in danger (on the road, in extreme sports, in unsafe sex…) and they will feel relief (anesthetization). Other life events could endanger a balance they worked hard to acquire and risk setting off traumatic memory. The events could be positive or negative (change of status, work, retirement, moving…), or any situation of significant emotional stress, again positive or negative (exams, competitions, first job interview, marriage, birth, divorce, separation, mourning, medical intervention, unemployment).

When victims of serious violence seem to be doing well and succeed in spite of it all, they are labeled resilient. Among them, some did not develop traumatic memory, either because they were able to modulate or shut down their emotional response and escape overload, or if disjunction did happen, they had specialized and effective care immediately so that psychotraumatic disorders could not set in. But in other victims who succeed in life and seem to be happy and fulfilled, many are wrongly considered resilient. They pay the price of enormous and exhausting efforts to seem to be doing well, but they live through incommensurate suffering, horrible solitude, and sometimes destructive dissociative behaviors that they hide and that those around them don't know about.

Others are true resilient: Having developed traumatic memory, they succeed through intense personal psychological work in discovering how to modulate and switch off their emotional response each time it is set off. This modulation is accomplished through putting words to their emotions, identifying and understanding the trauma they endured, making connections between their symptoms and the violence, establishing an internal dialogue, writing, exchanging, using art, literature, or philosophy, and never giving up trying to understand, seek, and reclaim the truth. Often these people are lucky to have more information about their past, sometimes with abusers who accept to talk about it and tell at least part of the truth. They also benefit from supportive people around them, which is perhaps the most important factor. They are encouraged and supported in their quest for truth. Finally, a very small number of victims have access to specific psychotherapeutic care centered on violence and treatment of traumatic memory, and they can thus heal—that is, demine—their traumatic memory through transforming it into autobiographical memory.

9.4 The Cycle of Violence

Most violence originates in childhood. Wars and political control are also considerable sources of violence during conflicts and long after due to the traumatic memory of former soldiers and civilian victims. Armed conflicts harm more and more civilians (murder, genocide, deportation, torture), especially women. Rape and other sexual violence are used as weapons and instruments of terror with increasing frequency in conflicts (rape of civilians has been recognized as war crimes and crimes against humanity by the International Criminal Tribunals of Rwanda and ex-Yugoslavia). Children are also increasingly harmed by armed conflicts and reduced to sexual and domestic slavery or used as child soldiers.

Childhood is where future violence originates. The vulnerability, immaturity, and dependence of children, the astonishing statistics on mistreatment, sexual violence (over 50% of sexual violence is committed against minors), childrearing violence, and the explosion of domestic violence make childhood a factory for the production of traumatic memory. This particularly virulent traumatic memory can provoke uncontrollable terror and is a reservoir of violent dissociative behaviors in adolescence and adulthood, especially as men benefit from a power dynamic accepted by a society that is profoundly masochistic and patriarchal. Mothers have the socially sanctioned "right" to dominate and control their children, who are not sufficiently protected or defended in their actual rights. Too often, raising children is a kind of breaking in. Children reduced to slaves, child soldiers, and trafficking victims exploited in pedo-pornography are in great danger. They must be identified, found, and saved, and then benefit from intensive specific care programs.

Wars (with massacres, torture, rapes), terrorism, and state-sanctioned violence also maintain the cycle. War has the power of making monsters and killing machines by rapid contamination. It is enough that there is an enemy, an authorization to kill, and an initial experience that is particularly atrocious (such as a massacre). This creates psycho-trauma with a dissociative state resulting from disjunction of emotional circuitry. This makes it seem that one is no longer active in the violence but coolly observing it (due to emotional anesthetization).

In such situations, reminiscences of atrocities committed impose themselves as pseudo-reality that competes with actual reality and recreates a state of terror, panic, and intolerable distress associated with rage and destruction of the abuser of the past. Flipping over into this "film" and replaying a scene of extreme violence experienced allows for disjunction either as a victim (danger-seeking, risk behavior, exposition) or as an aggressor (exercising extreme violence, a position favored by the authorization to kill enemies and the way society mostly tolerates war crimes).

9.5 Violence without Limits: A Contagious Illness

The more there are massacres, war crimes, and contamination from extreme violence, the more soldiers become extremely violent and powerful criminals. In Rwanda in 1994, during the genocide against the Tutsis, all the elements were there: Designation of internal enemies, civil war (after the attack that cost the lives of presidents of Rwanda and Burundi), a call for hatred, and a plea for genocidal murder of all Tutsis as well as moderate Hutus. This was constantly broadcast on the Radio of a Thousand Hills. The massacres amplified in a few days and the number of killers recruited into the Interahamwes and Impuzamugambis terrorist groups rose exponentially through contaminating dissociation. In a few weeks, emotional anesthetization was at its peak, which allowed murderers (in a state of total dissociation) to rape, torture, and kill with machetes men, women, and children. The genociders left home every day to go kill Tutsis as if they were going to work (Hatzfeld, 2003). In record time, almost 1 million Tutsis were massacred. This is similar to the Shoah, during which the Einsatzgruppen (mobile groups) were responsible for 1.5 million deaths, with the daily number of executions horrifying and unimaginable (during the Babi Yar massacre,

33,771 Jews were shot in two days), just as the daily numbers of deaths in gas trucks and then chambers where nearly 3 million Jews were assassinated.

To destroy human life with this terrible efficiency, total dissociation is necessary. Killers must be fully disconnected from the reality of victims, sometimes assisted by intoxication. No Nazi torturer was required to participate in the massacres: Those who couldn't take it were simply transferred. Benefitting from total superiority in being part of "the superior Aryan race" and being permitted to kill made it possible to very efficiently gain a feeling of "well-being" due to dissociation and anesthetization fed by the extreme violence available. This violence recycled and recharged traumatic memory endlessly as criminals became addicted, dependent, and totally adhered to the totalitarian and genocidal plans of Hitler. After the fall of Nazi Germany, the torturers pleaded their innocence by saying they had to obey orders and felt no regret or guilt. Few of them were condemned, and if we try to imagine their lives after the war, we can picture the reserve of dissociating violence they possessed and the hell they made those around them live. For the genocidal Hutus in the Democratic Republic of Congo, we can now see the considerable number of rapes committed, reported by Amnesty International. On the side of survivors of massacres and extermination camps, having confronted the unthinkable and unimaginable, the nameless horror was extremely traumatizing. It went beyond any representable limits. The violence was unspeakable, and the survivors are described as living dead as if they'd descended into a hell from which no return is possible. They look disincarnated like those in the Nazi camps called "Muselmanns." Along with survivors' guilt (why me?), there is the burden of having seen and heard what no person ever should, and they carry in them absolute horror. When they returned, no one listened to them. Everyone wanted to maintain the few illusions that remained about humanity and value the actions of the Resistance, and the victory of the Allies. Victims were condemned to solitude and the impossible task of mourning their massacred family and fighting the traumatic memory that haunted them every night with the worst nightmares; then, they had to start their day as if nothing happened. They were condemned to construct a new family as if nothing happened, at the price of avoidance and dissociating behaviors that were disabling, painful, and often ignored by those around them: Hell.

For the past 20 years or so, survivors of Nazi camps who are still alive can finally speak out, bear witness, and be heard, thanks to important historical, political, and media work, including commemoration and compensation, with many documentaries, articles, essays, films, and television programs. Before this, there were, of course, remarkable books and historical studies by Primo Levi, Elie Wiesel, George Semprun, and Robert Antelme, as well as the film *Night and Fog*, but these were not known to the general public or numerous enough to allow victims to finally risk speaking out. Now, many testimonies have been written or recorded, finally allowing survivors to leave behind a terrifying solitude that has lasted many decades and put words to the unprecedented violence they endured.

The Algerian war for France and the Vietnam war for the United States were the first occasions for significant studies of the psychological consequences of exposure to serious trauma (risk of imminent death, explosions, attacks, violent death of peers, seeing mutilated cadavers, and so on). The significant risk of developing post-traumatic stress was identified in almost 50% of cases with addictive behaviors (alcohol, drugs) and violent behaviors (fights, domestic violence, mistreatment of children, and sexual aggression).

9.6 The My Lai Massacre

With the My Lai massacre, the psycho-traumatic consequences of war were first studied, and this time on the torturers. The goal was to understand the explosion of extreme violence that made an entire company of soldiers perpetuate atrocities. On March 16, 1968, in a few hours, 504 defenseless civilians in the Vietnamese village of My Lai—women, children, and old people—were massacred in particularly atrocious conditions by the American contingent made of young recruits called Charlie Company, under the command of 24-year-old sublieutenant William Calley. Only the helicopter pilot Hugh Thompson and his team tried to stop the massacre, and they saved a dozen villagers by taking them on board the helicopter. The killing only spared a few survivors and was revealed in late 1969 by the journalist Seymour Hersh (the same journalist who later unveiled the torture at Abu Graib in Iraq), in a report with photos in *Life* magazine. This massacre radically changed American public opinion and led to massive protests against the Vietnam war, as well as awareness of concepts related to trauma and psycho-traumatic disorders stemming from wartime violence.

In a highly mediatized trial, Sublieutenant Calley was condemned for life (but only ended up spending three and a half years under house arrest). But America suddenly was aware of this war's horrors, with atrocities regularly committed by GIs and punctuated with extremely violent discourse (with phrases like "everything is prey" or "seek and destroy"). In only four months, young recruits were transformed into merciless assassins, torturers, and rapists acting in a hypnotic, dissociated state of murderous rage. The killing was sparked when the first soldier gratuitously abused an old man, which made the others switch off their awareness and one by one join the altered state of murder.

One soldier from Charlie Company recalled:

She was running… She was carrying something… I shot her. I turned over her corpse and saw she had a baby in her arms. My bullets had shot through the baby. Everything spun in my head. Then, the training program came back to me. So I did nothing but kill. I cut peoples' throats, hands, ears. I scalped them.

When everything flips at the moment a person discovers the horror of his acts, insufferable distress threatens him, but the memory of violent programming/training authorizes him to delve into extreme violence, which is highly effective for disjunction and dissociation. This means the hypnotic state of complete emotional anesthetization.

Following the massacre, the Company stood together in their lie, transforming it into a victorious operation against the

Vietcong. They received congratulations from the commander-in-chief of the army in Vietnam. The truth only emerged a year later, thanks to a GI who didn't participate in the massacre but heard several friends talking about it. He wrote to the Pentagon, the White House, and Congress, and this led to the inculpation of Calley and 46 soldiers of the company. The article in *Life* then spread the information internationally.

The soldiers of Charlie Company who were examined and treated all showed significant post-traumatic stress disorders due to the violence they committed, and this fact was used by the defense to show the harmful effects of war on the psychological integrity of soldiers.

9.7 What Help Is There for Victims? How Can They Survive?

Victims battling traumatic memory and its consequences find themselves isolated and abandoned. They are forced to manage alone their sufferings and psycho-traumatic consequences of violence with many questions without answers about it and their aggressor. The violence they endured created a rupture of meaning that blocked any possibility for mental representation. This rupture is associated with the powerlessness experienced when the violence happened, and this is the origin of traumatic memory as well as the endless suffering and loss of identity that go with it. Most victims deploy tremendous energy and determination to try to understand what happened, their symptoms, and their aggressor's behavior because their lives depend on it. It is necessary to anticipate violence and find strategies to avoid it, and also because they perceive that it is essential to understand it to recognize who they are and hope to feel a little better.

9.8 Vulnerability and Misunderstanding

It is important that victims find around them a support network of people who are reliable, kind, reassuring, understanding, and capable of speaking and acting out against the horror and injustice of what happened. This also includes professionals who must be good listeners, competent, available, and capable of assisting, informing, protecting, and caring for victims. This can make all the difference, attenuating feelings of solitude, insecurity, and vulnerability. Quality support has a positive impact on self-esteem, which is usually catastrophically low in victims. Violence, with instrumentalization and harm to human dignity, leads to a feeling of worthlessness, all the more so when endured in childhood. The child victim has not yet experienced the necessary unconditional worth that all children should have in the eyes of parents so they can construct themselves harmoniously and with healthy self-esteem. This is essential for adequate self-protection and self-care.

Most often, victims experience people around them, including professionals assigned to their care, as incapable of truly understanding what they experience, even if they can sometimes provide real support. As most professionals know little about survival mechanisms that emotionally anesthetize dissociated victims, they are incapable of giving them the necessary empathy. The dissociative symptoms lead professionals and those surrounding victims to underestimate victims' suffering and the intensity of their trauma and not feel any emotions when faced with them, as the usual mechanisms of empathy malfunction when a person has someone dissociated in front of them (unless aware of trauma's mechanisms). In other words, the mirror neurons required for empathy to spontaneously occur are disactivated by traumatic dissociation. It is often wrongly perceived as indifference or resilience, and people consider that there is no longer any trauma. This makes them less compassionate, more demanding, and even easily annoyed by the absence of reaction and the cognitive disorders that can be taken for indifference or lack of will. Dissociated people can then endure psychological harassment with unpleasant and hurtful remarks made constantly to try to get a reaction.

Most of what is said to victims seems far from reality and not at all adapted to the seriousness of their situation. They often get moralizing, educational lectures when professionals are not coldly indifferent or guilt-provoking. Victims find themselves almost always having to explain themselves constantly to be heard, believed, and helped, and they must fight if they hope for effective protection, justice, and a minimum of compensation. Above all, they are stuck with their suffering, pain, fatigue, unexplained symptoms, lack of consideration for the impact of all this on their lives, and without adapted medical care. They go from doctor to doctor hoping one day to find one who will listen, understand, treat, and relieve them.

9.9 Violence-Related Symptoms Not Recognized as Such by Care Providers

Many victims have tried to get help from psychiatrists, psychologists, psychotherapists, and psychoanalysts, sometimes endlessly, with the risk of being "psychiatrized" and labeled chronic depressive, manic depressive, or even psychotic, and overloaded with sedatives, mood regulators, painkillers, neuroleptics, and soporifics, which serve to kill pain and calm the biggest anxieties but disconnect victims from reality. These are chemical straitjackets that transform them into zombies. Heavy psychotropic treatments, repeated hospitalizations in psychiatric wards, and treatments of electroshocks that recreate disjunction are administered, locking victims into the status of chronically mentally ill and disabled, without hope of a cure. All this "care" ignores the violence at the origin of the disorders. It does not identify the symptoms as psycho-traumatic consequences but rather as psychological disorders that are endogenous (come from within).

9.10 Does Psychoanalysis Work for Victims?

In psychoanalysis, the history of the patient, and her relationship with her parents and those around her, is the focus. But the reality of violence endured will not be less ignored than in conventional psychiatry. The focus is on inner conflicts linked to desires, fantasies, and emotions incompatible with the superego. Centered on the Oedipus Complex, psychoanalytical talk therapy involves questioning the mind's inner functioning through defenses (repression, denial, projection) at the origin of suffering and symptoms. Even while ignoring violence endured, a devoted and well-intentioned psychoanalyst can help victims understand some aspects of self and have more contact with the outside world. But they are powerless to give satisfying explanations of symptoms and violence or to question strategies of domination in an unequal society.

Psychoanalysis centers on the subconscious and claims that people have mastery over their psyches and desires. It does not question domination and inequality in society or discrimination against women. As "father of psychoanalysis," Freud at first denounced violence but then linked its origins to unresolved conflicts between forces within the mind: Libido, superego, and the death impulse. Society was only mentioned as making the superego more or less effective in regulating these conflicts. According to Freud, each person battles original violence linked to subconscious destructive desires stemming from libido. Culture must muzzle these through "castrating" rules, sometimes at the price of several symptoms, or sublimate them through intellectual and cultural pursuits. In psychoanalysis, violence—especially sexual violence—is considered inevitable, and sexuality is traumatizing in itself due to subconscious desires. Symptoms in victims are considered psychological conflicts from within linked to the death impulse. In addition, much childhood violence is said to not have really happened but to involve fantasies linked to subconscious desires and the Oedipus Complex.

Psychiatrists and psychoanalysts usually do not link victims' symptoms to the abuse or violence they endured but rather to disorders originating in them (due to brain chemistry, etc.) and/or due to mental conflicts about an unresolved Oedipus complex. The treatment in both cases is not centered on the root cause: Violence and resulting traumatic memory. Traditional psychiatry tends to treat symptoms by provoking further dissociation through medication, shock therapy, isolation, and guilt, trying to scare anorexics, giving amphetamines to hyperactive children, and so on. These anesthetize victims but at the price of a reinforced traumatic memory. This makes its symptoms chronic, entailing lifelong treatment and dependence on psychiatric institutions. It also means it is difficult for victims to find a place in society since mental illness is equated with insanity. Unlike conventional psychiatry, psychoanalysis is only dissociating when therapists abuse their power. It is also less stigmatizing, but it can entail exhausting and endless guilt. In both cases, however, the human qualities of some therapists are useful and can relieve victims through support and denunciation of violence and power abuse and help them improve self-esteem and reconnect with belief in their abilities.

Not really finding answers to their questions from health professionals, victims search for people, testimonies, studies, articles, philosophical and sociological essays, psychology books, interviews, television programs, internet sites of organizations that assist victims, and blogs that offer pieces of information and explanation. All this at least allows for a little better understanding and feeling less alone. Victims are reassured to know that others feel the same suffering, have the same symptoms and behaviors, and survived more or less the same violence.

9.11 Lift the Veil of Illusion Through Art

For victims searching for their truth, artistic expression (literature, novels, theater, poetry, music, visual arts, cinema…) can provide elements of response and make them feel less alone through giving a faithful mirror that finally tells them they are right and clears away the fog. It tells them that what they suffer really exists and can even be the subject of a novel that can give them back their dignity. Art, contrary to the raw nakedness of testimony or memoir, opens many possibilities for connections and resonances with their own past. Art is a reservoir of representations, sensations, sensory perceptions, and feelings that touch us with their beauty—meaning their exactness—and allow us to gradually, through intimate channels of association, venture onto the minefield of traumatic memory without risking any explosions and therefore work at demining it. This perpetual motion between the thing represented (metonymy), and its metaphorical representation (described by Guy Rosolato) allows a dynamic movement of representations that prevents traumatic memory from flaring up. It is as if no overload can occur because the current is constantly deviated and modulated. The initial violence can be approached and viewed without risk. Through not lowering itself to demonstrating morals but by developing hypermorality (discussed by Georges Bataille in *Literature and Evil*), art finds authenticity and fidelity through internal coherence. It can even bring to the light of day the reality of violence without risking trauma and morbidity. Art is not Medusa's head. It is faithful awareness of violence and the aggressor's mind, but without guilty complaisance and thus without danger of petrification, fascination, or addiction. The horror becomes viewable and representable.

Well before doctors, psychiatrists, and politicians, artists have been aware of child abuse. Fairytales, children's literature, and 19th and 20th-century novels are full of horrific violence against children. The reality of violence against women, especially sexual and domestic violence, is present in many novels. Lacan noticed this in writing: "the only advantage that a psychoanalyst has a right to take from its position is to remember what Freud said, that the artist always precedes him and that he should not act as psychologist where the artist opens a path."

9.12 Artists' Truths Connect Victims to Life

If the artist alone has the potential or "right" to reveal the taboo reality of horrific, incongruous, and incomprehensible violence hidden where no one expects it, this is because the artist's social status allows for this. Except in totalitarian societies, artists and their subversive activities are tolerated because they act as the safety valve on the pressure cooker through revealing truths that link victims to life and avoid descent into nothingness, death, insanity, or violence. This truth is sufficiently made over by the functions of entertainment, with esthetic and intellectual pleasure or even (in a twisted way) have an elite function (as with classical music). The danger art could present through denouncing violence is considered an accessory, as is its revolutionary potential and questioning of inequalities and systems of discrimination.

Art makes connections on a background of truth and representations. It can help victims survive, denounce, understand, and heal. But to join the world of the living often remains difficult, and the mechanisms of self-destruction are lodged at the center of self.

9.13 Artistic Practice: Essential Support for Victims

Practicing a form of art can be a key asset for victims and give them a place to play out their emotions and psychological processes through words, sounds, and images. They can more or less consciously express and share truth through finding a sense of perfection that means finding oneself again. This exaltation can be shared and thus validated and even enriched by readers, listeners, or viewers of one's work.

Without necessarily having to become an artist, victims of violence can greatly benefit from writing their stories, describing what they lived through, and what they feel (testimony, diary), and translating emotions into poems, songs, instrumental music, drawings, or paintings. These representations help them understand and analyze what happened and give them better intellectual tools to modulate their traumatic memory and maintain a healthy and calming inner dialogue if anxiety is provoked by reminiscences.

9.14 What Are the Antidotes to Violence's Consequences?

Friendship, comradery, and true love can be antidotes for most consequences of violence. Victims know this and frantically seek love to give meaning and value to their lives. Finding true love, having children, loving them, being loved by them, and protecting them may appear to be the only valid reasons to live. But the experience of true and mutual love is rare. This is partly due to avoidance behaviors: Mistrust, lack of confidence, social phobias, fear of sexuality, pregnancy, and birth, and fear of doing harm… all this makes it so intimate relations are feared or even avoided. All intense emotions, even positive ones, are perceived as dangerous, and victims move forward most often masked. Also, traumatic memory and dissociative symptoms upset and parasite relationships, feelings, and reactions. They are responsible for the feelings of inferiority and of never being able to be oneself, a horrible self-image, hypervigilance, insecurity, and a need to control everything, making total relaxation and trust impossible. Everything is scary, and they feel alone and unworthy of love, having no self-confidence and little confidence in their partner. Victims are likely to be unsure of their own feelings and unable to project themselves into the future. It is very difficult to be authentic, so they do too much or not enough, seeming to play a role but badly acting, overacting or underacting the part of best friend, faithful lover, perfect partner, loving and attentive mother, or protective husband and father.

The usual discourse about love, sexuality, and relationships between men and women, parents and children, is based on a patriarchal worldview with power relations, dishonest scripts, imposture, and illusion, all of which parasite any attempt at authenticity in, relationships and families. This discourse propagates the idea of "true love" and "a nice family" as masquerades and tends to strip away genuine selfhood through fabricating and imposing caricatures for everyone. In spite of all this, relations can be authentic if victims' partners are not put off by the many difficulties in getting close to victims. Partners must understand and be empathetic no matter what happens and never use domination. If they can tame the victim, maybe little by little, the victim can love and be loved.

But the road will be rough with many pitfalls due to a traumatic memory always ready to blow up in the face and put everything into question, plunging victims into a black hole that it is difficult to get out of. If the companion can stick with it, always there when needed and in the right way: Fair, authentic, loving, attentive, respectful, helping to understand and be capable of hearing oneself and moving forward step by step, maybe then this love relation will help victims to slowly start to reconstruct themselves. If the family we make works well, with respect for each other and true shared feelings, if our children seem balanced and happy, then maybe we can reassure ourselves and believe a little in happiness and our worth. But this happiness remains fragile and vulnerable so that the slightest failure, conflict, or painful event risks calling everything into question. This restarts the self-destructive mechanisms rooted in the deepest part of us, never fully dismantled because never really treated.

9.15 The Danger of Falling Under the Abuser's Influence

Most often, decent people with whom a quality relationship would be possible run away discouraged and intimidated by victims' resistance or are too respectful to persist. Or perhaps the victim will flee, too scared and incapable of committing and making a decision, too scared to find a family, remaining instead alone and full of despair. If not careful, a dangerous person will find victims, a predator who has seen their vulnerability and strengths and who will not give up but will break into their lives and destabilize and scare them into his arms. This is not, however, because victims don't realize what's going on. He succeeds in dissociating or "hypnotizing" victims into a state of anesthetization, and they let the rest happen, in a way. They say "yes" and try to persuade themselves that they love him. That is made easier by the state of dissociation that rapidly generates dependence and makes the victim think she has him "under her skin." She accumulates with him a new traumatic memory that is added to the old one, with a reservoir of immense distress that makes her still more vulnerable, lost, and incapable of confronting life. He has the power to anesthetize her by his presence since he dissociates her through his personality, his worrying behaviors, and his displaced, humiliating, and unfair statements.

Often victims' friends and family cannot stand this person or understand why she seems to love him. This further isolates her and puts her at his mercy. Once at this stage, even more severe violence can happen without the risk of the predator being exposed.

He can now do anything since the mind-bindings on his prey prevent her from fleeing. He has a dissociating drug and slave subject to him until the spell is broken, either because the violence went so far that her survival instinct kicked in, or because someone succeeded in persuading her to leave him.

Perhaps someone close to her, maybe one of her children, was also harmed this time, so she will leave him, a fortunate awakening from the nightmare. Hopefully, their paths won't cross again, or else a simple gaze or word could plunge the victim once again into dissociation and being under his control, which is the only immediate cure for the state of insurmountable stress in which his presence puts her. She is in a state of emotional indifference, depersonalization—as if hypnotized—to the great despair of those who care about her and try to protect and save her; they really do not understand.

To avoid encountering any aggressors, victims often stay alone in a secure and predictable universe where only the least dangerous emotional relationships are cultivated, which are uniquely friendships or perhaps turned toward pets, perceived as much less dangerous, more authentic, faithful, predictable, and manageable since they do not lie, manipulate, or take control. Child victims may have imaginary friends, dolls, and stuffed animals for their main company, that they can love without any risk and attribute feelings to, emulating the responsiveness and love that they need. They may even create an entire imaginary or virtual world.

Searching for love at all costs to heal oneself can mean real risks of constructing illusionary spaces in one's own mind. The one designated as a love object, partner, friend, child, or pet risks being instrumentalized and having to play an imposed role in a healing scene that they don't really understand. They will fail to play the role correctly, no matter how hard they try. They will be confronted with endless psychological hemorrhages in themselves or the one constructing the "ideal" relational scene. It will be disappointing and will not fill the void of distress due to childhood violence and the anguish of dramatic abandonment. They will have to manage these hemorrhages however they can. This parental-type role will make them feel eternally guilty and can put them in situations similar to that of the torturer in their past, their violent parents, and reactivate traumatic memory in their partner, who might have outbursts and be violent to them.

9.16 The Need for Specialized Care

Without specialized care, victims of violence survive in swinging back and forth between two positions. They might lose themselves by letting life pass them by to suffer the least possible. They disconnect from reality, dissociate, anesthetize, and are most often absent from themselves and in a parallel world. On the other hand, they might bravely try to advance on the minefield, taking significant risks and enormous physical, emotional, and mental effort to control or avoid dangerous situations. This costs much suffering and exhausting mental labor to analyze, connect, and constantly search for truth. They take the risk to love, create, plan, and fight to find themselves again and live authentic lives.

10

How to Care for Victims and Cure Traumatic Memory

ACCORDING TO ALICE MILLER (2006), effective therapy must help patients become aware of the painful, repressed history of their childhood through awakening their emotions and dreams so that they no longer fear the dangers that really did threaten them throughout childhood but that no longer pose any threat today. Patients no longer need to fear or subconsciously repeat what happened at their tenderest age, because they are now aware and, with the therapist, lucidly testify to what happened. Only then will they cease to treat themselves cruelly and stop accusing or harming themselves with all sorts of addictions. At that moment, they will have developed empathy for the child who suffered severely from their parents' behaviors. If dangers are present in their adult lives, they will be better armed to face them because they are now more capable of understanding and relativizing their old fears.

Victims are almost always abandoned without any specific care or treatment. The vast majority of violence, including the most serious acts such as murder attempts and rape, are not brought to justice. Victims are not identified, and their voices are not heard. Their families, neighbors, teachers, social workers, colleagues, and doctors don't hear or want to hear. Victims remain alone, their psycho-traumatic disorders putting them through a living hell.

DOI: 10.4324/9781003497516-11

10.1 The Great Struggle

In spite of the colossal effort victims deploy just to survive, they are the ones questioned about their behaviors, not their aggressors. They are criticized for the survival strategies they put in place. Avoidance strategies are viewed negatively, and they are told not to be so "shy." Their lack of motivation and inability to move forward and "confront" life, "fight" (when that's actually all they do), take initiative, be brave, or succeed are not tolerated. They are criticized for isolating themselves, refusing contact with others, not paying attention or concentrating, and taking refuge in dreams or activities (except ones with high social value such as studies, music, or sports).

As for their dissociative strategies, these are very negatively judged when they are addicted to drugs or alcohol. Risk behaviors are bitterly criticized and totally misunderstood. Victims are blamed for their psycho-traumatic symptoms. Children are blamed for their agitation, irritability, aggressivity, and incapacity to adapt to social norms and expectations. They are criticized for their eating and sleep disorders, bad grades, and attention deficits. Adults are blamed for being sad all the time, depressive, apathetic, scared, anxious, phobic, insomniac, fatigued, in pain, sick, unpleasant, frigid, and "eternal victims." They are told that they understand nothing about life, are incapable of doing anything or of self-control, and lack willpower.

The AIVI-IPSOS investigation on incest showed that on average, incest victims wait 16 years before telling anyone what happened, and in most cases (74%), it is the victims who take the initiative to speak out. In spite of all the symptoms they show, almost no one ever asks them simple and obvious questions: "What was done to you to put you in such a bad state? Did someone abuse you?" The victim could then tell about aggressions in the first person, and the investigation suggests that they can do this if asked (for 98% of them); it is thus essential to take a step toward them.

It is rare that victims succeed in finding someone who will listen. When victims do speak out, others avoid the issue (34% of cases, according to the AIVI-IPSOS study) or impose silence (19%); they also might question what victims say and call them liars (18%). When victims do succeed in pressing charges (or the authorities or other professionals report an incident), they start an exhausting process full of dead ends. Our 2015 IVSEA study showed that 83% of sexual violence victims were never protected or recognized. Victims must fight to be believed and recognized and for the perpetrator (who usually denies guilt) to be examined and judged. Doubt benefits the perpetrator, but victims rarely are given good faith. Police and judges do not know about psycho-traumatic mechanisms. Because of this, post-traumatic symptoms harm the credibility of victims rather than confirm it. These should be concordant elements of evidence or even proof because they are pathognomonic.

2011 was the year of patients' rights, but the majority of victims still lack appropriate and specific care, which is absolutely essential, and even receive "care" that is actually additional violence. At best, care employees do not know the mechanisms of psycho-trauma, hold false beliefs rife with stereotypes, or are indifferent, negligent, emotionally anesthetized, discriminatory, and have the intention to harm (dominate, manipulate, and destroy).

10.2 Re-Traumatizing Victims Under Pretext of Care

Care given to victims that only treats symptoms ignores abuse and violence. This makes it ineffective in the long term. The expression of traumatic memory is often misleading and means errors in diagnosis. This is due to the diverse manifestations of symptoms. Invasive examinations and useless surgery are sometimes performed, diagnoses that are prejudicial to victims stay with them (such as psychosis), and they are subject to long hospitalizations in isolation and heavy, disabling treatments. Often, psychiatric treatments are anesthetizing and dissociating, such as sedatives, shock treatment (increasingly used today), isolation, and constraint.

Violence used against people in crisis (reliving trauma as their traumatic memory flares up) is unfortunately "effective" in the short term because it leads to disjunction and emotional anesthetization that calm the person. It is, however, catastrophic because it retraumatizes victims and recharges their traumatic memory. Such "treatment" could include verbal violence (insults or degrading remarks), psychological violence (manipulation, threats), or physical violence (restraint, isolation, privation, cold showers).

Care, by definition, is given to those who are vulnerable, whether this is permanent or occasional. It could be due to a temporary illness, trauma, or pregnancy, or it could be constant, such as chronic illness, physical and mental disabilities, or dependence due to being a child or very old. Such vulnerability exposes patients to an increased risk of violence from caregivers, family, or other patients. Sexual violence committed by health workers, especially doctors, is much more frequent than people think. They are much denied and covered by the law of silence. The position of authority that a doctor has, the abuse of implicit confidence, and the pretense of a debt owed allow doctors to commit violence and emotionally trick patients so that they cannot refuse or defend themselves, just as with parent-child incest. In the United States, around 10% of doctors, psychiatrists, and psychologists have had sexual contact with their patients, and 89% of these relations were between a male professional and a female patient. (In France, no study has been done on this form of violence and its serious consequences on victims; we have no numbers.)

A disabled person is three times more at risk of being abused than an abled person. A Canadian study has shown that 40% of physically disabled women are sexually abused at least once in their lives and that 39–68% of mentally disabled women are sexually abused at least once before they turn 18! Abuse increases the isolation and difficulties that disabled people—especially women—face.

10.3 Violence Is a Public Health Crisis

Why is there no health policy that takes into account the impact of violence on people's health, when it is a major risk factor? The large-scale U.S. ACE Study, with over 17,000 respondents, showed that violence in childhood is one of the main determining factors of health 50 years later (Felitti, 2004). It is urgent to develop a serious policy of public health regarding violence and protect all victims, giving them quality care by trained, accessible, and affordable specialists. Health professionals must be trained in prevention, detection, and treatment, with health centers that victims can access near where they live. There needs to be campaigns for information and prevention, more investigations and research on the subject, and the creation of major national and international organizations to study violence, its impact, and how to care for victims.

10.4 What Resources for Victims?

Victims need access to resources, and what is now offered is far from adequate. For several years, there has been some efforts in police and medical departments with specialists in violence, psychologists, and informative brochures on victims' rights created by France's Delegation for Women's Rights and Centers for Information on Women and Families, as well as the National Federation of Assistance for Victims, Feminist Collective to End Rape (CFCV), the European Organization Against Violence toward Women in the Workplace (AVFT), the World through a Gaze, which publishes a preventative booklet on incest and pedocriminality, the organization Traumatic Memory, and others. All these organizations have websites. National hotlines are active in France, 119 or 39-19, as well as free numbers for raped women and shelters for women victims of violence (though for minors, specific centers for care and shelter are rare). In the United States, RAINN has a sexual assault hotline (1-800-656-4673) and an online chat.

But government organizations do little to provide information to the public. As long as health professionals are in the dark about psycho-trauma and there are few centers for specific care, large actions in favor of the government funding for prevention and treatment are unlikely to succeed. There is almost no specific training on the mechanisms of psycho-trauma for any professionals (medical, social, or judiciary). Political effort is required to no longer abandon victims of violence without proper care. Benefits to the quality of life, health, education, and full social and professional participation would be so great that the cost of creating centers for care and training professionals would be very small in comparison.

10.5 Specialized Treatment

Care for victims—and this is essential—must be compassionate and empathetic. The victim must be protected, comforted, and surrounded with concern. It is important that all professionals be specifically trained and work together as a network.

In emergencies, victims need to be rescued, protected, kept safe, and comforted. They need help, information on their rights and on what to do next, and guidance about traumatic consequences and necessary care. It is essential that they not be left alone and that they can talk about the violence to trustworthy people, including from specialized organizations, health, social, and legal professions, and police and government officials.

Rape is a medical and judiciary emergency 24/7 because it requires medical and psychological care urgently for prevention (HIV, Hepatitis B and C, pregnancy), and legal medical examination to establish a medical certificate confirming the violence and evidence (samples, traces of violence). Some of this care and search for evidence need to be done as soon as possible, within the 48–72 hours following the rape. It is also necessary that victims know not to wash and to keep in a paper or cloth bag any clothing or objects that might help identify the rapist through DNA.

The earlier specialized care is given the more effective it is, and it can even avoid the onset of traumatic memory (in the 12 hours following the violence) and psycho-traumatic disorders by helping victims recover from the state of tonic immobility and dissociation. The health provider's role (or that of another professional or loved one) is to be a lucid witness who is active, comforting, and protective. They offer their cortical and emotional functioning to the victim, who is momentarily paralyzed and disconnected from her own emotional circuitry. This can involve a sort of mental resuscitation by diminishing stress and preventing traumatic damage through restoring meaning and coherence so that the thought process can start again. The therapist must translate into words, as accurately as possible, the reality of the traumatic experience and its effects. She must reintroduce meaning and coherence into what was unthinkable to get the victim's mind beyond the tonic immobility that paralyzes it and blocks all control and cortical treatment of sensory and emotional information. The elaboration of accurate mental images of the traumatic experience, violence, and intentionality of the aggressor are necessary to allow the memory to be encoded and thus avoid the onset of traumatic memory.

The treatment is essentially psychotherapy, but the priority for sexual violence victims is for them to be safe and to avoid new violence, as well as suicide attempts and to medically treat stress, mental anguish, and anxio-depressive symptoms from which the victim suffers. This will avoid the onset of traumatic memory while identifying and treating dissociating risk behaviors.

The specialized psychotherapy must be joined by a solid treatment plan with general and specialized doctors working together as a network of professionals trained in the consequences of stress, psycho-trauma, and treatment of addictions and eating disorders. To calm mental suffering and anxio-depressive symptoms, psychotropic treatment can temporarily be used (painkillers, tranquilizers, and antidepressants). These dim emotional responses, but it is important that they not cause emotional anesthetization and disinhibition. Physical therapy, relaxation techniques, and energy work can be beneficial forms of parallel treatment.

To avoid rising levels of stress (and of adrenaline) that can become too much (flaring up traumatic memory), victims can get a prescription for preventative beta-blockers (propranolol). This has the advantages of protecting the heart from stress and making the patient feel safe enough to do the psychotherapy, bringing calm and diminishing survival strategies (avoidance, control, and dissociation).

It is always necessary to treat more than the symptoms. Specialized psychotherapy is also needed. It is even more necessary to avoid using treatments that are dissociating and anesthetizing such as sedatives and heavy neuroleptics, shock therapy, and amphetamines (used to calm hyperactive children). The principle of specific therapeutic treatment consists of recognizing, analyzing, and denouncing violence and helping victims to make connections, understand what they are going through, and realize that the abuser fully intended to harm them and why (based on his own traumatic memory). A clear separation is drawn between what is traumatic in the perpetrator and how that infests the traumatic memory of the victim. The goal is to de-mine and dismantle traumatic memory progressively (preventative treatments for overdoses of stress can be used while waiting for the effects of psychotherapy to work).

The psychotherapy consists of formulating words and making connections, giving victims meaning so they can find their dignity and authenticity again while relieving their suffering, anxiety, and constant tension. It also sets victims free from feelings of shame and guilt and symbolically delivers the child or adult held prisoner of a violent past. It reintegrates this person into a life that regains its rightful course and meaning. The therapist helps the victim throughout this long path, tracing all violence endured and all abandonment, sharing her emotions and allowing her to identify them better, getting angry for her, opposing incoherent farces from the aggressor's system, and reintroducing rights, coherence, and respect for human dignity.

This specialized treatment also allows for neurological damage that occurred during the violence to be repaired (we observed neuronal and dendritic regrowth after loss of up to 30% of neurons in some brain structures such as the hippocampus or frontal cortex); cognitive disorders can be healed (memory, concentration, and attention); addictive avoidance and dissociating behaviors disappear because they become useless when traumatic memory no longer flares up (is de-mined) or shuts off again easily (is disarmed); less medical attention is needed because the cause of the problem is treated and not only the symptoms.

10.6 Psychotherapy Centered on Traumatic Memory

Specialized treatment of traumatized victims is centered on the traumatic memory of violence. It is above all psychotherapeutic. The earlier in life violence happened, the more victims were required to construct themselves with feelings and sensations of terror and perverse actions and words. They had to fight these without understanding and were unable to find the line between themselves and traumatic memory. Traumatic memory haunts them, takes possession, and prevents them from being themselves. Worse, it makes them believe that they are double: Dr. Jekyll and Mr. Hyde, or even triple: A normal person (which they are), someone worthless and guilty that they are ashamed of and who deserves to die (who the aggressor pretended they were and they internationalized), and a person who could become violent and perverse and therefore must constantly control and self-censor (the abuser in them, confused with self). Such psychotherapy frees victims from traumatic memory and dissociative processes so that who they really are can again express itself and simply live (Van der Hart, 2010). This liberation is accomplished by identifying traumatic memory and then shutting it off or diminishing it little by little. The identification of traumatic memory is done through understanding its mechanisms and recognizing all its parasitic and destructive manifestations: Emotions, sensations, thoughts, behaviors, and symptoms. The undoing depends on repairing and controlling traumatic memory as soon as it flares up to prevent it from invading the mind. Mine-removal consists of transforming traumatic memory into autobiographical memory, which is a more stable means of finally getting rid of and breaking free from it. The victim confronts the violence again so she can put it into words and connect the mental representation of violence with all the emotions she feels and therefore reconnect the emotional circuitry with the cortex. This de-mining work finally allows the hippocampus to integrate the traumatic memory by transforming it into conscious, autobiographical memory and making it useless to set off safety mechanisms of disjunction.

10.7 Reassure, Listen, and Explain

The therapist must reassure the victim that she is not alone, that she is no longer in danger, and that her reactions during and after the violence were normal. It is necessary to name and explain these reactions: Fright, emotional shock, tonic immobility, paralysis, dissociation, and emotional anesthetization. It is also necessary to recognize and precisely name the violence that occurred, remind victims of their rights, condemn and be enraged, and state that it is very serious and the perpetrator had no right to do it. Nothing the victim did or didn't do, said or didn't say, could justify the aggression. The traumatic memory of the perpetrator functions as an endless torture that stages the dehumanization of the victim and her reduction to a worthless object that the perpetrator can dirty and destroy, leading up to the idea that the victim doesn't deserve to live and should feel shame and guilt. Everything is false and incoherent, but the imposed role-play is integrated and, virus-like, infects the mind of the victim through the intermediary of trauma. The victim sees herself through the perverse, deforming mirror of the perpetrator and his violence, and she feels guilty and shameful. She scorns and hates herself, considering herself as having no worth and no rights, someone only good for harming, humiliating, destroying, and throwing away, just like a piece of garbage. A young patient who was an incest victim in childhood wrote to me when her distress was unbearable: "I'm even going to vomit on my head to prove to myself that I'm nothing but a shitty piece of barf and this is all I deserve—I hate myself worse than the Nazis—I don't know what to do anymore with my shitty ugly face—I'll take a knife and slit my wrists. Keel over! Die! I want to burn alive, to blow myself up, to kill, scar, torture, and hit myself, to tear out my hair. I haaaaaate you, die, slut, bitch, good for nothing..." And after she scarred herself: "That's what you deserve!! I deserve nothing more poor bitch, slut, idiot!" It was the abuser who, through her traumatic memory, was speaking to her and torturing her again.

The therapist has to get involved in setting things straight and putting coherence where there was none. She must speak out against the violations of the victim's rights and dignity

("It's very serious. No one had any right to do that to you, and it's punishable by law; it's a crime. You can press charges.") The therapist also needs to tell the victim what should have happened so that rights and justice were respected. This is important because the abuser's system has confused all the norms, especially when the violence recurred over a long period of time and if the victim was very young. The therapist must reveal that the perpetrator did this on purpose and shed light on his strategies, lies, and acting. The behaviors, gestures, and phrases of the abuser are to be collected and analyzed to show the manipulative and stereotypical character of it all. It is essential to show that the aggressor sought above all—deliberately—to do the most harm possible. This had nothing to do with the victim personally—victims are totally interchangeable, as long as they belong to a group that is compatible with the imposed role (woman, child, vulnerable, or racialized person). The abuser uses a pre-made script taken from his own history and supported by stereotypes that he reuses for the occasion and that have nothing to do with the victim. Nothing is true; it is all a lie and a farce, whether insults, venomous words, or compliments and destabilizing statements of love, which are an additional destructive strategy to get the victim's guard down and let in some hope, to make the subsequent assault more brutal.

The therapist must be capable of fully hearing and believing the victim's suffering. She must be aware of how difficult it is to talk about it. The victim's terror, despair, guilt, and urge to die must all be taken into consideration, and the therapist must reassure the victim that it is normal to feel so badly after all the violence she endured. The victim breaks the law of silence and the loyalty that was imposed on her as well as the threats that she might have received. She faces the risk of her traumatic memory exploding and the overwhelming distress this would entail. She must find the right words to represent her truths in spite of doubts and confusion about what happened stemming from her dissociative disorders, memory impairments, and faulty spatiotemporal orientation. It is necessary to ask the right questions and encourage her to speak so that she can allow herself to do so. It's also necessary to recognize her suffering to calm her better, and especially to seek to understand her and respect her needs (to speak or to be silent, to take more or less distance) and to really listen to her and not dismiss any of her thoughts or reactions. It is absolutely necessary to analyze with precision everything that happened and explain it constantly, recalling all the statements and emotions internalized from the aggressor, by force or manipulation through shame ("you love it, you little slut"), guilt ("you asked for it—you made me do it—you aroused me"), the feeling of being reduced to nothing, worth nothing, and only a thing that others can do what they want with, when they want, and so on. The therapist can always show that these are manufactured randomly and make no sense, so that they can be removed from victims' minds and stop colonizing them.

The therapist must give the victim tools to understand her emotions, sensations, and reactions by explaining the neurobiological mechanisms of traumatic memory and its consequences. It is also necessary to explain how treatment works, why it is necessary, its efficacy, and everything they need to know in terms of resources, organizations, and things they can do.

10.8 The Therapist's Duties

Any scorn, judgment, trivialization, denial, or moralizing goes against the victim and is another, additional violence. Victims must not be abandoned and condemned to silence. For victims, feeling protected, supported, understood, and not alone is already huge. To not be alone, to have their suffering recognized, to share emotions with someone able to get angry on their behalf—these are absolutely necessary to begin the healing process and be able to give up survival strategies accumulated since the violence began. Solid and adapted support, even if it is not medical care, is therapeutic in itself.

The priority is to stop the violence and make sure the victim is safe, using the law, and then giving information and explanations about psychological and neurobiological mechanisms of psychotrauma so that victims understand what happens to them and have a toolbox to better protect and care for themselves. They can be guided toward specialized care centers with doctors trained in psycho-traumatology. Then the healing can begin: Relieving the mental anguish as a priority, then helping to avoid dissociating behaviors and identify traumatic memory that takes the form of mines that need to be located, then patiently de-mine them by reestablishing neurological connections. This means making connections and reintroducing mental representations for each manifestation of traumatic memory.

The issue is "repairing" the initial psychological damage and the mental immobility linked to the irrepresentability of violence. This is responsible for the first mental shutdown that made the brain incapable of controlling the emotional response, and the overload of stress, disjunction, and installation of dissociation and traumatic memory. This repair work is about revisiting the lived experience of violence, this time accompanied by a professional mine-remover, with the safety of a specifically trained and caring professional. If necessary, medication can be given in addition to this. The goal is that the lived trauma can be integrated little by little through becoming more representable and understandable. This involves putting words to every situation, behavior, and emotion, and correctly analyzing and contextualizing reactions and behaviors of the aggressor. This profound analysis allows the associative brain and hippocampus to regain control over reactions from the cerebral amygdala and encode emotional traumatic memory to transform it into autobiographical memory that is conscious and controllable: The ultimate goal of therapy.

10.9 Cortico-Limbic Reconnection

The goal of traumatic memory–centered therapy is to never give up trying to understand everything and give it meaning. Every symptom, nightmare, and behavior that is not recognized as coherent with who you fundamentally are, and any incongruous thoughts, reactions, or sensations must be dissected and linked back to their origins. This sheds light on the violence endured through making connections. For example, bottomless despair that surges in spite of everything seeming to go well is linked to a reactivation of traumatic memory set off by a link with the violence, such as a significant date, gesture, or physical contact that can seem harmless. It makes the victim relive the violence in some way, such as having a period, when the sight of blood could subconsciously remind her of being raped, just as having her neck squeezed by a scarf or turtleneck can recall strangulation. A certain smell might make you nauseous and want to vomit because it reminds you of the aggressor, and a pain might make you panic because it is like that felt during an aggression. A sound might be unbearable and full of anguish because you heard it during the violence, such as the sound of rain if it was raining. A time of day could be routinely anguishing and lead to alcohol consumption, bulimic episodes, suicidal tendencies, or self-mutilation; it is the time of day when the aggression happened. A feeling of irritation, tickling, or heating of the genital region not connected to what is actually happening can recall being molested. "Sexual fantasies" that are violent and disturbing, that the victim doesn't want but that can impose themselves on her mind, are in reality traumatic reminiscences of rapes or sexual aggressions.

Quickly, this work of cortico-limbic reconnection becomes automatic and allows victims to make the world around them feel safer. During the flaring up of traumatic memory, the cortex can then control the emotional response and calm the distress, making the use of risk situations to gain (spontaneous or provoked) disjunction unnecessary. The victim becomes an expert mine-remover and continues the work alone. As traumatic memory discharges more and more, the feeling of permanent danger dissipates.

Each manifestation of traumatic memory is to work through and understand, working backward through a chain of associations. All symptoms, panic attacks, feelings of despair, harmful thoughts, addictions, compulsions, and risk behaviors are brought to light and become less and less scary. They appear logical, coherent, and predictable, therefore much easier to control. The person in therapy can reassure herself: She is not going crazy; her suffering makes sense and is legitimate, and what is happening in her is coherent and can be managed. If she is suddenly invaded by a flashback with unbearable distress, she can tell herself that a situation or sensation is at the origin and seek to find what set it off. This seeking is in itself a protection that avoids tonic immobility and generates cortical control that calms the feeling of panic. This calming can be obtained rapidly through a few therapy sessions, as with the 12-year-old girl who was abused by a brother ten years older. He no longer lived with her, but she was struck several times each day by flashbacks and feelings of panic and distress. After having understand the mechanisms of traumatic memory at work, she proudly announced at our third session that she had succeeded in blocking several flashbacks and avoiding any feelings of discomfort and anxiety. She succeeded in identifying immediately the origin of the reminiscence after stumbling on a family album while cleaning her room, or after being in a waiting room with a family that had a little girl and older brother.

If a victim suddenly feels compelled to harm herself, put herself in danger, drink, take drugs, or overeat, it is essential to immediately find what could be the cause and identify the association that set it off in order to control it more effectively. A 57-year-old patient who routinely got drunk every evening at 5:00 realized that that was the time her uncle sexually abused her, between the time she got home from elementary school and when her mother returned from work. A 30-year-old patient self-mutilated every Friday night and then had terrifying nightmares. At age seven, she was raped with acts of torture by a camp counselor on the last night of camp, a Friday. A 40-year-old patient panicked at the idea of being away from her mother for even a day, invaded by a feeling of strangulation and incapable of taking any food; she was mistreated and force-fed at age three by a nanny hired for several weeks when her mother went abroad to visit her husband. A ten-year-old boy who anxiously verified several times that the windows and doors were locked before going to bed was a witness at age four to his father trying to throw his mother out of the window.

Awareness of how traumatic memory functions allows patients to not adhere to the negative emotions, perceptions, sensations, invading compulsions, or denigrating phrases. Instead, they link these to the violent past. These manifestations of traumatic memory become for the patient an alarm that reminds her of past violence. It is enough to identify it to stomp it out. A good-looking patient, each time she saw herself in the mirror, found herself ugly and spat: "you are a fat cow, my poor girl, look at your head, you are so ugly it's scaring me!" With psychotherapy, she finally succeeded in seeing herself as she really was and not as her parents pretended she was during her childhood. She began to react right away when she'd look at herself in the mirror and find herself ugly by saying: "What's going on? Why is this statement of my parents coming back?" In seeking what could set off her traumatic memory, she found: Recent contact with family, a date corresponding to a family celebration, or a place. Having identified the toxic parental discourse and the link that reactivated it allowed her to reestablish her own interior discourse and find a present liberated from the traumatic past, which gave her a true feeling of freedom.

To do all this work of emotional reconnection, it is necessary to be the most precisely aware possible of what was endured. This is not easy, since violence is often subject to lacunary, neurological, and survival amnesia. There are also doubts cultivated by the silence and lies of abusers, and emotional and bodily anesthetization that trivializes violence. It is necessary to reestablish truth, find out what really happened, recognize the seriousness of the facts, get the law involved, and also reconstitute evidence and clues gathered in the psychotherapy. Emotional reactions, the intensity of suffering, the symptoms, the nightmares... all these are clues that can be attentively studied in order to allow scenes of the past to appear. Knowledge of this traumatic past improves through this work, thanks to the constant back and forth between precise memories of the patient that shed light on current symptoms and what is discovered about her past through studying symptoms. There is a back-and-forth between mental recognition and emotional recognition, which allows for step-by-step validation of the story in which the patient recognizes herself more and more. Each piece of the puzzle of traumatic events is put in place until the image of the past is finally clear and whole, and representations and emotions are finally reunited to give a feeling of rediscovered truth. This moment allows the patient and the therapist to be aware of witnesses and rescuers so that the terrorized victim encysted in the traumatic past can symbolically be found and reassured. The patient finds unity and liberation from her traumatic past and the colonizing presence of the aggressor.

As long as victims remain ignorant of the past, they cannot fully recognize the suffering endured or understand its consequences. The ghost-victim trapped in that past remains alone, abandoned, and outside the world of the living.

10.10 Collaborating with Loved Ones

Throughout therapy, it is important that those close to the victim and other professionals work together to assist victims by giving tools that allow them to better understand the mechanisms of psycho-traumatic disorders. This also allows them to actively participate in finding and identifying traumatic memory due to their status as witnesses of it or knowledge of current symptoms they are confronted with every day and that they can describe and help us analyze. This participation also allows them to feel less anxious and lost when faced with the reactions of their traumatized loved ones. It allows them to have more adapted behaviors and the victims feel less alone and misunderstood. This is in addition to adequate medical, social, and legal help and contact with victims' organizations.

10.11 Other Treatments

Other psychotherapeutic treatments have been successful, such as behavioral and cognitive therapies. These are useful for treating phobias and obsessional disorders that invade and disable victims, and some behavior disorders (Foa, 2012). Until specific therapy is more widely available, EMDR (Eye Movement Desensitization Reprocessing) is a therapeutic method created by Francine Shapiro. It consists of using rapid eye movements to reduce through soft dissociation the negative charge of associations due to traumatic memory and better integrate them. However, these useful therapies must be associated with more overall psychotherapy treating traumatic memory, and it is important to be careful that they are not dissociating.

Lifespan Integration by Peggy Pace is a technique for reabsorption of dissociative and post-traumatic disorders. It reintegrates all the aspects of self-dissociated by traumatic memory. Systemic therapies help with awareness of the context at the origin of violence and better understand how they are played out again. Psychoanalytic therapies should be used wisely and centered on the violence. In any case, the therapist should be considerate, ethical, and positioned strongly against violence, making connections and helping piece together the victim's shattered world. For incest, transgenerational analysis and investigation of family secrets sheds light on which parental models incestuous sexual violence is based on and originates from (Le Dréau, 2011). Whether the therapists are medical doctors, psychologists, or others, they must be trained in psycho-traumatology and center their care on violence and traumatic memory.

Energy work and physical therapy can also be of precious help (when associated with overall treatment of traumatic memory) to find how traumatic memory is expressed in the body and help with emotional reconnection in the body, reembodying the victim to find a bodily model free of violence and farce, and a representation of their own body that is no longer that of the aggressor, so that they can reinvest their own body and reinhabit it. These practices are useful to handle outbreaks of stress through relaxation techniques.

Art therapies (drawing, painting, sculpting, crafts) and therapies through singing, mime, theater, dance, and writing (novels, stories, testimonies, poems) are useful for expressing emotions of trauma endured and recreating meaning through creation, as well as discovering one's hidden talents and unimagined abilities in a way that is safe.

For traumatized children, play therapy is important, with tools such as game boxes that can help children verbalize and act out their trauma as well as construct their own emotions.

10.12 In a Victim's Own Words

Written for the conference on sexual violence held by the organization Traumatic Memory, November 10, 2010:

November 7, 2010, three days before this conference and still nothing: impossible write anything, as fall is always a difficult season for me, and then suddenly this need to speak out, scream, and bear witness.

I am a little boy, 8 years old, and my mother "the old witch" as I call her ever since I knew, uses by fingers and mouth for her pleasure in her bed, and has already been doing this for several years.

It is so hard to say this—victims always feel alone, dirty, and guilty.

Here we go: that has been going on a long time already—now I'm 11 or 12, and that autumn

Suddenly, she raped me with an object in my anus and left me half-dead after strangling me with her hands.

Alone in the room, on the floor against a table, my anus hurts, and the air enters with difficulty into my lungs. I want to go back in time to just before I passed out from her squeezing my neck—that calmed the pain.

I couldn't just stay there. I had to move and get the object out of my anus, then put my underwear back on, tuck in my shirt, move, and above all not cry, not cry… get up to go where?

In the next room, she is there, back turned, and the air weighs a ton. I go into a corner. She turns and her gaze is of rage, insanity, death, and threat. In any case, nothing happened; the child is dead. Tomorrow, he will forget everything: post-traumatic amnesia.

The child is dead. The man is 50 years old. He met women, he loved, and a little girl was born. His most recent partner suspected the unspeakable and insisted that he get help. For the past 15 years, he's been in therapy, since in spite of the love that's there, their relationship has been disappointing.

The man is 50 years old, and since the child died, he lives outside of his life. Since he's started examining himself, he feels there are things he really doesn't want to know that are beyond words and even more frightening than death. These things stab him in the heart, grab his soul, and destroy him physically. The truth emerges.

What I'm telling you is commonplace. This destruction of self, this anguish in the body, this rotting of the soul, this doubling, this absence, this solitude, this physical pain without explanation, this unease with sexuality... all incest victims experience these.

Survival or suicide—that's often the only decision to make. Real living disappeared, but we must never, ever give up. I have to fight—to fight against the big mess, the incredible disorder that the wicked witch made of me.

When the amnesia disappeared, it was horrible...

I couldn't even see life anymore, the pathways of possibility being cut off, nothing left but void and insanity. So many times, I wanted to ask my therapist to have me institutionalized...

And then, as more and more pieces were put together, my strength came back. I had to choose between love and nothingness, hope or anguish, passion for life or nothing, and I chose life, love, and hope.

I don't lead a peaceful life, but it has flavor. It is not the love of a simple heart—everything is complicated, delicate, fragile! And hope in all this? It's often despair but it's experienced as happiness: *to live in spite of it all!*

All of you women and men, organizations, therapists, social workers, judges, lawyers, and police officers who listen to us and help to liberate us from our personal prison, and for all victims of incest—the triple murder of innocence, the soul, and our body's intimacy—I want to give you a message of hope:

These horrible things from our childhood are the messy canvas on the easel of our sad story. Give us the strength to look at them and to show them and we become the hand, brush, and colors of the artist. Finally, we can have a future full of light that will allow us to make the painting come alive.

Without all of you who listen to us and seek to change society's tolerance of intimate violence, our lives as victims would stay old snowballs that are dirty and muddy, bleeding under the sun.

The words of victims only exist if heard. And then, from being painful, they become rich with promise. Thank you!

Conclusion

THE HORRIFIC STATISTICS on sexual violence and the severity of its consequences on health and quality of life for victims show at what point it is a major social and public health problem. Current knowledge about the neurobiological mechanisms of violence gives us tools to fight against it, prevent it, and protect and care for victims. It is scandalous that the majority of victims, in spite of the remarkable work of many organizations, are still abandoned without help, justice, or appropriate care. This is above all a political problem.

We still live in a profoundly unequal world, in spite of progress toward greater equality in Western societies. There are too many who cling to their privileges, including the exorbitant privilege of committing acts of violence and even rape. In democratic societies, these privileges are disguised as freedom, love, childrearing, sexuality... It is necessary to speak out against this falsification. These ideals must always take into consideration rights to the dignity and mental and physical well-being of others and never take it as a "natural right" to possess, consume, or instrumentalize another person. This includes possessing a child, partner, body... Spheres such as the family, couple, love, and sex should not entail giving up fundamental human rights and should not be totalitarian realms with privileges that transgress these. To paraphrase Orwell, "War is peace, freedom is slavery, ignorance is strength." We can apply this confusion of words and totalitarian vision to what happens in many families and couples, and in the spheres of love and sex: "love is hatred, freedom is slavery, pain is pleasure, transgression is law, crime is happiness!"

Some people self-proclaim above ordinary mortals due to their power, wealth, supposed intelligence, and worth because they are artists, stars, athletes, politicians, and warriors: They

DOI: 10.4324/9781003497516-12

have access to privileges and can choose not to submit to the same laws as everyone else. Worlds beyond law are thus created, in which violence is a necessary tool to feed the illusion of all-powerfulness and where people designated as inferior are chosen to be forcefully enrolled in this masquerade of power. The omnipotence is such a lie that it must endlessly use more and more transgressive scenarios, consuming an increasing number of victims to continue.

Freedom can only flourish where the rights of all are guaranteed and universal. These universal rights, when respected, are a powerful protection against violence. In the absence of fundamental rights to dignity and wholeness, consent is not a conceptual tool sufficient to define if there is violence or not. Consent of a person to give up their rights, to be killed, harmed, sequestered, tortured, humiliated, contaminated, enslaved... that would not be acceptable. The eroticization of hatred, domination, and submission would not be tolerated. A society that recognizes universal human rights should make the political decision not to tolerate any violence and to rescue and assist all victims, protecting, caring for, and giving justice to them.

To fight against violence and its transmission from person to person and generation to generation, it is time to guarantee equal rights to everyone. It is also time for "psychological wounds" of violence victims and their neurobiological reality be finally recognized, understood, addressed, and treated. It is now time to finally consider these wounds as the logical consequences of intentionally harmful acts perpetrated with the goal of generating the most possible suffering in victims and deliberately orchestrate trauma in them that is useful for the aggressor to anesthetize himself and uphold his domination. It is time for victims to finally be rescued, protected, and supported. It is time to have solidarity with victims and be angry about what they endured, denouncing the perpetrators. It is time to give victims back their dignity and worth, which the aggressor denied them. It is time to give them justice and care.

Today, all this is possible, thanks to progress in recognition of violence and understanding of psycho-traumatic mechanisms. I truly hope to contribute with my own research to the articulation of how traumatic memory corresponds with a range of behaviors used to escape it, such as control and avoidance behaviors, usually not identified by care providers, and the risk behaviors previously seemed paradoxical, which I have named dissociative behaviors. Once these psycho-traumatic consequences are understood, they can be treated effectively. The psychological, neurobiological, and self-treating responses make sense and follow a predictable, consistent pattern. It is therefore possible to liberate victims so they are no longer colonized by the aggressor and the violence. They can find their rightful path and place again, once again safe and in harmony with themselves in their mind, body, and life.

This recent knowledge can be used as a tool for primary, secondary, and tertiary prevention, showing how the struggle against all forms of violence and not tolerating any of it, including the forms usually shrouded in silence, such as those under pretext of love, childrearing, and sexuality. Identifying, protecting, and healing all victims, especially children who were victims or witnesses to sexual violence, has a considerable impact in avoiding the onset of new violence while preserving the health of these children short, middle, and long-term. It is essential to spread the information as much as possible to everyone and gain training for all professionals who might be in contact with victims. I hope that this book can participate in this effort and help pave the way for better justice for victims and denunciation of stereotypes and false representations of violence and of victims, along with general complicity or compliance with the law of might makes right. It is time that the fundamental rights of every human be respected.

A

Appendices

A.1 A Victim's Letter to Professionals Working with Victims of Violence

November 2012: "I've been a victim of physical, psychological, and sexual violence as a child and adult, and it is as a victim that I address you today. We, the victims of childhood and adult violence, are usually unseen and said to be silent, but that is false—it's totally false. When we try to speak out, no one listens. They are afraid of us and what we might say, and they quickly shut us down. But we speak out anyway, a lot, through our behaviors and our bodies, yet we are not understood. Instead, we are judged about what we are and how we are. We end up thinking we are not normal, not really part of the human race; we are outside the world, shut up in our homes, in front of our computers, and we slink along the walls to avoid your gaze. Of course, sometimes we succeed in pretending to live like you live. We can smile, be polite, and share a fleeting moment of joy, but we are only pretending. We are not living; we are just surviving with our pain and suffering inside, in a solitude that you cannot imagine.

Yes, you try to help us. You talk about us—for us—and you tell what we go through, what we feel. You try to think for us, but you don't reach us; you don't ask us what we need, and we are not included in your decision-making or your information campaigns. Your world is not accessible to us. Very few doors are open for victims of violence, really very few, and these doors are only partially opened and can close in front of us at any moment, without any particular reason. Our lives are difficult. We've endured so many inhuman situations that we live in hell.

A simple word in a conversation with you switches our brains and makes us live through violence again in our body and mind while we listen to you. We lose all means and cannot communicate in a normal way, and you don't understand or stop following. This can also happen with a noise, gesture, smell, place, or object. This is real torture, so we shut ourselves up in our houses. It's very hard to go out and try to communicate with you.

We need true solidarity from society and full respect as human beings just like you. We need support so that we can start living and not only surviving. There is some help available, such as hotlines, addresses, and websites, but we can't always access these. Some of us have no phones, are uncomfortable writing an email to an unknown person, or cannot go out for a meeting with a professional for safety reasons, to avoid reliving violence in mind and body and because all our energy goes into our inner struggle to survive. But we can, from our homes, read, write, and exchange in secure spaces. We can do that.

We need a specialized platform on the internet for victims of all ages and all types of violence, for information and exchange, where every victim belongs. There should be specialists who converse with us openly and reassuringly and also a space for victims only. This is terribly lacking.

We need the media to get involved in spreading awareness of the psycho-traumatic consequences of violence and the mechanisms of traumatic memory. This is necessary for victims to understand ourselves and no longer think we are crazy, panic when our brains switch, or feel guilty when we seem to behave strangely. We also need others to understand us so that we are no longer ashamed to be victims.

We urgently need professionals who are easy to reach, respectful, and trained in psycho- traumatology, so that we can get real treatment. This involves more than just moral support. And we don't need them to tell us we are the problem or that it's about our personalities. Too much of the "care," when offered at all, is a disaster, and we don't want that anymore. We need to be taken seriously and respected by medical, social, police, legal, and state institutions. Our rights must be real and not simply words on paper.

Finally, education in respecting other's bodies seems necessary to us. However, this education must begin with a law that forbids, without any hesitation or exception, any violence committed against the bodies of infants, babies, children, teens, and young people: a law that makes it illegal for parents to use physical punishment on their children's bodies. When children are finally respected in their bodies and spirits, they will respect the bodies and spirits of others, no problem. Thank you for your attention."

A.2 Excerpt from the Play "Solinge" by Pia Divoka

The following is an excerpt from the play Solinge by Pia Divoka, staged during the conference on sexual violence held by the organization Traumatic Memory and Victim's Rights on November 10, 2010.

> Delphine just moved in and Ludile hasn't come yet. The building is 10 meters away. She opens the glass door of the hall. The new smell contrasts that of the street. She wrinkles her nose. She presses the door phone button. No one. Of course. She turns to leave. A man is there. He says: "I forgot my keys… would she please, the young lady, press the button? A woman's voice would work better, right?" She presses a random button. A voice answers her and the door clicks open. At the same moment, when she hears the click, Ludile's senses freeze. She is only 20 and just realizes she made a terrible mistake.

The metal of the blade is cold on the skin of the neck. A lack of saliva is added to the freezing of the vocal chords. In any case, the insane look of the man holding the knife against her leaves her no choice but to be silent. The pressure of the blade removes the small amount of sound with which she could have said no.

In her late 20s, she is fragile and she stumbles. She hasn't known fear, not much, not right there, unexpected, that is meaningless, she is meeting with her friends that she's with every day for so many years her legs don't carry her anymore she can't get past it she tries to reason with herself not him there's no reason in her gaze she repeats it's not real not real not real not real not real not real not real…

She doubles over and is close to fainting. The man yells that it's not time for that. The situation if violently unreal, because she's never heard of it before.

It has no connection with reality, this intolerable contact of the blade. The man pushes her to the other side. The other side of the glass door.

The smell of detergent is even stronger. Two doors. That of the elevator and the other. He acts quickly.

He talks quickly. Makes no sense. He tears off her pink plastic watch and her not heavy purse. Her earrings that she made herself and her ring, a souvenir from Brittany.

Nothing else…

Can she leave now?

The man panics. With his free hand, that isn't holding the knife against her throat, he grabs the handle of the second door, which opens to the stairs leading to the basement.

He starts a stopwatch that begins to tick. Time stops.

The brain searches. This resembles nothing and goes beyond all understanding. The insanity read in the stranger's eyes forbids any communication. No possible escape. Total submission.

Forced intrusion into intimacy. Total annihilation of being… Destruction of soul.

Ludile knows "right hand or left hand?" but what to answer when he asks which of your breasts he should cut.

The game is rigged. No, it's not a game when there are no rules… He is in full hallucination.

The threat is so great that the only possibility for survival is to disconnect everything. Short- circuit.

Whack! right on the skull.

He doesn't follow through to the end of his arm, his hand, his gesture.

He stops and gets annoyed skin too white neck too smooth, at the too-smooth breast. He doesn't go all the way into his insanity. He impales her with his penis and keeps his knife grazing her neck. And she, she, she, she is without herself. She is finished, fragile, taboo, immobile, and useless.

In 4 letters.

It's just like in the movies but without the music. Ludile thinks about it right then but the painful red wound screams out all else. In a fog of teeth and tongue not really hers and a voice that she doesn't recognize she hears herself say, "Don't kill me." (…)

She is dead now.

"Don't kill me" she remembers whispering.

Then she ran her finger around the emptiness of her skull. A thick new emptiness; Naked, she puts her clothes scattered on the gray concrete steps back on. She pushes the door that leads to the hall. She no longer remembers the moment when the attacker decided to leave and abandon her to this huge void.

This immensely void void.

References

For more information, consult the blog devoted to this book: lelivren oirdesviolencessexuelles.wordpress.com and the sites of the organization Traumatic Memory, of which I am the founder and president: memoiretraumatique.org and stopaudeni.com. Here you will find much information, brochures, our research reports (IVSEA, IPSOS), along with articles you can download, testimonies, other resources, and videos describing psycho- traumatic mechanisms.

The reader can also refer to the books, studies, and articles that follow. The main ones were cited in the text. Several of these are major references in the field of sexual violence. The articles of the Felitti and Anda study in the United States formally establishes that violence should from now on be recognized as a serious public health problem.

References

Abraham H.C., Contribution à la psychanalyse des névroses de guerre, in *Œuvres complètes*, tome II, Paris, Payot, [1918] 1966; 173–180.

Abraham N. and Torok M., *L'écorce et le noyau*, Paris, Flammarion, 1987.

American Psychiatric Association, *DSM IV*, Paris, Masson, 1996.

Amnesty International, *Les Violences faites aux femmes: une affaire d'État*, Paris, Autrement, 2006.

Antelme R., *L'Espèce humaine*, Paris, Gallimard, coll. Tel, [1957] 1999.

Arcan N., *Putain*, Éditions du Seuil, 2001.

Attac, *Mondialisation de la prostitution*, Paris, 1001 nuits, 2008.

Aubry I., *La première fois j'avais 6 ans…*, Paris, Oh! Édition, 2008.

AVFT, *Violences sexistes et sexuelles au travail/Faire valoir vos droits*, 2nd ed. 2011.

Baccino É., *Médecine de la violence. Prise en charge des victimes et des agresseurs*, Paris, Masson, 2006.

Bajos N. and Bozon M., *Enquête sur la sexualité en France*, Paris, La Découverte, 2008.

Banon T., *Le bal des hypocrites*, Paris, Au diable Vauvert, 2011.

Barrois C., *Les névroses traumatiques*, Paris, Dunod, 1988.

Bataille G., *La littérature et le mal*, Paris, Gallimard, 1990.

Berger M., *L'échec de la protection de l'enfance*, Paris, Dunod, 2nd ed. 2004.

Brison S., *Après le viol*, Nîmes, Édition Jacqueline Chambon, 2002.

Browning C.R., *Ordinary Men: Reserve Police Battalion 101 and the Final Solution in Poland*, New York, HarperCollins Publishers, 1992.

Bourdieu P., *La domination masculine*, Paris, Seuil, 2002.

Cacho L., *Trafics de femmes. Enquête sur l'esclavage sexuel dans le monde*, Paris, Nouveau Monde, 2010.

Cabrol C., *Blessures de femmes*, Paris, Atlantica, 2009.

Cauderlier M., *Berceaux maudits*, Wavre, Mols, 2010.

Ciavaldini A., *Psychopathologie des agresseurs sexuels*, Paris, Masson, 1999.

Cordelier J., *La dérobade*, Paris, Phébus, 2007.

Coutanceau R., Smith J., Lemitre S., *Trauma et résilience*, Paris, Dunod, 2012.

Coutanceau R. and Salmona M., *Violences conjugales et famille*, Paris, Dunod, 2016.

Cornet J., *Faut-il battre les enfants? Relations entre les accidents et la violence éducative*, Revigny, Hommes et perspectives, 1997.

Crocq L. *et al.*, *Traumatismes psychiques: prise en charge psychologique des victimes*, Paris, Masson, 2007.

Danziger N., *Vivre sans douleur*, Paris, Odile Jacob, 2011.

Darves-Bornoz J.M., *Syndromes traumatiques du viol et de l'inceste*, Paris, Masson, 1996.

Davoine F. and Gaudillière J.M., *Histoire et trauma. La folie des guerres*, Paris, Stock, 2006.

De Clercq M. and Lebigot F., *Les traumatismes psychiques*, Paris, Masson, 2000.

Delphy C., *Classer, Dominer, Qui sont les autres?*, Paris, La fabrique, 2008.

Delphy C., *Un troussage de domestique*, Paris, Syllepse, 2011.

Demongeot I., *Service volé*, Paris, Michel Lafon, 2007.

Devroede G., *Ce que les maux de ventre disent de notre passé*, Paris, Petite bibliothèque Payot, 2003.

Dworkin A., *Woman-Hating: A Radical Look at Sexuality*, New York, Penguin, 1974.

Amnesty International, *En chemin elle rencontre...*, t. 1 et 2, Paris, Des ronds dans l'O, 2010 and 2011.

Eustache F. and Desgranges B., *Les nouveaux chemins de la mémoire*, Paris, Les éditions du Pommier, 2010.

Eiguer A., *Le pervers narcissique et son complice*, Paris, Dunod, 1996.

Fassin D. and Rechtman R., *L'empire du traumatisme: Enquête sur la condition de victime*, Paris, Flammarion, 2007.

Ferenczi S., *Confusion de langue entre adultes et l'enfant*, Paris, Payot, coll. Petite bibliothèque Payot, [1932] 2004.

Ferenczi S., *Le Traumatisme*, Paris, Petite Bibliothèque Payot, [1935] 2006.

Freud S., *Beyond the Pleasure Principle*, English translation: New York, Norton, [1921] 1975.

Freud S., *Group Psychology and the Analysis of the Ego*, English translation: New York, Norton, [1921] 1990.

Freud S., *Inhibitions, Symptoms and Anxiety*, English translation: London, L. & V. Woolf, [1925] 1936.

Freud S. and Breuer J., *Studies in Hysteria*, English translation: London, Penguin Books, [1895] 2004.

Foa E.B. and Rothbaum B.O., *Revivre après un viol*, Paris, Dunod, 2012 (Introduction by Salmona, M.).

Foa E.B. and Rothbaum B.O., *Traiter le traumatisme du viol*, Paris, Dunod, 2012.

Fromm E., *The Anatomy of Human Destructiveness*, New York, Holt, Rinehart and Winston, 1973.

Gamet M.L. and Moïse C., *Les violences sexuelles des mineures. Victimes et auteurs: de la parole au soin*, Paris, Dunod, 2010.

Godart M.O., *Rêves et traumatismes ou la longue nuit des rescapés*, Ramonville Saint- Agne, Erès, 2003.

Gouardo L., *Le silence des autres*, Paris, Michel Lafon, 2008.

Gryson-Dejehansart M.C., *Outreau, La vérité abusée*, Paris, Hugo et Compagnie, 2009.

Guiller A. and Weiler N., *Le viol un crime presque ordinaire*, Paris, Le Cherche midi, 2011.

Halimi G., *Viol, le procès d'Aix*, Paris, Gallimard, 1978.

Hatzfeld J., *Dans le nu de la vie*, Paris, Seuil, 2000.

Hatzfeld J., *Une saison de machettes*, Paris, Seuil, 2003.

Henrion R. *et al.*, *Les femmes victimes de violences conjugales. Le rôle des professionnels de santé*, Paris, La documentation française, 2001.

Henry N., *Les filles faciles n'existent pas*, Paris, Michalon, 2008.

Herman J.L., *Trauma and Recovery: The Aftermath of Violence - From Domestic Abuse to Political Terror*, New York, BasicBooks, 2015.

Hillis S., "Global prevalence of past-year violence against children: a systematic review and minimum estimates". *Pediatrics* 2016; 137(3): e20154079.

Hirigoyen M.F., *Femmes sous emprise: Les ressorts de la violence dans le couple*, Pocket, Paris, 2006.

Horassius N. and Mazet P., *Conférence de consensus de la FFP, Conséquences des maltraitances sexuelles: Reconnaître, soigner, prévenir*, Paris, John Libbey (ed.), 2004.

Hurni M. and Stoll G., *La haine de l'amour: La perversion du lien*, Paris, L'Harmattan, 1996.

Janet P., *L'automatisme mental*, Paris, Alcan, 1889.

Janet P., *L'évolution de la mémoire et de la notion du temps, Leçons au Collège de France 1927-1928*, Paris, L'Harmattan, 2006.

Jaspard M., *Les violences contre les femmes*, Paris, La Découverte, 2005.

Jehel L., Lopez G. *et al.*, *Psychotraumatologie*, Paris, Dunod, 2006.

Katz C., *Victimes de harcèlement sexuel: se défendre*, Lormont, Le Bord de l'eau, 2007.

Kédia M., Sabouraud-Seguin A. *et al.*, *L'aide-mémoire de psychotraumatologie*, Paris, Dunod, 2008.

Lacan J., *Hommage fait à Marguerite Duras, Du ravissement de Lol V. Stein, in Marguerite Duras*, Paris, Albatros, 1975, pp. 7–15.

Lassus P., *L'enfance du crime – Tous les grands criminels ont été des enfants maltraités*, Paris, Bourin, 2008.

Lassus P., *La violence en héritage. Le tragique paradoxe des relations parents-enfants*, Paris, François Bourin, 2011.

Le Boulaire M.A., *Le viol*, Paris, Flammarion, 2002.

Le Goaziou V., *Le viol, aspects sociologiques d'un crime*, Paris, La documentation française, 2011.

Legardinier C., *Les trafics du sexe, femmes et enfants marchandises*, Toulouse, Milan, coll. Les essentiels, 2002.

Le Dréau N., *Après l'inceste. Comment je me suis reconstruite avec la psychogénéalogie*, Paris, Interédition, 2011 (preface by Salmona, M.).

Lempert B., *Désamour*, Paris, Seuil, 1989.

Lempert B., *Le tueur sur un canapé jaune. Les rêves et la mémoire traumatique*, Paris, Seuil, 2008.

Levi P., *Les naufragés et les rescapés. Quarante ans après Auschwitz*, Paris, Gallimard, 1989.

Masson J.M., *The Assault on Truth: Freud's Suppression of the Seduction Theory*, English translation: New York, Ballantine Books, [1984] 2003.

Louboff F., *J'aimerais tant tourner la page*, Paris, Les Arènes, 2008.

Matokot-Mianzenza S., *Viol des femmes dans les conflits armés et thérapies familiales. Cas du Congo Brazzaville*, Paris, L'Harmattan, 2003.

MacKinnon C.A., *Feminism Unmodified: Discourses on Life and Law*, Cambridge, Mass., Harvard University Press, 1987.

MacKinnon C.A., *Only Words*, Cambridge, Mass., Harvard University Press, 1993.

Maritée, *Ma vie en pièces détachées*, Publibook, 2012.

Maurel O., *Oui la nature humaine est bonne! comment la violence éducative ordinaire la pervertit depuis des millénaires*, Robert Laffont, 2009.

Marzano M., *Malaise dans la sexualité. Le piège de la pornographie*, Paris, J.C. Lattés, 2006.

Miller A., *For Your Own Good: Hidden Cruelty in Child-Rearing and the Roots of Violence*, New York, Farrar, Straus, Giroux, 1990.

Miller A., *Banished Knowledge Facing Childhood Injuries*, London, Virago, 1990.

Miller A., *Breaking Down the Wall of Silence: The Liberating Experience of Facing Painful Truth*, New York, Dutton, 1991.

Miller A., *The Body Never Lies: The Lingering Effects of Cruel Parenting*, New York, W.W. Norton, 2005.

Moore M., *La force d'avancer*, Paris, Les Nouveaux Auteurs, 2011.

Morbois C. and Casalis M.F., *L'aide aux femmes victimes de viol*, Paris, Le Bouscat, L'Esprit du Temps, 2002.

Mukwege D., *The Power of Women: A Journey of Hope and Healing*, Short Books, Hachette UK, 2021.

Nathan T., "Tuer l'autre ou tuer la vie qui est en l'autre. Ethnopsychanalyse des crimes contre l'humanité". *Nouvelle Revue d'ethnopsychiatrie* 1992; 19: 37–54.

Nguyen S., *Comment aider une victime de viol*, Paris, Hachette, 2011.

Nisse M. and Sabourin P., *Quand la famille marche sur la tête: inceste, pédophilie, maltraitance*, Paris, Seuil, 2004.

Orwell G., *1984*, London, Secker & Warburg, 1949.

Poiret A., *L'ultime tabou: Femmes pédophiles, femmes incestueuses*, Paris, Patrick Robin, 2006.

Portelli S., *Le viol, un crime, vivre après*, Paris, Collectif féministe contre le viol, 1995.

Poulin R., *La mondialisation des industries du sexe: prostitution, pornographie, traite des femmes et des enfants*, Paris, Imago, 2005.

Prazan M., *Einsatzgruppen: sur les traces des commandos de la mort nazis*, Essai, Seuil, 2010.

Racamier P.C., *L'inceste et l'incestuel*, Paris, Dunod, 1995.

Rivière A., *La petite fille et la dame en rouge*, Paris, published by the organization Traumatic Memory and Victimology, 2012, (postface by Salmona, M.) distributed for free by the organization memoiretraumatique.org.

Rizzolatti G. and Sinigaglia C., *Les neurones miroirs*, Paris, Odile Jacob, 2008.

Romano H., *L'enfant et les jeux dangereux. Jeux post-traumatiques et pratiques dangereuses*, Paris, Dunod, 2012.

Romito P., *Un silence de mortes, la violence masculine occultée*, Paris, Syllepse, 2006.

Rosolato G., *Essai sur le symbolique*, Paris, Gallimard, 1969.

Rush F., *Le secret le mieux gardé: l'exploitation sexuelle des enfants*, Paris, Denoël, 1980.

Sabouraud-Séguin A., *Revivre après un choc. Comment surmonter le traumatisme psychologiqu*, Paris, Odile Jacob, 2001.

Sadlier K., *L'état de stress post-traumatique chez l'enfant victime d'agression*, Paris, PUF, 2001.

Salmona M., La mémoire traumatique, *in* Kédia M, Sabouraud-Séguin A (eds.). *L'aide-mémoire en psychotraumatologie*, Paris, Dunod, 2008.

Salmona M., Thérapie post-traumatique, *in En chemin elles rencontrent…*, tome 2, Paris, Amnesty International et les éd. Des ronds dans l'O, 2010.

Salmona M., Les conséquences psychotraumatiques des violences: les mécanismes neurobiologiques, *in Violences envers les femmes, le NON des femmes handicapées*, Paris, L'Harmattan, 2010.

Salmona M., Mémoire traumatique et conduites dissociantes, *in* Coutanceau R, Smith J (eds.). *Traumas et résilience*. Paris, Dunod, 2012.

Salmona M., La prise en charge médicale des enfants victimes *in Le parcours judiciaire de l'enfant victime* sous la direction de Attias D. et de Khaïat L., Eres, 201.

Salmona M., Dissociation traumatique et troubles de la personnalité post- traumatiques, *in* Coutanceau R, Smith J (eds.). *Les troubles de la personnalité en criminologie et en victimologie*, Paris, Dunod, 2013.

Salmona M., *Violences sexuelles. Les 40 questions-réponses incontournables*, Paris, Dunod, 2015.

Salmona M., Le changement dans les psychothérapies de femmes victimes de violences conjugales, *in* Coutanceau R, Smith J (eds.). *Psychothérapie et éducation: la question du changement*, Paris, Dunod, 2015.

Salmona M., Le respect des droits des enfants à être protégés de toute forme de violence, et à recevoir tous les soins nécessaire quand ils en sont victimes devrait être un impératif absolu pour les pouvoirs publics, *in Les enfants peuvent bien attendre: 25 regards d'experts* publié par l'UNICEF France, 2015, book that can be downloaded at the UNICEF website.

Salmona M., *Châtiments corporels et violences éducatives. Pourquoi il faut les interdire en 20 questions réponses*, Paris, Dunod, 2016.

Salmona M., Comprendre l'emprise pour mieux protéger et prendre en charge les femmes victimes de violences conjugales, *in* Coutanceau R, Salmona M (eds.). *Violences conjugales et familles*, Dunod, 2016.

Salmona M., Comprendre et prendre en charge l'impact psychotraumatique des violences conjugales pour mieux protéger les femmes et les enfants qui en sont victimes, *in* Ronai E, Durand E (eds.). *Violences conjugales: le droit d'être protégé*, Paris, Dunod, 2016.

Searles H., *L'effort pour rendre l'autre fou*, French translation: Paris, Folio essais, [1965] 1977.

Sellier H. and Garde S., *Enquête sur une société qui consomme des enfants*, Paris, Les Éditions du Survenir, 2008.

Semprun G., *L'écriture ou la vie*, Paris, Gallimard, 1994.

Sironi F., *Bourreaux et victimes. Psychologie de la torture*, Paris, Odile Jacob, 1999.

Talmont V., *Inceste: Récit*, Paris, J'ai Lu, 2005.

Ternon Y., *L'innocence des victimes au siècle des génocides*, Paris, Desclée de Brouwer, 2001.

Thomas E., *Le viol du silence*, Paris, J'ai Lu, 2000.

Thurin J.M. and Baumann N., *Stress, pathologies et immunité*, Paris, Flammarion, 2003.

Van der Hart O., *The Haunted Self: structural dissociation and the treatment of chronic traumatization*, New York, W.W. Norton, 2006.

Van der Kolk BA., McFarlane AC., Weisaeth L., *Traumatic Stress: The Effects of Overwhelming Experience on Mind, Body, and Society*, NY, The Guilford Press, 2006.

Tursz A., *Les oubliés – Enfants maltraités en France et par la France*, Paris, Seuil, 2010.

Vaiva G., Lebigot F., Ducrocq F., Goudemand M., *Psychotraumatismes: prise en charge et traitements*, Paris, Masson, 2005.

Vigarello G., *Histoire du viol. XVIᵉ-XXᵉ siècles*, Paris, Seuil, 1998.

Vila G., Porche L.-M., Mouren-Siméoni M.C., *État de stress post-traumatique chez l'enfant et l'adolescent*, Paris, Masson, 1999.

Villiers, L. de, *Tais-toi et pardonne!*, Paris, Flammarion, 2011.

Waal Frans De, *L'âge de l'empathie. Leçon de la nature pour une société solidaire*, Les Liens qui libèrent, 2010.

Welzer H., *Les exécuteurs. Des hommes normaux aux meurtriers de masse*, Paris, Gallimard, 2007.

Wiesel E., *La nuit*, Paris, Ed. de Minuit, 2007.

Zajde N., *Guérir de la Shoah*, Paris, Odile Jacob, 2005.

Zagury D., *L'énigme des tueurs en série*, Paris, Plon, 2008.

Articles

Alami K.M., Kadri N., "Moroccan women with a history of child sexual abuse and its long-term repercussions: a population-based epidemiological study". *Archives of Women's Mental Health* 2004; 7: 237–42.

Afnaïm A. and Salmona M., Mémoire traumatique *in Mémoires*, n° 44, décembre 2008.

Anda R.F., Felitti V.J., Bremner J.D., "The enduring effects of abuse and related adverse experiences in childhood a convergence of evidence from neurobiology and epidemiology". *European Archives of Psychiatry and Clinical Neuroscience* 2006; 256: 174–186.

Astin M.C., Ogland-Hand S.M., Coleman E.M., Foy D.S., "Posttraumatic stress disorder and childhood abuse in battered women: comparisons with maritally distressed women". *Journal of Consulting and Clinical Psychology* 1996; 6: 308–312.

Baldeck M., Les mots pour dire les violences sexuelles, ou le minutieux travail de falsification de la réalité par le langage, 2010, downloadable on the site www.memoiretraumatique.org.

Bremner J.D., Vythilingam M., Vermetten E. *et al.*, "MRI and PET study of deficits in hippocampal structure and function in women with childhood sexual abuse and posttraumatic stress disorder". *American Journal of Psychiatry* 2003; 160: 924–932.

Breslau N., Davis G.C., Andreski P., Peterson E.L., "Traumatic events and posttraumatic stress disorder in an urban population of young adults". *Archives of General Psychiatry* 1991; 48: 216–222.

Brown D. *et al.*, "Adverse Childhood Experiences and the Risk of Premature Mortality". *American Journal of Preventive Medicine* November 2009; 37(5): 389–396.

Brown-Lavoie S.M., Viecili M.A., Weiss J.A., "Sexual knowledge and victimization in adults with autism spectrum disorders". *Journal of Autism and Developmental Disorders* 2014.

Desmedt A. *et al.*, "Glucocorticoids Can Induce PTSD-Like Memory Impairments". *Mice, Science* 23 March 2012; 335(6075): 1510–1513.

Dong M., Giles W.H., Felitti V.J., Dube S.R., Williams J.E., Chapman D.P., Anda R.F., "Insights into causal pathways for ischemic heart disease: adverse childhood experiences study". *Circulation* 2004; 110: 1761–1766.

Dvir Y., "Childhood trauma and psychosis". *Child Adolescent Psychiatry Clinic of North America* 2013 Oct; 22(4): 629–641.

Fall S., *L'éternel détournement de Dolorès Haze,* 2010, available on the site www.memoiretraumatique.org.

Fall S., Causalité circulaire et coresponsabilité – pour une autre approche des violences, 2012, available at www.memoiretraumatique.org.

Farley M., Baral I., Kiremire M. *et al.*, "Prostitution in five countries: violence and post-traumatic stress disorder". *Feminism & Psychology* 1998; 8: 405–426.

Farley M., Cotton A, Lynne J. *et al.*, "Prostitution & trafficking in nine countries: a update on violence & posttraumatic stress disorder". *Journal of Trauma Practice* 2004; 2(3–4).

Favre D. *et al.*, Empathie, contagion émotionnelle et coupure par rapport aux émotions, *Enfance* 4/2005; 57: 363–382.

Finkelhor D., "The international epidemiology of child sexual abuse". *Child Abuse and Neglect* 1994; 18: 409–417.

Felitti V.J., "Long-term medical consequences of incest, rape, and molestation". *South Medical Journal* 1991; 84: 328–331.

Felitti V.J. and Anda R.F., "The Relationship of Adverse Childhood Experiences to Adult Health, Well-being, Social Function, and Health Care", *in* Lanius R, Vermetten E, Pain C (eds.). *The Effects of Early Life Trauma on Health and Disease: The Hidden Epidemic*, Cambridge, Cambridge University Press, 2010.

Ferrand A., Quand une femme est agressée, le doute n'est pas permis. 2011, available on the site www.memoiretraumatique.org.

Ferrand A., Rien de ce qui est sexuel ne serait criminel, 2011. available on the site sisyphe.org.

Foa E.B., Keane, T.M., Friedman, M.J., (eds.), "Effective Treatments for PTSD: Practice Guidelines", International Society for Traumatic Stress Studies. New York, Guilford Press, 2000.

Fulu E., Mediema S., Roselli T., McCook S., "Pathways between childhood trauma, intimate partner violence, and harsh parenting: findings from the UN Multi-country Study on men and violence in Asia and the Pacific". *Lancet Global Health* 2017; 5: e512–e522.

Garcia-Moreno C. *et al.*, "Prevalence of intimate partner violence: findings from the WHO (World Health Organization) multi-country study on women's health and domestic violence". *Lancet* 2005; 368: 1260.

Gilles C. *et al.*,: "Audit on the management of complainants of sexual assault at an emergency department". *European Journal of Obstetrics & Gynecology and Reproductive Biology* 2010.

Goodwin R.D. and Stein M.B. "Association between childhood trauma and physical disorders among adults in the United States". *Psychological Medicine* 2004; 34: 509–520.

Heim C.M., "Decreased cortical representation of genital somatosensory field after". *American Journal of Psychiatry* 2013 Jun; 170(6): 616–623.

Jewkes R. and Fulu E., "Prevalence of and factors associated with non-partner rape perpetration: findings from the UN Multi-country Cross-sectional Study on men and violence in Asia and the Pacific". *Lancet Global Health* 2013 Oct; 1(4): e208–18.

Ledoux J. and Muller J., "Emotional memory and psychopathology". *Philosophical Transactions of the Royal Society of London B* 1997; 352: 1719–1726.

Lee C., White H.R., "The effects of childhood maltreatment on violent injuries and premature death during young adulthood among urban high-risk men". *Archives of Pediatrics & Adolescent Medicine* 2012 sept 1: 814–820, doi; 10.1001/archpediatrics.2012.244.

Louville P. and Salmona M., Traumatismes psychiques: conséquences cliniques et approche neurobiologique *in* dossier: Le traumatisme du viol dans la Revue Santé Mentale de mars 2013 n°176.

McFarlane A.C., "The long-term costs of traumatic stress: intertwined physical and psychological consequences". *World Psychiatry* 2010 Feb; 9(1): 3–10.

McLeod et associées, 1992, Réseau d'action des femmes handicapées du Canada (RAFH), cité dans le Rapport du groupe de travail sur les agressions à caractère sexuel, 1995, Ministère de la Santé du Québec.

Mehrabian A., "Relations among personality scales of aggression, violence and empathy: validational evidence bearing on the Risk of Eruptive Violence Scale". *Aggressive Behavior* 1997; 23: 433–445.

Möller A., Söndergaard H.P., Helström L., "Tonic Immobility during sexual assault – a common reaction predicting post-traumatic stress disorder and severe depression". *Nordic Federation of Societies of Obstetrics and Gynecology* 2017; 96: 932–938.

Nemeroff C.B., Douglas J., Bremner Foa, E.B., Mayberg H.S., North C.S., Stein M.B., "Posttraumatic stress disorder: a state-of-the-science review influential publications". *American Psychiatric Association* 2009; 7: 254–273.

Perroud N., "Increased methylation of glucocorticoid receptor gene (*NR3C1*) in adults with a history of childhood maltreatment: a link with the severity and type of trauma". *Translational Psychiatry* 2011; 1: e59; doi:10.1038/tp.2011.60 Published online 13 December 2011.

Potterat J.J., "Mortality in a long-term open cohort of prostituted women". *American Journal of Epidemiology* 2004; 159: 778–785.

Putman F.W., Research update review: "Child Sexual Abuse". *Journal of the American Academy of Child & Adolescent Psychiatry* 2003; 42(3): 269–278.

Rauch S.L., Shin L.M., Phelps E.A., "Neurocircuitry models of posttraumatic stress disorder and extinction: human neuroimaging research–past, present, and future". *Biological Psychiatry* 2006; 60: 376–382.

Rice M.E., Chaplin T.C., Harris G.T., Coutts, J., "Empathy for the victim and sexual arousal among rapists and nonrapists". *Journal of Interpersonal Violence* 1994; 9: 435–449.

Rodriguez N. and Ryan S.W., "Posttraumatic stress disorder in adult female survivors of child sexual abuse: a comparison study". *Journal of Consulting and Clinical Psychology* February 1997; 65(1): 53–59.

Salmona M., Lutter contre les violences passe avant tout par la protection des victimes publié sur le blog *un monde en partage*, December 2009.

Salmona M., Mécanismes des violences: quelles origines? published on the geopolitical blog *Diploweb*, November, 2010.

Salmona M., Les violences envers les femmes et les filles: un fléau mondial encore trop ignoré, November, 2010, site www.memoiretraumatique.org.

Salmona M., La nausée… et La victime c'est la coupable… published on the blog of *Médiapart*, July and September, 2011. www.memoiretraumatique.org.

Salmona M., Des violences traumatisantes et dissociantes, avant, pendant et après la situation prostitutionnelle, 2012, published on the site www.memoiretraumatique.org. and regardsdefemmes.

Salmona M., L'impact psychotraumatique des violences sur les enfants: la mémoire traumatique à l'œuvre, *in La revue de santé scolaire et universitaire* 6, Elsevier, 2013.

Salmona M., Le viol, crime absolu *in* Le traumatisme du viol, *Santé mentale*, mars, 2013, n° 176.

Salmona M., L'impact psychotraumatique de la violence sur les enfants: la mémoire traumatique à l'œuvre *in la protection de l'enfance*, La revue de santé scolaire & universitaire, janvier-février, 2013, n°19, pp 21–25.

Salmona M., En quoi connaître l'impact psychotraumatique des viols et des violences sexuelles est-il nécessaire pour mieux lutter contre le déni, la loi du silence et la culture du viol, pour mieux protéger les victimes et pour que leurs droits soient mieux respectés? 2016, downloadable on the site http://www.memoiretraumatique.org/assets/files/2016-Necessaire-connaissance-de-limpact-psychotraumatique-chez-les-victimes-de-viols.pdf.

Salmona M., Impact des psychotraumatismes, sur la santé et la scolarité *in* Dossier: Les blessures de la vie, *La revue de santé scolaire & universitaire*, mai-juin, 2016, n° 39.

Salmona M., Le changement dans les psychothérapies de femmes victimes de violences conjugales, *in* Coutanceau R, Joanna S (eds.). *Psychothérapie et éducation: la question du changement*, Paris, Dunod, 2015.

Salmona M., Pour en finir avec le déni et la culture du viol en 12 points, 2017, téléchargeable sur le site https://stopauxviolences.blogspot.fr/2017/03/pour-en-finir-avec-le-deni-et-la.html.

Schmidt A., La correctionnalisation du viol: la négation d'un crime, 2012, published on the site memoiretraumatique.org.

Shin L.M., Scott L., Rauch S.L., Roger K., Pitman R.K., Amygdala, "Medial prefrontal cortex, and hippocampal function PTSD". *Annals of the New York Academy of Sciences* 2006; 1071: 67–79.

Spataro J., Mullen P.E., Burgess P.M., Wells D.L., Moss S.A., "Impact of child sexual abuse on mental health". *British Journal of Psychiatry* 2004; 184: 416–21.

Steele K. and Colrain J., "Abreactive Work with Sexual Abuse Survivors: Concepts and Techniques", *The Sexual Abused Male, Volume 2, Applications of Treatment Strategies*, Lexington MA, Lexington Books, 1990, 1–55.

Tabet P., "La grande arnaque, l'expropriation de la sexualité des femmes". *Actuel Marx* 2001; 30: 131–152.

Trinquart J., La décorporalisation dans la pratique prostitutionnelle: un obstacle majeur à l'accès des soins, thèse de doctorat en médecine, Paris, 2002, downloadable on the site www.memoiretraumatique.org.

Van der Hart O. and Friedman B., "Trauma, Dissociation and Trigger: Their Role in Treatment and Emergency Psychiatry". *Emergency Psychiatry Today*, Amsterdam, Elsevier, 1992, 137–142.

Van der Kolk B.A. and Van der Hart O., "The intrusive past: the flexibility of memory and the engraving of trauma". *American Imago* 1991; 48: 425–454.

Widom C.S, "Accuracy of adult recollections of childhood victimization: Part 1; childhood abuse". *NCJRS Psychological Assessment* 1996; 8(4): 412–421.

Williams L.M., "Recall of childhood trauma: a prospective study of women's memory of child sexual abuse". *Journal of Consulting and Clinical Psychology* 1994; 62(6): 1167–1176.

Woolley C.S., Gould E., McEwen B.S., "Exposure to excess glucocorticoids alters dendritic morphology of adult hippocampal pyramidal neurons". *Brain Research* 1990; 531: 225–231.

Yehuda R. and Ledoux J., "Response variation following trauma: a translational neuroscience approach to understanding PTSD". *Neuron* 2007 Oct 4; 56: 19.

Other Research and Reports

CEDAW Convention sur l'élimination de toutes les formes de discrimination à l'égard des femmes. Adoptée en 1979. Entrée en vigueur: September 3, 1981.

Déclaration de Varsovie Sommet de Varsovie – Déclaration de Varsovie (16 and 17 May, 2005). Strasbourg Conseil de l'Europe, 2005.

Convention on the Rights of the Child, 1989, downloadable on the site of UNICEF: https://www.unicef.org/child-rights-convention.

Council of Europe Convention on preventing and combating violence against women and domestic violence. https://rm.coe.int/168008482e.

Enquêtes Cadre de vie et sécurité CVS Insee-ONDRP, de l'Observatoire National des réponses pénales, 2010-2016. Downloadable on the site inhesj.fr.

Enquête sur le comportement sexiste et les violences envers les jeunes filles (CSVF) en Seine Saint Denis, France, 2007. Downloadable on the site www.memoiretraumatique.org.

Contexte de la sexualité en France (CSF) de 2006, Bajos N., Bozon M. and CSF., Les violences sexuelles en France: quand la parole se libère, *Population & Sociétés (Bulletin mensuel d'information de l'Institut national d'études démographiques)*, 445, May 2008.

IVSEA Impact des violences sexuelles de l'enfance à l'âge adulte, 2015, conducted with 1,200 victims of sexual violence, by the organization Traumatic Memory and Victimology with the support of UNICEF France: Salmona, Laure author, Salmona, Muriel coordinator, report and summary downloadable on the sites http://stopaudeni.com and http://www.memoiretraumatique.org.

Les français-e-s et les représentations du viol et des violences sexuelles, 2016, IPSOS for the organization Traumatic Memory, Salmona, Muriel, director and Salmona, Laure coordintor and author of the report and press file downloadable on the sites http://stopaudeni.com/and http://www.memoiretraumatique.org.

Study of rape and sexual aggression in 2013 and 2014 in the courts of Bobigny by the Observatoire des violences envers les femmes du 93 and the TGI of Bobigny.

Étude analytique de la mise en œuvre effective de la Recommandation Rec 2002 sur la protection des femmes contre la violence dans les États membres du Conseil de l'Europe.

Étude de mortalité des sans abris à Marseille de Médecins du Monde et de l'équipe mobile santé mentale et communautaire, Marseille, January, 2009.

Hagemann-White C. and Bohn S., Université d'Osnabrück, Allemagne, Protéger les femmes contre la violence: Conseil de l'Europe 2007.

Les lettres numéro 4, 8, 10 et 12 et de l'Observatoire National des violences faites aux femmes de la MIPROF (Mission Interministérielle de Protection des Femmes Victimes de Violences et de Lutte contre la Traite des Êtres Humains) all reports and studies on violence against women, as well as organizations and what they are doing to prevent it, available on the site http://stop-violences-femmes.gouv.fr.

Rapport national enquête nationale sur les violences envers les femmes en France ENVEFF Jaspard M, Brown E, Condon S, Fougeyrollas-Schwebel D, Houel A, Lhomond B, Maillochon F, Saurel-Cubizolles M, and Schiltz M. (2003). Les violences envers les femmes en France: une enquête nationale. Paris, La Documentation Française.

Rapport de Véronique Le Goaziou: rapport final de la recherche "Les viols dans la chaîne pénale" 2016 consultable sur le site de l'ORDCS.

Rapport de la Mission d'information sur la prostitution en France, rapport présenté à l'Assemblée Nationale en 2011, downloadable on the site memoiretraumatique.org.

Rapport des Nations Unies sur toutes les formes de violences à l'égard des femmes, 2006.

Rapport du Conseil économique social et environnemental CESE: Vion, Pascale, Combattre toutes les violences faites aux femmes, des plus visibles aux plus insidieuses, Les éditions des Journaux officiels, novembre 2014.

Résolution A/RES/48/104 adoptée le 23 février 1994 par l'Assemblée générale des Nations Unies. Déclaration sur l'élimination de la violence à l'égard des femmes.

Review on national systems of statistics and registration on child abuse in European Network of National Observatories on Childhood, 2007, site www.childoneurope.org.

United Nations Children's Fund, *Hidden in plain sight: A statistical analysis of violence against children*, New York, UNICEF, 2014.

World Health Organization and London School of Hygiene and Tropical Medicine. Preventing intimate partner and sexual violence against women: Taking action and generating evidence Geneva: World Health Organization, 2010.

World Health Organization, *Global Status Report on Violence Prevention*, Geneva, WHO, 2014.

For Product Safety Concerns and Information please contact our EU
representative GPSR@taylorandfrancis.com
Taylor & Francis Verlag GmbH, Kaufingerstraße 24, 80331 München, Germany

9 781032 802619